THE CELT AND THE CHRIST

Another Look at the Letter
to the Galatians

By
Dorothy Minchin-Comm
&
Hyveth B. Williams

2008

Order this book online at www.trafford.com/07-1665
or email orders@trafford.com

Most Trafford titles are also available at major online book retailers.

© Copyright 2008 Dorothy Minchin-Comm, Hyveth B. Williams.
All rights reserved. No part of this publication may be reproduced, stored in a retrieval system, or transmitted, in any form or by any means, electronic, mechanical, photocopying, recording, or otherwise, without the written prior permission of the author.

Note for Librarians: A cataloguing record for this book is available from Library and Archives Canada at www.collectionscanada.ca/amicus/index-e.html
Cover design adapted from Dover Pictura,
Letters and Alphabets (New York: Dover Publications, 2004), p.43.

Printed in Victoria, BC, Canada.

ISBN: 978-1-4251-4068-7

We at Trafford believe that it is the responsibility of us all, as both individuals and corporations, to make choices that are environmentally and socially sound. You, in turn, are supporting this responsible conduct each time you purchase a Trafford book, or make use of our publishing services. To find out how you are helping, please visit www.trafford.com/responsiblepublishing.html

Our mission is to efficiently provide the world's finest, most comprehensive book publishing service, enabling every author to experience success. To find out how to publish your book, your way, and have it available worldwide, visit us online at www.trafford.com/10510

www.trafford.com

North America & international
toll-free: 1 888 232 4444 (USA & Canada)
phone: 250 383 6864 ♦ fax: 250 383 6804
email: info@trafford.com

The United Kingdom & Europe
phone: +44 (0)1865 722 113 ♦ local rate: 0845 230 9601
facsimile: +44 (0)1865 722 868 ♦ email: info.uk@trafford.com

10 9 8 7 6 5 4 3 2 1

The Celt and the Christ

This book is dedicated

to

Our family, friends and colleagues, with love and gratitude.

You are all the rich soil in which this seed

was allowed to germinate

and to bring forth

the fruit of our research.

The Celt and the Christ

TABLE OF CONTENTS

Dedication	iii
Table of Contents	iv
Foreword	vi
Preface	xi
Synopses of Chapters	xiv
Introduction to the World of the Galatians	1

PART I
I. Tradition & the Law

1. Departing from Tradition	17
2. Ceremonial Obligations	28
3. Inalienable Rights or Restrictive Regulations?	36

II. Contending for Identity

4. Breaking Down Barriers	43
5. Face-off with the Judaizers	53
6. Liberty or Death?	62

PART II
III. Spiritual Practice

7. The Solitary Way	68
8. The Journey-Quest	81
9. The Discipline of the Rule of Three	91

IV. Belligerence & Instability

10. Raiding and War	100
11. Passion and the Virtues of Commitment	107
12. Boasting and Challenging	116

PART III
V. Mentoring and Devotion

13. The Ties that Bind	122
14. Help with the Heavy Load	130
15. Love Never Fails	139

VI. The Brand-marks

16. A Flair for Design	153
17. Bewitched?	162
18. The Painted People	170

EPILOGOS 178

ENDNOTES 180

APPENDICES
I. A Chronology of Galatia	201
II. A Survey of Indo European Languages	206
III. Index to Topics	207
Authors' Page	220

The Celt and the Christ

FOREWORD

In the swelling current of publications on things Celtic, two types predominate: There are the treatments of Celtic religious sensibility, early Christian or pre-Christian, as such can be traced primarily in Scotland, Wales and, above all, Ireland. And there are the studies of more ancient pagan Celtic roots, through archaeological and historical investigations across Europe and the Near East, as far as Iran. Missing from this pattern are attempts to explore the Christian Gospel's first encounters with Celtic peoples, as the nascent mission first spread across Asia Minor.

This study addresses that gap. Concentrating on the Apostle Paul's initial overtures in the Roman province of Galatia, it mines his follow-up letter to "the churches of Galatia" that he had there established. The results are fresh and helpful—not only for shedding important historical light on this earliest wellspring of Celtic Christianity, but also for the lessons that we still can learn today. How did this small, assertive movement present itself in terms meaningful to these tribal groups, so different in culture from either Judaism or the larger Roman world? How did these clans adapt the strange proclamation to their own understandings? How, and to what extent, did the Gospel preserve its own core of integrity in this process of adaptation and appropriation? And what lessons can we draw for our own sharing of Jesus in this world of clashing cultures?

The Celt and the Christ

For present purposes, we need not resolve the vexed question of whether the "Galatians" of Paul's letter are inhabitants of north central Asia Minor, or of the Roman province of Galatia, that additionally embraced the southern cities of Pisidian Antioch, Iconium, Lystra and Derbe. But while largely in the north, the Celts were a people who defined themselves ethnically and culturally, not geographically. Paul's audience is not simply the churches of a locale, as might be inferred from his salutation in Galatians 1:2. His outburst "You foolish Galatians!" (3:1) may well echo a disparaging ethnic snub common to the day. If we need textual warrant for the possibility of a visit by Paul to the northern part of Anatolia, where the population was more densely Celtic, Acts 16:6 and 18:23, with their regional rather than political designations of Phrygia and Galatia, will suffice.

In Paul's day and setting, these striking people had been making their presence felt across Europe for seven centuries and more. By the third century BC, three great tribal groups (Tolistobogii, Trocmi and Tectosages) had occupied much of northern and central Asia Minor through migration, conquest and agricultural settlement. These comprised sub-divisions of the great swath of Celtic peoples arching across the northern bounds of the Hellenistic and, eventually, the Roman empire. Here these *Keltoi* were known as *Galatai*. Certainly Paul knew something of them from his own upbringing in Tarsus, principal city of Cilicia, Galatia's neighboring province.

As appreciative of the powerfully spoken word as they were disdainful of its written form, they leave us only the mute specimens of their finely-wrought material culture from which to surmise their meanings. These, plus snatches of oral tradition and the none-too-sympathetic characterizations by foreign interpreters give us the picture we have: of a people tall, fair of hair and complexion, adorned, skilled in crafts, agriculture, oratory, and in individual combat. More often at conflict among themselves than collaborating against any other powers, they seem to have inspired a grudging mixture of fear, respect, intrigue and disdain from their more conventional neighbors across the Roman empire.

We cannot know to what extent Paul might have sought initial contact with Celtic hearers in his Galatian travels, in the course of his first or second missionary journey. There were certainly Greek and Jewish populations throughout the province of Galatia, including its Celtic north. Given his deliberate pattern of reaching out first to his Jewish brethren, we may assume the same strategy there. And beyond Judaism's pale, the language barrier would have favored his evangelizing Greek-speaking communities. Even so, among those of Gaelic tongue there was certainly enough competence in the vernacular "Koine" Greek of the marketplace for commerce. And where trade and transactions led, the Gospel regularly found its way. Whether Christ was "publicly placarded" (3:1) among them by Paul himself or by workers who arose in his wake, there is every likelihood that the Gospel's adherents in Galatia came early to include Celtic people.

By the time Paul is writing his Letter to the Galatians, accordingly, he can craft his appeal in terms that can apply to many, but that seem especially suited to what we can know of the culture and consciousness of Celtic peoples. If, with the preponderance of recent scholarly opinion, we regard the Galatian letter as written during the later stages of Paul's life, there is ample time for the Gospel to establish itself among Celtic populations, as well as for the judaizing influences he mentions, even as he marvels that they are "so soon" led astray (1:6).

The epistle perhaps tells us more about Paul than about his addressees. The Apostle's exasperation overrides his usual diplomatic style; only in this letter does he violate his practice of opening with a prayer of thanksgiving for the spiritual strengths of his readers. Here he plunges directly from his salutation into reproof. His intense re-telling of his showdown with Peter (2:11ff), his zeal to shelter his hearers from those who would confuse them (5:10), his passionate sign-off in his own hand (6:11ff), as he seeks to connect as directly as possible with these congregants—all of these features reveal more of his burning, yearning spirit than do any of his other writings. Paul cares profoundly about these people.

And this, in turn, can tell us something about them. For Paul's paternal, almost proprietary sense toward these people speaks of his desire to protect them from corrosive notions that are new to them: the sophistries of the debate within the Christian movement that would undermine their wholehearted trust in Christ's atonement. That they are susceptible to such is already clear. Are they a people who too readily trust visiting authorities from a larger, somewhat foreign world? Do they need help in seeing that what comes as a further development of the Gospel is in fact a "different Gospel" (1:6ff)? That the very terms of the debate are unfamiliar may contribute to their diversion. So too may a certain self-doubt in the face of external ecclesiastical authority. Centuries later, even after generations of maturation in the faith, Christendom's Celtic branch would yield to the Roman tradition simply on the basis of appeals to uniformity. "What thing more perverse can be felt of our church," Abbot Cummian would argue to his own Celtic brethren in 664, "than if we say . . . only the Irish and Britons know what is right?"

The Celt and the Christ

Without psychologizing unduly, how better to appeal to a people who may see themselves as marginalized from the dominant culture, than by assuring them of their full sonship in Christ (4:1-7)? And how better to counter the new enslavements of Christian legalism, than by painting it as a return to pre-Christian superstitions such as these Galatai had known in their previous lives (4:8-11)?

As we read between the lines of Paul's letter, we too come to care about these people, for in their struggles we see what is most human in ourselves. We can grant them their particular idiosyncracies: If, unlike the wisdom-seeking Greeks (I Cor 1:22), these people are more impressed with the manifestations of the Spirit, Paul is quite prepared to call them back to that level of Christian experience. Faith-based miracles, at least, are better than "works of the law" (3:5). And if, over subsequent centuries, the lives of the Celtic saints are recounted as little more than concatenations of wondrous deeds, we find an echo of their earliest Christian life.

Admittedly, miracle is the cousin of magic. If Celtic devotional exercises reflect a certain talismanic sense, always re-weaving the web of protection in the face of dangers known and unknown, we can understand the impulse even if we abjure the practice. How different, after all, are the prayers of Saints Patrick and David from the practice of some of today's Christians, for whom the "prayer of Jabez" (I Chron 4:10) serves as a mantra? We do understand.

The mentality behind such practices lends itself to the keen observance of sacred rites, as demarcations between the holy and the profane. If Paul finds consonance between the Galatians' previous devotion to solstice and equinox, and their recent observances of day and month, season and year (4:8-11), it is because the former prepared the way for the latter. So naturally did such judaizing tendencies take root in their Celtic soil, that they were blind to the threat to their faith. And again, we understand.

In sum, we can envision a people whose instincts for freedom were coupled, paradoxically, with a certain vulnerability to suasion from those who could tap into their sincerity. Rhetorical skills could work with them. Paul could have played to their impressibility, as his opponents seem to have done. Instead, he goes for the freedom. The bald, stunning word of their liberation in Christ came once again to them as the core of the good news, for it spoke to the core of their souls. If their drive toward individual freedom was their military and political undoing in the face of the Roman legions' disciplined ranks, it was their spiritual deliverance from the claims of legalistic religion.

It is hardly surprising, then, as we trace Celtic Christian spirituality over the

The Celt and the Christ

following centuries, pressed up as it was against the margins of the Western world, to see how many spiritual nightingales it produced. And if, by Whitby's convocation, the ecclesiastical ravens prevailed as sooner or later they always must in this world, the solitary nightingale's song is never fully silenced. For it carries forward in our own hearts: "It is for the sake of freedom that Christ has set us free."

In today's heated discussions concerning the meaning and propriety of "contextualization," as the good news makes its way across cultural bounds, we do well to examine the strategies of Paul's Galatian epistle. For here is the earliest clear demonstration of the principle that the core of the Gospel, even as it cuts across the norms and canons of every culture it encounters, can still be couched in terms meaningful to the people it addresses. Here we learn afresh how to avail of the Spirit's guidance in expressing truth in the mold of others' thought. And here we learn again the lesson of faithfulness to the Gospel's essence.

For this reason, this present study accomplishes more than shedding light on an important early chapter in one current of early Christianity—valuable as that is. It also gives us a paradigmatic case study of creative mission from which we can draw lessons still valid today. Both of these accomplishments come from the devoted effort of two friends who have brought expertise and insight to their task. We are all the richer for it.

John R. Jones. PhD
Dean, School of Religion (Ret.)
La Sierra University
Riverside, California
2008

The Celt and the Christ

Preface

Using religion as a means of controlling others is a power trip as old as human history. The Apostle Paul, however, came on the scene preaching the Gospel of freedom in Christ while founding several churches in Galatia. Hearing of the Judaizers' attempt to undo his work infuriated him. These religious leaders of the "old school" had herded the "freedom-loving Christians" back into the corral of religious rules and regulations.[1] He wrote a lively letter to them. A letter wonderfully relevant to the needs and personality of these Gaelic people.

Members of the Indo-European family of languages, the Celts and their culture have survived from ancient times until the present. They make up a colorful remnant of the first lords of Europe—those fiercely independent founders of Western culture. At the perennial risk of generalizing about an ethnic group, we must define some of their basic characteristics. They were inventive, flamboyant and vain. Volatile and given to reckless courage, they loved fighting. Yet, they prized eloquence, music and learning, strictly observing the responsibilities of hospitality and kinship. This could be a thumbnail sketch of the Bretons, the Irish, the Scots, or the Welsh today. It also describes the New Testament Galatians of Asia Minor (Turkey).

The Celt and the Christ

Galatia lay at the extreme end of the eastern migrations of the European Celtic tribes. These Gaelic tribes gained international experience through their widespread migrations, their marauding raids and far-flung trade routes. Yet, wherever they settled they remained fundamentally different from their neighbors. They retained their personality, language and philosophy far into Christian times—and beyond.

As founder of the Galatian churches, the Apostle Paul was the first to introduce the Christian Gospel to Celtic peoples. Scholars have argued for and against the "Northern" and the "Southern" theories. Some claim that Paul did not travel beyond the southern Hellenized regions. Others maintain that he penetrated into the more remote Celtic north. Since the Celts were compulsive migrants and raiders, and since their society dominated wherever they went, we see no difficulty. The apostle would have met basic Celtic culture wherever he went in the province. Externally Hellenized, yes. Yet, inwardly loyal to their ancient roots.

The book of Galatians—the charter of Christian freedom—was purposefully addressed to the Celts. Is there evidence, then, that Paul understood the unique nature of this community to which he ministered? Does he use illustrations and motifs which would be particularly comprehensible to a Celt? The tone of the letter is unusually harsh. Why? Does the history and ethnic mix of Galatia indicate that the local culture contributed to the problems Paul addressed?

It is the purpose of this book to explore these questions. We draw from a variety of sources of "Celticism"—ancient to modern, pagan to Christ. We must consider the premise: "Once a Celt, always [and everywhere] a Celt."

To those who may wonder how this book should be classified, we simply say: "It is neither theology nor criticism, devotion nor doctrine. Rather, it grows out of the vagaries of human personality. As such, it is simply an invitation to think of creative possibilities. Possibilities which may enrich our understanding of Paul's ministry and his letter to the young churches in Galatia. It has been said that the only excuse for writing a book is that one has something to say that has not been said before. We claim this rationale as we offer you yet *another* book.

The reader will see that each of our chapters begins with an illustration drawn from Celtic culture. These narratives then flow into discussions of the experiences of the young Galatian churches. This back-ground study, then, should provide us with the opportunity for a new reading of Paul's letter to the Galatians.

We are indebted to Richard Weismeyer for his invaluable artistic and technical contributions. Thank you to Heidi Ford for giving our manuscript a careful reading.

The Celt and the Christ

Dorothy Minchin-Comm, PhD
Professor of English (Ret)
La Sierra University
Riverside, California

Hyveth Williams, DMin
Senior Pastor
Campus Hill Church
Loma Linda, California

> The members of the Celtic Tour of 2001 (directed by Dorothy Minchin-Comm and John Jones) of La Sierra University proved to be an enthusiastic company of travelers. They were: James Choi, Robert Coffee, Mary Dodge, Janet Gray, Cherrie Heidenreich, Kelly Heidenreich, Heather Holloway, Carl Jones, Lisa Minchin, Donna Peck, Michele Pongvarin, Jean Read, Nancy Rider, Christy Robinson, Lydia Roda, Penny Shell, Dolores Stuart, Catalina Vizcarra, Ester Vizcarra, Kit Watts.
>
> Together we reached out to our spiritual forebears, the Christian Celts of Ancient Britain,
> - studying their lives, wisdom, and worship habits,
> - walking the same green fields that once knew them,
> - honoring their earthy independence, selfless courage, and utter devotion to God,
> - viewing the misty bays and lonely coastlines where they sailed, and exploring the stone ruins of their communities.

Synopses:
The Celt and the Christ

THE WORLD OF THE GALATIANS

As a background to our theme, we surveyed the basic characteristics of the Celtic tribes and their migrations over Europe. (Ireland, west; Turkey/Galatia, east; Northern Italy and Spain, south; and the German clans, north.) Three crucial influences prevailed: (1) The bond of Celtic languages, (2) Asia Minor's geography and culture, and (3) the establishment of the Kingdom of Galatia and its ultimate Hellenization as it evolved into a Roman province. Attached is a chronology of Galatian history from 1900 BC to 714 AD (Appendix I).

PART I
TRADITION AND LAW

1. *Departing from Tradition*

By the time of the Apostle Paul, Galatia had become a Roman Province. In material, political, and commercial ways, the astute Galatian Celts had become thoroughly Hellenized. Their tribal culture (shaped by Druidism) and their lan-

The Celt and the Christ

guage, however, prevailed in their religion, both then and now. Their ethnic characteristics had remarkable staying power. Having stated his apostolic qualifications and defined the crisis, Paul set about trying to persuade the Galatians to change their minds.

2. Ceremonial Obligations

Rituals, both Celtic and Judeo-Christian, had many purposes—material, social, and spiritual. Dismayed by the extreme Gaelic devotion to ceremony, Paul endeavored to lead the zealous Galatians into a balanced understanding of Christian rites.

3. Inalienable Rights or Rules and Regulations?

Paul's discussion of Law and Grace was particularly important to the Galatians. As Celts they had almost 2,000 years of skillful lawmaking behind them. The rights they guaranteed for both property and persons were just and amazingly democratic. This chapter discusses their sense of honor that naturally demanded the keeping of very specific regulations.

CONTENDING FOR IDENTITY

4. Breaking Down Barriers

In the hierarchical ancient world, Christianity became the "Great Leveler." Whatever class differences might prevail, all people became equal as they met together in worship before God. The Celts could be very generous in this matter. Even their women enjoyed privileges unmatched anywhere else at the time. Unfortunately, centuries of Christianity actually eroded women's rights, both in and out of the Church. Paul deals with the problem of prejudice and describes its cure.

5. Face-off with the Judaizers

This is an examination of the origins and teachings of the Judaizers who infiltrated the early Christian churches. The Judaizing love of ostentation was at odds with their legalistic restrictions, a difficult dilemma for the new Christians. Therefore, Paul had to address the serious issue of circumcision which had created a crisis among the early-influenced Galatians.

6. Liberty or Death?

Some of the most significant Celtic gifts to humanity are the determination to be free, individualistic and authentic. Their constant drive for liberty often turned out to be more important than life itself. Therefore, it must have been mind-boggling to the Apostle Paul that the Galatian Christians so quickly capitulated to the restraints imposed by the Judaizers. He appealed to their deep, ethnic sense of freedom as a way of distinguishing between the ceremonial law and the Gospel of grace.

PART II
SPIRITUAL PRACTICE

7. *The Solitary Way*

Paul makes a point of telling the Galatians about his three years of "exile" in the Arabian Desert. As the Celtic Christian church developed in the 3rd century AD, the religious leaders (unlike those of the Roman Church) practiced and encouraged solitude. Celtic monks and nuns required individual cells rather than "dormitory living" for their prayer and meditation. Here is a discussion of the inherent Galatian tendency to isolation and extreme independence. The three martyrdoms of Gaelic Christianity relate to Paul's personal experience.

8. *The Journey-Quest*

The life-changing journey-quest is a timeless picture of the spiritual life. The Celts were perpetual migrants, adventuring and settling new lands, wandering in voluntary exile, and searching for the "Otherworld." Thus the Galatians would have had no difficulty understanding the itinerant Paul on his hazardous missionary journeys.

9. *The Discipline of the Rule of Three*

Their ancient poetic triads (verse forms) revealed the Celtic penchant for "threes." Aware of this aspect of Celtic intellectualism, Paul addressed the Galatians in a complex, three-fold appeal which climaxes in a celebration of the glory of the Christian Trinity.

The Celt and the Christ

BELLIGERENCE AND INSTABILITY

10. Raiding and War

The Celts loved fighting. Marauding raids were threads that held the fabric of their society together. When they had no wars, they hired themselves out as mercenaries and paid-assassins. Paul's Hebrew heritage as a Benjamite also embraced a warlike disposition. Yet, he labored to transform the Christian Galatians from a natural to a spiritual warfare, expressed by a passion for spreading the Gospel.

11. Passion and the Virtues of Commitment

Strong emotionalism was a major characteristic of Celtic life and culture. It earned them the Greco-Roman designation of "barbarian," because at first they were not literate in the languages of the Empire. Also their battle frenzy and uncontrolled passions terrified their enemies. Melancholy moods of despair and their capacity for rash decisions were unmatched among other ancient tribes. Paul's challenge was to inspire his Galatian converts to rise above demonstrations of their "lower nature" in acts of unbridled anger.

12. Boasting and Challenges

Paul was astonished at the in-fighting and arrogance among the Galatians. Realizing that he had to deal with the innate Celtic zeal for heroism and personal glorification, the Apostle advised them against the destructiveness of blustering speeches and the irrationality of confronting one another with challenges. Nothing, he said, is worth boasting about, except "the cross of our Lord" (Gal 6:14).

PART III
MENTORING AND DEVOTION

13. The Ties That Bind

Kinship was a significant, time-honored kind of social cement in the Celtic world. They honored four kinds of relationships: adoption, fosterage, clientage, and hostage-taking. This chapter explores Paul's use of these cultural elements to impress upon the Galatians the true meaning of their relationship as born-again and bought-anew children of God.

14. Help with the Heavy Load

The powerful bonds within Celtic society made mentoring a natural obligation. The Irish *anam-chara* (soul-friend) functioned in both pagan and Christian communities. For example, this one-to-one relationship opposed "assembly-line" counseling. The intimacy of a trusted friend was preferred over confession to a priest or group therapy. More than once Paul offers himself to each believer as a concerned parent and soul-friend. As Celts, the Galatians responded best to individual attention.

15. How Love Works

Hospitality was a patriarchal practice and a sacred trust, widely understood throughout the ancient world. Europeans, both pagan and Christian, had stringent rules about the care and entertainment of guests and strangers. Paul's tribute to the Galatians, as his hosts, segregate their practices from the less generous customs of the Jews. Although the latter exercised a regulated kind of hospitality, they were quite exclusive and nationalistic in their religious customs.

BRAND-MARKS

16. A Flair for Design

The love of style, color, ornamentation and display is a well-recognized Celtic characteristic. So important was fashion that both ancient and modern Celts were often willing to fight to maintain their customs. Paul defines the Galatians as "vainglorious and self-praising" (Gal 5:26). He takes the opportunity to examine the advantage that the flamboyant Judaizers took of these vulnerable Christians.

17. Bewitched?

With their Druidic heritage, the Galatians were highly susceptible to the power of the spoken word and the practices of magic. A major practitioner of the occult among the early Christians, Simon Magus, disrupted the church with Gnostic heresy. Paul's message to the Galatians is surprisingly harsh in this connection.

18. The Painted People

Human-body art and painting is as old as time. Tattooing has worked its way through many cultures from ancient Egypt to downtown New York—and

The Celt and the Christ

everywhere in between. God warned the Jews not to practice body-modification. The Celts so loved body art that the Romans dubbed them the "painted people." In a surprising metaphor, Paul (an avowed Jew) declared that he also bore brandmarks, but he did it for Jesus. This chapter examines his claim and his invitation to the Galatians to do likewise.

The Celt and the Christ

A Chronology of the Life of Paul

The exact order of events in Paul's life and the dates of his epistles can only be estimated. An ongoing dispute, however, prevails among scholars. For instance, some regard the date of 30 AD as certain for Christ's ascension (Acts 1:9–11). Others assign this event to 29 AD. At the same time, all seem to agree on the date of 44 AD for the death of Herod Agrippa (Acts 12:23). Yet, neither of these dates helps determine the absolute chronology of Paul's life and letters. Nonetheless, to put things in some kind of perspective, probable dates are offered in the following table.*

Death, resurrection, ascension of Christ	30 AD
Conversion of Paul	c 35
First visit to Jerusalem (Gal 1:18)	37
Paul at Tarsus	37–43
To Jerusalem with Gifts from Antioch (Acts 11:30)	44 or 45
First Missionary Journey (Acts 13)	c 46 or 47
Council at Jerusalem	50
Second Missionary Journey (Acts 15:40–41)	54–58
I & II Letters to Thessalonians	52–53
Third Missionary Journey (Acts 18:23–28)	54–58
Letter to the Galatians	55
I Corinthians	56 or 57
II Corinthians	57
Letter to the Romans	57–58
Arrest at Jerusalem (Acts 21)	58 AD
Imprisonment in Caesarea (Acts 23:25–35)	58–60
Arrival at Rome (Acts 28:11–21)	61
First Impisonment in Rome (Acts 28:30)	61–63 or 64
Letters to Colossians, Philemon, Ephesians	62
Letter to Philippians	63
Release from first Roman Imprisonment	63 or 64
I Timothy	64 or 65
Letter to Titus	65 or 66
II Timothy	67
Death of Paul	67–68

Henry Snyder Gerhan, ed., *The Westminister Dictionary of the Bible*, (Philadelphia: The Westminster Press, 1944), p. 464.

INTRODUCTION TO THE WORLD OF THE GALATIANS

I. THE SPIRITUAL

When men and women are converted to Christ, certain rather predictable events follow. The spiritual journey of the Apostle Paul is an exemplar of this progression. After his stunning experience on the Damascus Road (35 AD), Saul of Tarsus had a name-change. The new name "Paul" ("lent of God") reflected the deepening transformation in his life. God, he discovered, was not an impersonal force to control believers and make them conform to the demands of Judaism.

1. Sharing. Finding a personal Savior in Jesus truly set Paul free. His new lease on life propelled him far a-field, into the Gentile lands of the Roman Empire. (It has been estimated that during his thirty-five years of ministry, Paul walked at least 2,000 miles!). He could not have been more eager to share this glorious experience and invite others to partake of the wonders of his new-found faith.

2. Challenges and Paul's Reaction to Them. On his first missionary journey (46 AD) the Apostle founded a series of house churches in Galatia. As soon as he left on other missions, however, Christian leaders of the old school—the Judaizers—undercut Paul's ministry. They even questioned his authority as an apostle (1 Cor 1:1). They also imposed their legalistic traditions upon the freedom-loving Galatians. Indeed, the false teachers had deceived a large segment of the church membership in the province (Gal 1:6). Their impact on the people threatened a general apostasy. The ease with which the Galatians had capitulated to the Judaizers shocked Paul.

This interference infuriated him, and he dispatched a letter to the Galatians (55 AD). With the authenticity of his ministry in question, Paul boldly set out to vindicate himself and defend his flock (Gal 1:11, 2:14). He reprimanded them but also offered the restoration of freedom—freedom to love, to accept, and to forgive themselves (and others) in Christ.

3. Special Preaching Techniques for Gentiles. First, he restated the principles of the Gospel he had previously given to them. Then he contrasted the concepts of the Judaizers (righteousness by compliance with regulations or "works") with the beauties of faith in Jesus Christ. By exalting Christ's part in the free gift of salvation for humanity, he readily dismissed the interfering Judaizers' theory that one could be justified by one's own merits.

Then Paul enhanced his presentation by skillfully alluding to the common culture of the Galatians. For instance because they loved paint and tattoos, Paul explained that he himself bore the "brand-marks of Jesus" (Gal 6:17). In many other ways Paul also employed his knowledge of Celtic culture to make his message relevant to the Galatians. This fact has inspired this study and commentary on Paul's letter, as seen through the prism of the history of the Celtic people.

4. Application to Paul's Ministry. Not only was he sensitive to the Galatian personality, but he also was fully aware of the benefits of using these insights to reach the new converts. He declared: "To the Jews I became as a Jew, so that I might win Jews; to those who are under the Law, as under the Law though not being myself under the Law, so that I might win those who are under the Law" (1 Cor 9:20). Likewise, he observed Gaelic influences to win the Galatians.

5. Results. Amid all of these concerns, Paul never lost sight of the most important lessons for the Galatians as well as for our contemporary church. These include:
- Salvation comes only by faith in Christ (Gal 2:16; 3:2 5:1).
- The Gospel teaches the legitimacy of justification by faith, without the works of the law.
- The importance of standing fast in their Christ-given liberty.
- Directives on living a Godly life.
- A detailed case study of the character of the conniving Judaizers.
- An intense appeal to the Galatians not to abuse their new found liberty in Christ nor to abandon the true Gospel.
- All must be accomplished by their living a holy life in brotherly love, a natural attribute of the Galatians (Gal 6:1-10).

6. Paul, a Model. Many Christians have depended upon Paul for their picture of a Spirit-led life. Actually, the Apostle urged the Galatians and other new Christians to imitate him as he followed Christ.

Philip Yancey cautions believers by pointing out that Paul "was hardly a typical Christian with his miraculous conversion and other supernatural interventions." He also notes that Paul had another remarkable ability—once he understood a concept intellectually, his "emotions lined up quickly and obediently." This, indeed, is a "very lofty ideal for the Christian life."[1]

Paul's letter to the Galatians demonstrates exactly what one old professor said to his class of young seminarians: "Preach the word to comfort the afflicted and to afflict the comfortable!" This the ancient Apostle did. On the one hand he castigated the Judaizers. On the other he passionately urged the Gospel of Jesus Christ as the means to recover and restore those seduced by the false teachers.

II. THE MATERIAL

The Celts. The first Europeans north of the Alps to enter recorded history! To the Mediterranean World they presented a lively, often inexplicable combination of contradictions. Feared for their "barbarism" and passion for fighting. Admired as skilled artisans and agriculturists. Appreciated for their intelligence and artistic talents. Patronized for their vanity and superstitions. These colorful, high-spirited people became the first converts to the Apostle Paul's special Christian mission to the Gentiles.

Peaking in the 3rd century BC,[2] the long period of Celtic expansion did not produce an empire, in the usual sense of the word. The people were too headstrong and independent for that. Chronically unstable, the Gaelic tribes constantly sought solidarity and security. The talent for political unification, however, always eluded them and led to their ultimate decline. At the same time, wherever the Celts spread throughout the ancient world, they quelled their opposition. They settled in as the dominant, elite class in the region and imposed their culture upon the native population. Mixed into the multiple nations of Asia Minor as they were, the Galatians produced a non-Semitic, non-classical society--and retained it far into the Christian era.[3]

Born to travel, the Celtic tribes moved in search of fertile new lands to provide themselves with more living space. Thus, they created new pastoral and farming communities. When the hereditary clan land was exhausted, they were just two solutions. The superfluous population had to be drained off into an army. Or a colony needed to be founded. (Frequently these mother-tribe and daughter-tribes shared a common name.) One Roman writer claimed that their lands "so abounded in men and in the fruits of the earth that it seemed impossible to govern so great a population."[4] Along with these peaceable endeavors, however, a lust for raiding and conquest always boiled in the Celtic blood.

THE TRAILS OF THE MANY KINGDOMS

United by language and culture more than race, the Indo-European Celts cut a wide swath through central Europe, from Iberia (Spain) and Ireland in the west to the borders of the Ukraine and Black Sea in the east. From the Po Valley

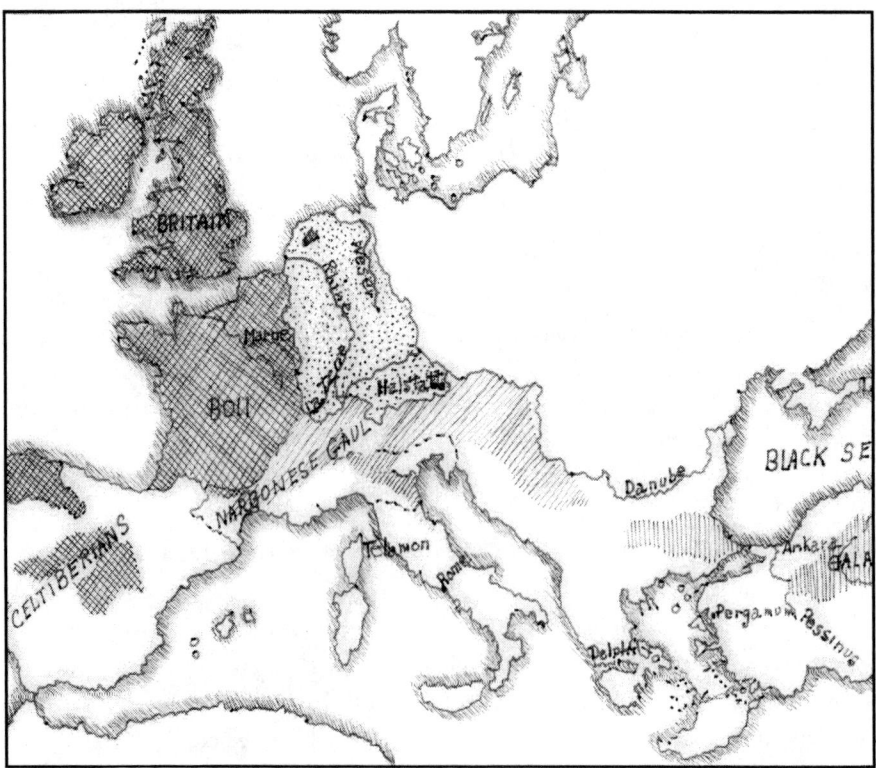

Map showing the expansion of the Celts throughout Europe. A distinctive Celtic culture began to evolve about 800 BC. By 450 BC, migrating tribes reached northern Italy. The isolated, most easterly settlement of Galatia (Central Turkey) was established in 270 BC. Seventy years later, the Celts had spread through the British Isles, as well as Brittany, France, the Netherlands, and Belgium. (Map by Eileen Minchin-Davis).

in northern Italy to the British Isles (Caledonia) and the Elbe River in the north.[5] By the end of the 4th century BC, Celtic communities were well established in the lands of the Middle Danube. Galatia represented the most easterly outpost of Celtic colonization.

In Asia Minor the Celts established their society upon a very ancient base. Anatolia (modern Turkey) began its recorded history about 1900 BC when the first Hittite Kingdom united the local tribes, centering their government in Bogazoy. Next came the Phrygian Empire in the first millennium BC, with Gordium as its capital. Finally, the roving Celtic tribes rallied in the high country around Ancyra (Ankara). Constantly fighting for their freedoms, the Galatians enjoyed just a brief, eighty-year period of independence (270-189 BC) before Rome annexed them.[6]

During the early 4th century BC, the Macedonian Empire curtailed the expansion of the Eastern Celtic tribes, confining them to northwest Hungary and southwest Slovenia. Following the death of Alexander the Great (323 BC), the Celts took advantage of the confusion to swarm through the remnants of his fractured empire.[7] Riddled with endless conflicts, the land was simply there for the taking.

Recognizing their military usefulness, both the King of Macedonia and Ptolemy of Egypt saw wisdom in employing thousands of Celtic mercenaries in their armies. Then, having established his kingdom only twenty years earlier, Nicomedes of Bithynia needed help in fighting his quarrelsome brother. At the same time, Seleucid Antiochus I of Syria was harassing him.[8]

For one gold piece per warrior, Nicomedes recruited 20,000 Celts from three tribes: the Tolistoboii, the Tectosages, and the Trocmi. At his invitation (in 278 BC), they crossed the Hellespont (Dardanelles) into Asia Minor. These people became the "Galatians" who settled primarily in north Phrygia. As usual, they arrived with their women, children and flocks.[9] With typical astuteness, the Celts realized that they could use the conflicts among the petty Greek kingdoms to their own advantage.

Unbeknown to these ancient kings, they had let the proverbial camel into the tent. The feisty Galatians refused to be contained in the land allotted to them. For many decades to come, they carried on their raids throughout Asia Minor. No one could foresee the problems these newly imported "Galatians" would create.[10] Although they were now cut off from their European roots, their strong individuality seemed to enable them to retain their Celtic customs and language well into Christian times.

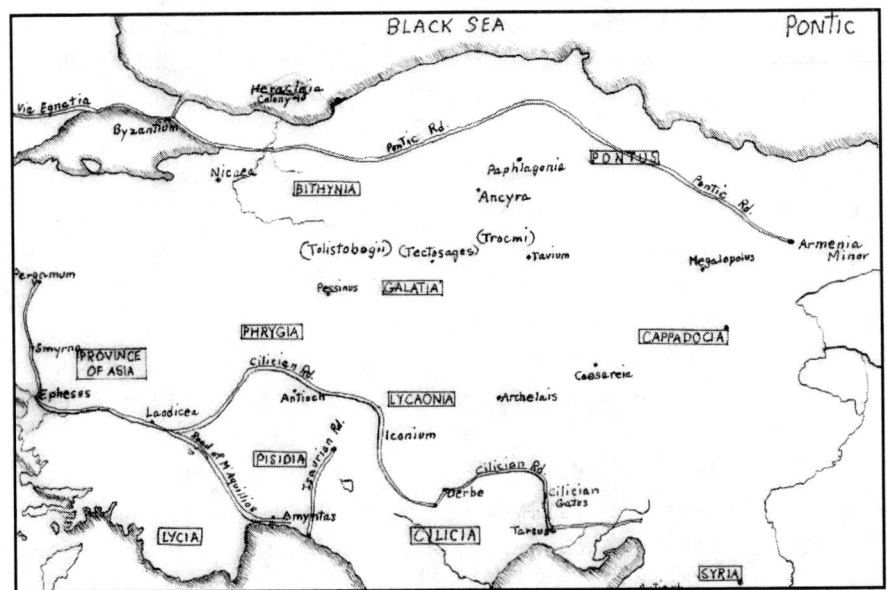

Map of the Hellenistic Kingdoms of Asia Minor. Notably, the southernmost of two Roman roads in Asia Minor passed directly through Tarsus, the home of the Apostle Paul. Thus, he had easy access to the most populous part of Anatolia. (Drawing by Eileen Minchin-Davis)

THE GALATIANS' NEIGHBORS

The Galatian tribes settled down among four small Hellenistic kingdoms.[11]

1. **Bithynia** stretched from the Bosporus along the coast of the Black Sea. Founded by 301 BC, this kingdom had remained independent within the Persian Empire. Nicomedes reigned from 278-250 BC and was chiefly instrumental in bringing the three Celtic tribes into Asia Minor.
2. **Pontus**, founded by Arionarzanes in 363 BC, survived Alexander's conquests and did not submit to Rome until 47 BC. It included the small kingdom of Paphlagonia.
3. **Cappadocia**, founded by Ariarthese I (331-322 BC) retained its independence until 15 AD.
4. **Pergamum** lay on the Aegean coastline, founded by Philetaerus (281-263 BC). It rose to power in the turmoil between Syria and Macedonia.

For the next 150 years, the Galatians lived on the margin of civilized (Mediterranean) life. They plundered far and wide, sacking cities, desecrating temples and inspiring fear wherever they struck. True, they provided Hellenistic

The Celt and the Christ

kings with vast numbers of mercenary soldiers and "for-hire" assassins. Their constant depredations, however, far outweighed any other usefulness they had to offer. They ranged over the countryside in carts, on horseback and on foot. For them, violent migration would be the rule, not the exception.[12]

THE LAND

As the bridge between Europe and the East, Asia Minor stretches from the Mediterranean coasts to the forests by the Black Sea, from the Euphrates to the Syrian Desert. In the 5th century BC, the Ionian Greeks referred to the central plateau where the roving Celts first settled as "up-country," 2,000–5,000 feet above sea level. This dusty, monotonous landscape makes one feel that the steppes of Central Asia had reached a long, naked arm toward the color and sophistication of the Mediterranean coastline.

History has shown that few cities flourished among the Galatians. From the start, they preferred to build their traditional hill-forts and farms, living with the indigenous population. The Greeks referred to the Celtic settlements as *Koinon Galaton*, "The Commonwealth of Galatia." A too-sophisticated title, perhaps. Actually, no overall leader emerged among them for a very long time. In fact, their druidic electoral system insured that no despot could easily arise among the Gaelic tribes.[13] At the same time, this political arrangement prevented any unification of power.

The Roman historians, Strabo (63 BC–21 AD) and Livy (59 BC–17 AD), both described the barrenness of the Galatian plateau, ringed by mountains. It contrasted unfavorably with the "rich woodland cover" of the fertile lowlands

Left: The "fairy chimneys" are unusual rock formations in Cappadocia. Early Christians took refuge in the caves of this moon-like landscape. Right: As they have done for millenia, sheep, goats, and a lone donkey graze along a roadside near Gordium. (Photos by Forrest Hannon, Sherman Oaks, California.)

and valleys. Travelers have marveled that men could even find the means to live there.

With their technological skills in agriculture, however, the resourceful Celts literally forced crops out of the ground. They pastured animals. In time, grain, wool and salt brought much wealth to Galatia. Among the best metal craftsmen in the ancient world, the Celts actually created Europe's first "Industrial Revolution" with their inventions: seamless iron rims for chariot wheels, shoes for horses, iron plow-shares, handsaws, chisels, chain armor. Even a rotary flour mill for the housewives.[14]

Recent scholarship has shown that the Celts were also the great road-builders of Europe—even though the Romans have reaped most of the credit for this engineering feat. Julius Caesar's account of his Gallic campaigns show him moving rapidly across Gaul on an already well-constructed road system. Furthermore, upon arrival in Britain, he found himself opposed by the heavy, four-wheeled war-chariots of the native Britons. They had built roads over the bogs with wooden logs—roads well engineered to sustain weighty traffic. Not only did their warfare call for efficient transportation, but the Celts, keenly interested in commerce, knew that they had to link their trade centers together.

Not surprisingly, then, two of Rome's best provincial highways passed through Galatia. With their brisk love of trade and their flamboyant material tastes, the Galatians took advantage of the two important overland routes that passed through their territory: the Royal Road from Sardis to Susa, Persia, and the Common Road between Ephesus and the Euphrates. In addition to carrying military traffic, the roads joined the frontiers to the hinterland. Eventually, Anatolia's network of roads would extend for 5,600 Roman miles.[15]

THE CELTIC LANGUAGES

The Celts were a really remarkable *mélange* of different tribes and ethnic groups. The Gallic elite conquered and enslaved indigenous people, and then fused all together with a common language, culture and religion. For instance, the Celtic imprint lives on in Europe, preserved in such place names as: London ("Fortress of Lugh," a chief Celtic god); Paris ("Parisii," a migrant Gaelic tribe); the Danube River (for the Celtic Goddess Danu);[16] and many more.

The Greek name for the Celts, *Keltoi*, means "hidden or secret." This may refer to the Celtic reluctance to put any of their vast store of knowledge into written form. Julius Caesar observed that the druids (Celtic priests) forbade the people to commit their knowledge to writing. Therefore, wisdom, history, phi-

The Celt and the Christ

A Galatian Tomb near Gordium.[17] **Many ancient Galatians died as they lived—isolated on the high plateau.**

losophy, science and the entire justice system had to be committed to memory and transmitted orally. Reliance on written documents, the druids believed, only impaired the mind and the memory.[18] No wonder it took up to twenty years to be educated as a druid.

Hence, we have no written record of the Celts before their collision with Mediterranean civilizations. Those writers were naturally biased observers of the Celtic scene.[19] The Mediterranean powers viewed the Celts with both fear and fascination. Greco-Roman writers concentrated on the differences between Celtic society—so unlike Rome's rational state-controlled civilization. With the coming of Christianity, however, no one seized upon learning and literacy more eagerly than the converted Celts.

A huge diversity of languages persisted in Asia Minor. It is said that Mithradates the Great spent eight years mastering all twenty-five of the languages his subjects spoke, including Gaelic.[20] Both Strabo and the poet Lucan attest to the fact that, like their fellow Gauls in Europe, the Galatians left no written documents in their own language. They did, however, speak their native tongue. To be sure, they were never illiterate. They used Greek and (later) Latin for secular and business affairs. And did so very correctly.

Even as the Galatian tribes scattered throughout the southern areas of the province, they preserved their language and traditions for a surprisingly long time. More than 300 years after Paul wrote his letter to the Galatians, St. Jerome declared that the language he heard around Ancyra in Galatia closely resembled that spoken by the Treveri tribe at Moselle, in Gaul (France).[21]

CELTIC ADMINISTRATION IN GALATIA

Strabo[22] described the three groups of Celts who settled Galatia. From him, we have our first picture of how Celtic government worked.[23] He observed that they all used the same language and were alike in every way. Their tribal organization called for a division of four. Each "tetrarchy" was governed by the tetrarch himself, with a judge, a military commander, and two junior commanders, all of them subordinate to him. The council of twelve tetrarchs consisted of 300 men. They assembled in the Drynemetos (Celtic druidic "grove of oak trees").[24]

The **Tolistoboii** came from the area of the Danube to settle the upper Valley of the Sangarios, claiming as their centers Pessinus and Gordium,[25] the strongholds of the long-dead Phrygian kings. On the way to Asia Minor, however, Chief Brennus of the Tolistoboii detoured with his elite troops to sweep through Macedonia and attack the Oracle of Apollo at Delphi, Greece. Gifted craftsmen in metals, the Celts were always ready to seize a hoard of gold and treasure. Such as would have been readily available at Delphi.[26] Legend has it that the god Apollo appeared in a thunderbolt and prevented the looting and desecration of his shrine. Another version avows that the Celts did indeed carry much treasure back to Gaul. In any case, Brennus himself died in the battle. His clansmen pressed on into Asia Minor.

Still further east, the **Techtosages** appropriated the area adjoining Phrygia, around Tavium, with Ancyra as their stronghold. The **Trocmi** occupied the most easterly territory, from Pontus to Cappadocia. In 281 BC another detachment of Celts gained a temporary foothold in Thrace and established the Kingdom of Tylis on the Black Sea. Eventually, however, they had to retreat into Bulgaria.

Although the Celts made no more attacks on Greece, groups of warriors still wandered about seeking mercenary employment. Wherever a fight was brewing, that is where they wanted to be. Indeed, no one made a better mercenary than a Celt, and they willingly served in whatever army would hire them. For the next

The Celt and the Christ

fifty years these Celts raided the countryside. Apart from agriculture, warfare was their most natural occupation. Thus the Gaelic tribes spread from the Atlantic to the Balkans, firmly planting their culture as they migrated. They meddled constantly in the affairs of neighboring states, until no one knew what to do with them. Early on, the Galatians, to a man, became *persona non grata*.

THE FIRST KINGDOM OF GALATIA

The fundamental Celtic lack of political unity naturally left the Galatians vulnerable to the Greek kingdoms around them. To say nothing of the power of Rome. In the Battle of Olympus, near Pessinus, the Roman general, Volso slaughtered the Tolistoboii and the Trocmi. Some 40,000 more of them (including women and children) were sold into slavery. Then he defeated the Tectosages at Ancyra and (technically) turned Galatia over to the Kingdom of Pergamum.

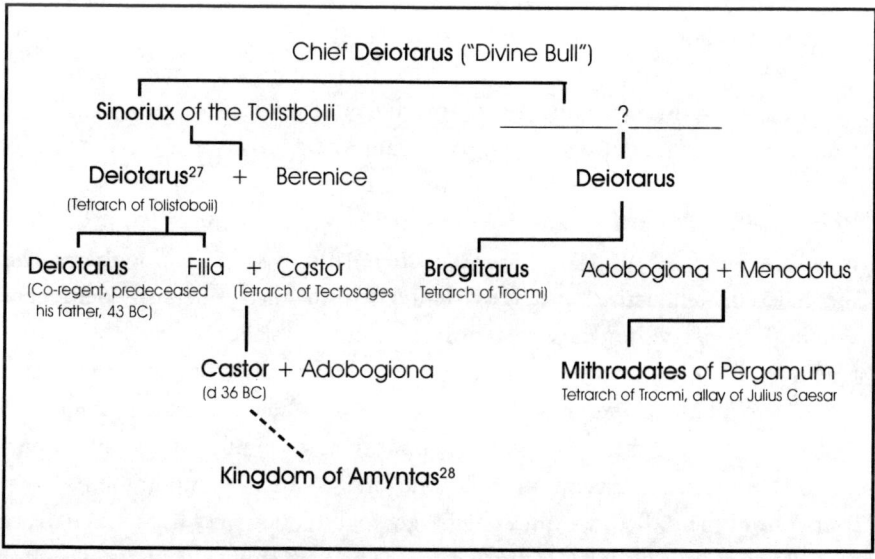

The Galatian Dynastic Family of Deiotarus. This diagram demonstrates how the three tribes in Galatia intermingled, despite the fierce inter-familial violence that raged among them.

In 189 BC, Ortagion made the first attempt at unification of the three Galatian groups. A charming, highly intelligent chieftain of the Tolistoboii, he tried to form a loose confederation of tribes. He achieved, however, only a fleeting success. We have a list (181 BC) of many chieftains of the Galatian septs[29] who refused to give up their tribal form of government. Their proud tradition dictated that the Celts should gain leadership positions by personal bravery and charisma alone, not by birth. Ortagion disappeared suddenly. Polybius records an interview he had with Chiomara, the chief's wife. Apparently, at that time, she and her husband lived in exile in Sardis.[30]

THE GALATIAN FACTIONS

Prior to Roman rule, little Hellenization had occurred in the interior of Anatolia. Still, the Galatians, who had settled in neighboring areas had "civilized" themselves, as was needful to insure their prosperity. The Celts were, after all, the archetypal enemies of Mediterranean culture.[31] While the Seleucids and Attalids strove to confine the Galatians to the area around Ancyra, these volatile tribes never rested from trying to maintain their independence and migratory habits.

Thus, for some 250 years the Galatians survived among their neighbors. Sometimes negotiating alliances, sometimes being overwhelmed. Sometimes conquering and collecting tribute. In any case, they were always manipulating and spoiling for a fight. No wonder the Apostle Paul found the Galatian Christians embroiled in factions and given to fragmentation.

By 123 BC the Celtic tribes became strong enough to ally themselves with Rome itself and to make a pact for the overthrow of the King of Pontus. Within thirty-five years (88 BC), however, that friendship ended in a bloodbath. Then the Galatians fell victim to their own integrity and their inherently democratic system. Mithradates V (The Great) of Pontus and Paphlagonia invited sixty major Galatian chieftains to dine at his court and discuss his war plans. Hospitality being such a basic principle of Celtic society, Mithradates counted on all of the Galatians' entering the feasting hall without their weapons. An easy situation to exploit. Just as the guests began to eat, the king's soldiers fell upon them, slaying every one of them. Because three chiefs had not attended the banquet, the treacherous Mithradates dispatched his assassins to pick off those last three tetrarchs in individual attacks.[32]

Deiotarus, son of Dumnorix of the Tolistoboii, was the sole survivor of this mass murder. Naturally, he knew that such a violation of the laws of hospitality had to be avenged. Therefore, fourteen years later, Deiotarus unseated the governor whom Mithradates had installed in Galatia. His patience paid off. Wisely, he fortified his position by making friendship treaties with Rome. Indeed, Cicero sang the praises of Deiotarus as an ally to every commander in the province.[33] Rome, however, had a complicated task sorting out the allegiances among their

The Celt and the Christ

neighbors in the colonies. Indeed, for a considerable time after Asia Minor came under Roman power, the stubborn Galatians held out, still retaining enough political freedom to maintain their tetrarchies.

Meanwhile, having accrued a great empire of his own, Mithradates made the strategic mistake of declaring war on Rome. For once the Galatians were on the right side. With the help of Rome, Deiotarus unseated the great King of Pontus and drove him into exile in the Crimea. Finally, in 63 BC, the Galatians must have enjoyed sweet satisfaction when they learned that Mithradates (in the middle of a suicide attempt) had been slain by a Celtic chieftain named Bituitus![34]

GALATIA AND ROME

What did it really mean to become a Roman Province?

Much weakened by Mithradates' murder of the tetrarchs, the Galatian elite class faced inevitable changes in their social order. Obviously, a divided leadership posed too much of a risk. Therefore, Deiotarus, ever the astute politician, moved Galatia firmly into the Roman orbit where the kingdom became more pro-Roman and less Greek. He adopted Roman methods of military training and learned the Roman art of estate management. At the time, in the old Celtic way, he never made an important decision without consulting the augurers. The Galatian leaders and Roman authorities, however, seem to have been linked mainly by political interests, a situation which prevailed to the time of Christ and beyond.[35]

By the middle of the 1st century BC, the Galatian aristocracy had become much Hellenized. Their kings had honors in Athens, Nicaea, Laodicea and Ephesus.[36] From 29 AD onward the Imperial Cult of Emperor Worship prevailed. The Romans had shrines in Ephesus and Nicaea, and the Greeks had the same in Pergamum and Nicomedia. A clever policy, this, for bonding with the provincials, insuring loyalty, and sustaining civic life.

A portrait of the King of Pontus, Mithridates Eupator VI (131–63 BC), taken from a contemporary coin. In his attempt to win the political game in Asia Minor, he treacherously murdered a large embassy of Galatian Celts.[37]

This strong "Emperor Cult" also worked in Galatia where Augustus was regarded as both man and god. Evidence exists to show that Celtic leaders participated in the cult. The Galatian aristocracy freely blended Greek, Roman, and Celtic traditions. This included animal sacrifices and augury, and gladiatorial competitions. Also, distributions of grain and oil exhibited the generosity of the wealthy families.[38] In time, the large Galatian landowners merged with the major Greek cities and colonies. Most of these aristocrats, however, could still proudly trace their origins back to the Celtic tribal chieftains.

Under Augustus, Roman annexation also produced the emergence and growth of cities and colonies in Asia Minor. In the more backward regions of northern Galatia, for example, three newly fortified cities appeared as part of the new urbanization of the province. They covered this heartland of the Celtic tribes: Pessinus (Tolistoboii), Ancyra (Tectosages), and Tavium (Trocmi). Thus, a complex, two-way flow of influence passed between Ruling Rome and Provincial Galatia. Politicians in Asia Minor quickly learned to draw on Galatian manpower and to benefit from its thriving rural economy.[39]

As usual, the Galatians established trade centers, to serve their flamboyant tastes. They suffered, however, from banditry. The Romans had reason to fear rural Galatia for both man-made and natural dangers. Moreover, city-dwellers despised and mistrusted the villagers, exploiting them whenever they could. City life was based on an elaborate, artificial culture and aristocratic ambitions. The resilient country people, on the other hand, had to survive on the land, using traditional peasant crafts and skills.[40] Diet, lifestyle, language, names, and patterns of government differed radically. Nonetheless, while Greek was widely (but unevenly) adopted in the countryside, Celtic languages were spoken for many centuries, into late Antiquity.[41]

The early Roman Empire laid heavy administrative requirements on the province. Eventually, however, she could not efficiently manage her more distant provinces. Harassed by the Norsemen, Rome had to withdraw from Britain between 410 and 442 AD. In the east, the irascible Celtic population of Galatia (along with their neighbors) posed a similar problem.

THE COMING OF CHRISTIANITY

The Apostle Paul lived in these "fluid times" of the early Roman Empire. He, perhaps, did not reach Ancyra, but he is believed to have visited the important religious center of Pessinus. Also, a number of obviously Christian funerary texts have been found on tombs on the plateau between Ancyra and Iconium. Because they date from the mid-1st century AD, Paul's preaching must have been carried through the region quickly.[42] The main cities he would have visited within

The Celt and the Christ 15

the Galatian area would have been Iconium, Lydia, Derbe, and Pisidian Antioch (Acts 13:14, 51, 14:6).

"If studies had been taken in the Roman Empire in 65 AD on religious preferences, they would have shown: 51% for Jupiter, 30% for Zeus, 9% for Mithra, and 1% for Jesus. So, St. Paul, who was promoting Jesus, might have just gone home said the heck with it. But St. Paul stayed—and that made the difference" (Harry Golden, Religious News Service).

On the edge of the Galatian Plateau, Psidian Antioch at first welcomed Paul and Barnabas and then stoned them (Acts 13:44–51). Afterwards the Apostle fled to Iconium and then on to Lystra in Lyconia (the home of Timothy) (Acts 14:3–7).

Mitchell observes that Christianity did not take firm hold of the rural population before the 3rd century AD. Paul's epistle to the Galatians, he says, threw "an intense spotlight" on a very restricted area, southern Galatia. At the same time, however, Anatolian pagan beliefs "were accompanied by a severe moral code" (of Celtic derivation). They provided soil "where Judaism and Christianity readily took root." These ideals persisted in Pergamum, Smyrna, Sardis, Philadelphia—and particularly Phrygia.[43] Indeed, once the Celtic spirit was broken, moral standards became quite depleted.[44]

Being far from their original homelands, the Galatians naturally underwent changes from Hellenism. Yet, certain basic characteristics emerged wherever the wandering tribes settled. Practices and personality traits that the "civilizing" influences from the Mediterranean did little to dissipate. As an isolated enclave within Anatolia, the Galatians exemplified a "Celtic Community." Throughout its checkered career in Asia Minor, Galatia still retained its ethnic identity. At the same time, they astutely adopted the material culture of their new homeland.[45] Paul's epistle reveals several of their distinctive weaknesses: Idolatry, sorcery, jealousy, hatred, murder, drunkenness, vanity, and so forth. They also exemplified good traits: Hospitality, spirituality, inventiveness, sense of justice, love of learning, and celebration of beauty.

At grass-roots level, what made a Celt a Celt never changed very much. Neither here nor there, then or now! Wherever they went their culture tended to dominate rather than be absorbed. We cannot ascertain just when Galatia's Celtic language, customs and historical traditions ceased to exist. It occurred, however, centuries after Paul's visit and long after he wrote his feisty letter to the Galatian Christians.[46]

Celtic Character Traits

1. Artistry, Love of the Beautiful
2. Vanity in Dress

3. Love of Celebration and Drinking
4. Cleanliness

5. Skilled Agriculturists
6. Invention of Tools

7. Love of Nature
8. Appreciation of the "Every Day"

9. Individuality, Love of Freedom
10. Instability and Passion

11. Exploration, Travel, and Adventure
12. Love of Competition and Fighting

13. Love of Learning (from Druids)
14. Love of Solitude

15. Law, Just and Practical
16. Earth versus the Otherworld

17. Spritiuality, Mysticism, Superstition

Part 1

1. Departing from Tradition

"I was outstripping many of my Jewish contemporaries in my boundless devotion to the traditions of my ancestors (Gal 1:14).... It is men of faith who are Abraham's sons [for] God would justify the Gentiles through faith" (Gal. 3:8,9).

The life of the Greek biographer, Plutarch (46–120 AD), overlapped with that of the Apostle Paul. A master of incisive storytelling, Plutarch introduces us to Camma, the wife of the Galatian Chieftain Sinatos. Of a devout turn of mind, she also served as a priestess to the Goddess Brigantu, the Celtic equivalent of the Greek "Virgin Huntress," Artemis.

In the customary turmoil of Galatian tribal politics, another leader, the Chieftain Sinorix ("King of Storms") murdered her husband. Then, to consolidate his power, he demanded that Camma marry him. She appeared to acquiesce to his will, and the wedding went forward. At the crucial point in the ceremony when the bridal couple was to drink wine from a common cup, Camma managed secretly to drop poison into the drink.

Sinorix reached for the cup, his privilege as the bridegroom. "Wait!" Camma restrained his hand. "I will drink first."

The bridegroom stepped back. All suspicions at rest, he watched Camma drink. Obviously, she had wholly given her allegiance to him. Then, he himself took a long draught from the cup. Within moments, both bride and groom lay dead before the altar. As dead as the unfortunate Sinatos who had already been sent to his grave by treachery.[1]

No one should underestimate the fierce loyalty a Galatian could give to tribe and family.

TRIBAL LOYALTY

Even after Asia Minor came (nominally) under Roman rule, the Galatians enjoyed a considerable amount of political freedom. Both Greeks and Romans found it expedient, insofar as possible, to let them live according to their traditions. In face of these powerful Hellenistic forces, the Celts tried to maintain their independence by forming various alliances among themselves and with their neighbors. Some advantageous and others disastrous.

The requirements of kinship held Gaelic society together. Kinship came by natural (genetic) means or by adoption and fosterage. A Celt had but one allegiance, to his/her family. The tribe, however, was one vast, extended family, made up of groups (to four generations) descended from one common ancestor.

So solid was this organization that the Celts tended to dominate wherever they conquered. Remnants of their tribal organization lasted well into the Christian era. This, long after we would have expected the powerful influences of the Mediterranean world to have overwhelmed them.

Most ancient societies were strictly hierarchical, and one usually had scant hopes of ever escaping to a higher standard of living. That basic three-fold structure is to be found in many places—Judaism included. First came the **elite/priestly class**, followed by the **warrior/aristocracy**, and then the **farmers** (followed by slaves who had no standing at all). These same basic class lines also prevailed in Celtic cultures where seven distinctive levels of talent evolved.

THE TRIPARTITE SYSTEM OF CELTIC SOCIETY

The Aristocratic Intelligentsia. This elite, priestly class maintained their high lifestyle by constant battles and raids.

1. **The Sacred King/Chieftain** (Irish, *tuath*). The king of the tribe/clan came from this warrior-elite class and had powerful "divine rights" over his people. A ritual leader, he had to practice three virtues: piety, bravery, and generosity. He also had to display physical, mental and spiritual perfection. He surrounded himself with advisers (mostly his close relatives). To disgrace himself or to fail in any of the above capa-

Departing from Tradition

bilities could result in his being deposed and even sacrificed. Or, if old age destroyed his mental and/or physical powers, he could be executed.[2] Many of the "saints" of the early Celtic Christian Church came from this top social rank.

2. **The Druids** (L *druidae*) held equal status with the chieftains, attending to religious rites, the administration of the law, and the education of the youth. They also maintained the genealogies of the clan, as well as its myths and legends. Although they sometimes appeared as characters of terror, the druids functioned chiefly as sages and philosophers.

3. **The Bards** (Gr *bardoi*). These gifted people excelled in the complicated techniques of self-expression, so dear to the Gaulish heart. In satisfying the Celtic hunger for music, eloquence, and the beautiful, they could pretty well "name their price." As "wordsmiths," musicians, and guardians of the language, they (like the other craftsmen) also enjoyed great social advantages. Their practice of conveying messages in verse-form made ideas easier to remember.

4. **The Seers/Diviners**. Masters of astrology and magic, the Celts allegedly required ritual human sacrifice, on occasion, to facilitate the making of predictions.

The Equites. Unlike some other Indo-European cultures (India), the Gallic tribes did not have a caste system. Any equite could aspire to the professional classes. These included: (1) The nobility, barons, and knights; (2) The warriors charged with defending the clan, and (3) The landowning free men, responsible for feeding the tribe.

5. **Craftsmen**. The Celts had extraordinary gifts in art and engineering. Living by their talents, blacksmiths, metalworkers and carpenters enjoyed many privileges and made up an honorable middle-class.

A stone head of a Celtic diety, from a sanctuary in Bohemia. In addition to his torc, he has another distinctive indicator of high rank—a huge moustache covering his mouth. Aristocrats shaved their cheeks and cultivated heavy moustaches. Peasants either shaved entirely or had short beards.[3]

The Plebes. These people became the foundation of Celtic society, supplying the needs of their chief. Because their culture was co-dependent, the king became father, protector and provider for his people. Landowning was the measure of a man. All of the landless people stood at the bottom of the social ladder, automatically "unfree." Thus forced into servitude, they mixed with slaves and the captives collected from raids and battles.[4]

6. **The Farmers**. In pre-historic times, the Celts discovered agriculture to be superior to the old "hunting and gathering" modes of their ancestors. As a result, wherever Gaelic settlements arose, we find planting, harvesting, crop rotation, and so forth. Indeed, most of today's farm implements and domestic conveniences are of Celtic invention. They also became pastoralists, grazing cattle, sheep, and goats. Despite all of these civilized pursuits, at a moment's notice, they were ready to travel, to migrate, and to fight.

A Farmer. The Celts depended on farming and cattle for their tribal survival. As inventors of metal tools, they added an iron point to the simple wooden plow, a design still in use. (Drawing by Eileen Minchin-Davis)

7. **Servants and Slaves**. Landowning was the measure of a man. All of the landless people stood at the bottom of the social ladder, automatically "unfree." They included drovers, hired laborers, servants and other people required to sustain the tribal system. Forced into servitude, they mixed with slaves and the captives collected from raids and battles.[5] Slaves remained as they were until the maturing of Christianity.[6]

The Celtic tribal hierarchy, however, had some forward-looking features unique to itself. The relationship between the aristocracy and those below them was not entirely negative. Moreover, the legal system allowed people (both men and women) to learn, to aspire to higher callings, and by diligence rise above the place where they had been born.

Departing from Tradition

To such a strong, but oddly flexible, society as this, the Apostle Paul brought the Christian Gospel.

THE FOUR QUARTERS OF THE GALATIAN STORY

As Paul faced the task of evangelizing the Galatians, he seems to have related to them in four distinct ways. First, by his own admission, the Apostle knew more about being ethnic—about being a Jew (Phil 3:4-5)—than almost anyone else we can think of. Through personal experience, he knew the rigors of the religious disciplines of being both a Jew and an Apostle. Then, he took on the still-greater challenge of leading believers from Judaism to Christianity.

Second, when he went to carry the Christian Gospel to the Galatians, Paul encountered this closely bonded tribal society, thoroughly imbued with the beliefs and customs of a 2,000-year history. These people acquired a heritage, first from the Hittites and later absorbed by the Celts from Central Europe. Fortified by common language and religion more than race, they tended to remain homogenous. Their traditions would endure centuries of political disasters, and strong remnants are to be found in Gaelic Britain and France today. Paul, therefore, faced an enormous cultural "wall."

Third, we may add to these elements, pressures from Rome. By Paul's time, the Galatians (along with neighboring kingdoms) lived as the most easterly province of the Empire. They "Hellenized" themselves, but only insofar as the new customs served their practical purposes. Otherwise, their own customs prevailed.

The fourth component of the Apostle's mission was the fresh, new message about Christ. Paul and his fellow-evangelists had taken up the challenge to "go into all the world" (Mk 16:15). And, wherever they went, they managed to turn that world "upside down" (Acts 17:6). The experience of the Galatians would be equally upsetting. Paul would come to them with a new doctrine, to be sure, but he would wisely customize his presentation to suit their character traits. Appreciatively he would appeal to their best qualities and would also fearlessly denounce their weaknesses.

With his customary astuteness, Paul understood his audience more clearly than we might initially suppose, on a first reading of his letter. Not only did he have insight into their social mores, but he also chose metaphors, illustrations, and patterns of argument familiar to their inquiring minds and cultural tastes. Moreover, with his own Hebrew insights, he knew that the Celts lived by laws more comprehensive (and often more humane) than even those of the Romans.

The intermingling of these four elements is the subject of this book. These lines opposed and crisscrossed one another in various times and places, and then finally blended into a whole—the Christianizing of the first Europeans.

THE FOUNDATION OF ANCIENT CELTIC LAW

A common culture, language, law, and religion linked the Gaelic tribes. Therefore, since the experience of the British Celts has been much more fully preserved than that of the Galatians, we shall make the continental leap from Asia Minor back to Ireland.

When Christianity first came to Britain, the missionaries found the Celtic tribes observing very ancient and sophisticated laws.[7] The regulations omitted nothing: Rank and status in kinship, personal relationships, and property ownership, offenses and punishments, contracts and pledges, and provisions for the teaching and maintenance of the system.[8] In Ireland, a chieftain, Ollamh Fodhla, seems to have been the first to codify the legal system in 714 BC.

Arriving in Ireland, fresh from his education in Rome, St. Patrick brought with him the five books of Moses. The High King of Tara, Laoghaire (Leary), affirmed the Brehon (*breaitheamh*, "the judge") legal system.[9] Now Patrick had a well-developed foundation of justice on which to build his Christian message. One that carefully defined each person's place in society. Indeed, several of the sophisticated Brehon laws ran contrary to Roman policy. Unique in at least three areas, they favored the needs of women, children and the elderly.

In council, Patrick adapted these ancient pagan precepts to Christian uses (428-436 AD). Indeed, he felt that they had been inspired by the Holy Spirit and needed only small modifications. The Brehon Laws prevailed through the 7th- and 8th centuries, until the Celtic Church gave way to the Roman.[10]

A sampling of a few cases will give a sense of the meticulous care the Celts invested in their society.

Interestingly, the earliest laws of "Sick Maintenance" go back to the Hittites,[11] a distinctly local connection for the Galatians. Among the many regulations regarding Gaelic views on healthcare is instruction about a person who was either accidentally or purposefully injured. The one causing the wounds was required to take his victim home to his house and care for him until he recovered. Or until he died. At the same time, he had to look after the relatives who had been thus deprived of support. Also he cared for the victim's retinue, which (if he had high status) might be large. The aggressor's kinfolk had to help care for the injured, even in his own house, if necessary. Moreover, they had to pay all medical expenses and fulfill the patient's work responsibilities during the convalescence period.[12]

The Gaelic tribes also had a carefully administered retirement plan. An elderly working man had to notify his chief when he could no longer work. The

Departing from Tradition

tribal council then provided him with a house (17 paces in diameter) and bread. He received one cow to provide milk. He was required to bathe once a week and wash his hair every Saturday. Socially, he could advise the elders and tell stories at the firesides on long winter nights.[13]

Brehon Law protected the poor. For instance, needles were very important to women. If someone stole a needle from a poverty-stricken woman, it deprived her of her living. Therefore, the fine would be higher than if the needle had belonged to the Queen.[14] The laws were not so much interested in retribution for the victims as in fines. The latter measure enabled restitution to be made.

Further on the domestic scene, a husband could legally hit his wife to "correct her." If the blow, however, left a mark she was entitled to the equivalent of her bride-price in compensation. If she wished, she could divorce him. Actually she had several grounds for divorce, including her husband's impotence or homosexuality.[15]

The committing of non-capital crimes, such as lying, perjury, and fraud, could be costly. Even if the offender was allowed to live, he completely lost his tribal status. The Gauls generally favored the enforcing of fines over purely retaliatory measures. In fact, they used six kinds of fines, including the loss of the Honor Price (Irish *Einachlan*), a devastating social and financial event. Nonetheless, preserving life took precedence over the simple punishment of crime.

Some Features of the Celtic/Irish Brehon Law[16]

1. Purposeful. Designed to prevent mayhem among a vigorous, volatile people.
2. Democratic. Not decreed by the king but agreed to by the people.
3. Communal. Kinship valued above financial or social institutions.
4. Flexible. Reviewed and updated at the Festival of Tara, every 3 years.
5. Compassionate. Concerned for the weakest in society.
6. Punitive. Administered both capital punishment and fines.
7. Truthful. Strictly managed pledges, loans, and contracts.
8. Selective. The succession of power determined by ability and election, not birth.
9. Personal. Provided rules for every relationship in life.
10. Conservative. Held to the old ways, changing only slowly.

Obviously, in Paul's time, the Galatians did not have access to the Irish laws described above. Assuredly, however, they did have the druidic code on which the Brehon Laws were based. That was a truly enlightened rule of life reaching back untold centuries into their heritage and providing a substantial bond linking the migrating tribes all over Europe.

THE GOSPEL CHALLENGE

The preponderance of evidence shows that the Galatians were first converted to the Christian faith by Paul's ministry. He was also instrumental in nurturing and "strengthening" the churches established in Anatolia (Acts 18:23). While he was with them, they expressed strong affection and great esteem for his person and his work. As soon as the Apostle left Galatia, however, Judaizing

A Jewish baptism. Note that the leaders (with staff) and spectators on the bank watch while the candidates immerse themselves in the river.[17]

teachers came with insinuations that drew the new converts from the truths of the Apostle's teaching. Grossly perverting the great doctrine of justification by faith, they declared that those who embraced faith in Christ should also observe the law of Moses. Finally, they slandered Paul, assassinating his character and reputation.

Departing from Tradition 23

Departing from Tradition 25

This kind of interference, known as Judaizing, was not a new phenomenon. It had a long history among Gentiles wherever Jews settled (Es 8:17). Plutarch tells of a freed Gentile slave who was accused of "Judaizing," or living like a Jew. The renowned Jewish historian, Josephus, reported that the Gentile Metilius saved his own life by promising that he would Judaize, even to circumcision. He also described a time when Syrians had some of their citizens "under suspicions [of]... Judaizing."[18] Even the Roman Governor Pilate told the Jews that his wife was "god-fearing and more than ever Judaizes with you."[19]

It is apparent that the word "Judaizing" encompasses Gentiles who, for political, economic or religious reasons, converted to Judaism. They then lived like Hebrews in every facet of their experience. They went further than sympathizing with their Jewish neighbors. They persisted in "out-Jewing" the Jews. Only by baptism and circumcision, these teachers said, could the Gentiles become the actual spiritual children of Abraham. Only thus they could be recognized as heirs of the promise in Genesis 15 (v. 5-6).

THE MISSION OF THE JUDAIZERS

In Scripture, the word "Judaizing" appears exclusively in the book of Galatians (2:14). There, Paul rebukes Peter for refusing to eat with the Gentiles at Antioch. The latter had been intimidated by the faction who compelled "the Gentiles to Judaize."

The profession of teaching and transforming Gentiles into Jews was the vigorous mission of the Judaizers. Gentile adherents to Judaism, they said, must fully accept the Mosaic law and must observe all Jewish customs, especially the rite of circumcision. The latter ceremony completed their participation in the Abrahamic promises and secured their positions as "spiritual sons."

In the early years of Christianity, some of these strict adherents to all things Hebrew wore the Judaizing nomenclature like a badge of honor. They transferred their loyalty to "The Way," the name assigned to the first Christian believers after Pentecost (Acts 19-9). These Hebrew converts, however, did not forego the practice of their ceremonial laws. In time, they became "a thorn" in the Apostle Paul's flesh as they doggedly followed him from region to region "correcting" his presentation of the Gospel of Jesus. Everywhere they imposed a mixture of Judaism and diluted Christianity on those whom Paul had won to Christ.

In due course, the Judaizers arrived in Galatia, where they seized the affections and minds of the fledgling congregations, with all of their gullibility. Paul's converts quickly abandoned the gospel he had taught them. They eagerly engaged in the legalistic rituals of the false teachers.

In his letter to the Galatians Paul faced the challenge of redressing the counterfeit influence of these intruders. To score points successfully with the unstable Galatians and, at the same time, counteract the depredations of his detractors, Paul resorted to a "confessional didactic." In raw, vivid detail he gave testimony of his past. He told them how he had railed against the first believers in Christ and persecuted them (Acts 7:54-8:1). In fact, he even admitted that back then, he "was outstripping many of [his] Jewish contemporaries in [his] boundless devotion to the traditions of [his] ancestors" (Gal 1:14).

PAUL'S QUALIFICATIONS AS AN APOSTLE

The Greek word "apostle" literally means "one who is sent." The corresponding Hebrew word describes the role of an "ambassador" or a messenger who functions with the full authority of those who sent him. For example, the majority of the twelve post-crucifixion apostles had been chosen by Christ. As "servants of the circumcised" (Rom 15:8; Gal 2:7), they were sent with the full authority of Jesus to preach the Kingdom, heal the sick, and cast out devils (Mt 10:7-8; Lk 9:2; 10:9). Paul, on the other hand, had been "made an apostle" with a particular mission to the Gentiles (Gal 1:16; I Cor 9:16).

The brilliant pupil of the esteemed Hebrew teacher, Gamaliel, Paul confessed that he was not only among the leaders of those bent on destroying the early church, but also that he "went beyond" his fellow-students in his practice of Judaism (Gal 1:13-14). His sole object, at that time, had been to protect the faith and preserve the traditions of the fathers. Ultimately, however, it became the "good pleasure" of God to separate him [Paul] from his legalistic past (Gal 1:15-16). He now taught the Good News about Jesus, the Son of God and founder of this new faith—even if it should require his death.

Recalling Jesus' strong sense of mission, Paul fearlessly announced the coming of God's Kingdom. He simply lived for the coming of that Kingdom, repeatedly calling on others to join him in his mission. He echoed Jesus' bold declaration: "As the Father has sent me, so send I you" (John 20:21). Paul was personally convicted that his call to be an apostle was both extraordinary and divine (Gal 1:17). His mission to the Galatians, he pointed out, confirmed this high calling (Gal 2:1-10).

The Gospel, as far as Paul understood it, charged him to be "determined to know nothing among you, except Jesus Christ, and Him crucified" (1 Cor 2:2). He would never "boast except in the cross of our Lord Jesus Christ" (Gal 6:14). In the Good News he brought to the Galatians, Jesus alone would be central.

Departing from Tradition

Since Christ died for their sins, that made salvation available to them through faith alone (1 Cor 15:3-5). Therefore, Gentiles joined the family of Abraham by faith, not by the works of circumcision.

PAUL'S PROPOSITION

In order to accomplish this monumental task of changing the minds of the wavering Galatians (again) Paul resorted to two effective methods. First, he rebuked them for embracing the perverted gospel of his opponents (Gal 1:6-10). Sparing no words, he announced emphatically that theirs was the "gospel according to man... received from man" (Gal 1:11-12). He engaged them with the very scriptures that had been used to enslave them to the ceremonial laws of Judaism. Herein lay "The Way" into the grace-filled world of Christ's Gospel.

Second, he astutely pointed to the passage underscored by those who had taught them "another gospel." (And a most reprehensible one!) Drawing from the *Torah*, Paul declared:: "Even so Abraham believed God, and it was reckoned to him as righteousness" (Rom 4:3). Moreover, that scripture revealed God's long-range plan: "All the nations will be blessed in you"(Gal 3:6-8).

Up to that point, Paul's message to the Galatians had several themes. First, his Gospel (as opposed to that of the Judaizers), had authority. He had received it personally from Jesus Christ (Gal 1:15-20). Second, that his version of the Gospel demonstrated that God offered salvation freely through Christ. Hence, there could be no obligation to the Mosaic laws. Third, believers became children of Abraham by *faith* and not works.

The Galatians had been distracted "from faith to works, from grace to law, from spirit to flesh." They had come to believe that their ancestry somehow went back to their "Father Abraham." Not so, Paul said. The righteous Abraham himself was a true worshipper, not because of circumcision but because he had already received the Gospel in the promise.

He had, in fact, risen above all tradition and blazed the true trail of faith.[20] He enlarged the scope of Christianity—magnificently.

2. CEREMONIAL OBLIGATIONS

You are observing special days and months and seasons and years! I fear for you, that somehow I have wasted my efforts on you. I plead with you, brothers, become like me, for I became like you" (Gal 4:10-12 NIV).

To better understand the Galatians, we look, again, at the Irish Celts to find a template for ritualized religion. After twenty years' absence, St. Patrick (390–461 AD), a Romanized British Celt, returned to Ireland. He went back to the place where, as a teenager, he had been taken into slavery. Then he spent the rest of his life evangelizing Ireland, codifying the ancient Brehon Laws and trying to adapt Christianity to Irish society.

In his own person, Patrick demonstrated a powerful Celtic temperament: Impetuous anger against tyrants, tenderness toward the weak, and passion for saving souls. Of the many stories relating to the life of Eire's most honored saint, one in particular points up the stubborn, dogged devotion that the Celts gave to the practice of ritual.

Late in life, Patrick journeyed to Cashel, County Tipperary, to visit Aengus, the Over-King of the Province of Munster. One can imagine the old saint climbing the rugged trail up to the palace, atop the Rock of Cashel. There, in the royal stronghold of the ancient lords of Eoghanachta, Patrick fearlessly challenged the King to receive the Gospel of Christ.

King Aengus, Queen Eithne, and many courtiers (out of loyalty to the king) accepted Patrick's teachings. Then came the baptism. As Aengus came to

Ceremonial Obligations

The Rock of Cashel, County Tipperary, Ireland, a 19th century drawing.

be baptized, the aged Patrick inadvertently set his staff down on the young king's bare foot. The wound bled extensively. Only after the rite was completed, however, did St. Patrick realize what he had done.

He apologized profusely for causing such great pain. Stoically, the King brushed the whole event aside. He had simply assumed that the injury was a necessary part of the ritual and had accepted it as such. So the story goes. Traditions and loyalties have always lived long among the Celts. Thus, they were both receptive to Christian ritual and vulnerable to its abuses.

CELTIC RITUAL

What ritual heritage did the new Christians bring into the Galatian churches? Julius Caesar, unabashedly prejudiced against his enemies, wrote[1] in 55 BC, "The whole nation of the Gauls is greatly devoted to ritual observances." He accused the druids of being the "ministers" of human sacrifices to appease the gods. "They believe, in effect, that, unless a man's life be paid, the majesty of the immortal gods may not be appeased." Moreover, he claimed, when they ran out of criminals to execute, they turned to the innocent. By nature, the Celts had to be enslaved to religious ritual.

Despite their fierce devotion to marauding and fighting, the Gauls practiced advanced methods of agriculture. Along with other days to honor individual gods, they had four equinoxes/solstices and four major Sabbaths.[2] Moreover, they used the lunar cycle so that their day began at sunset. Indeed, the Celts believed the moon to be so sacred that it could scarcely be mentioned by name.

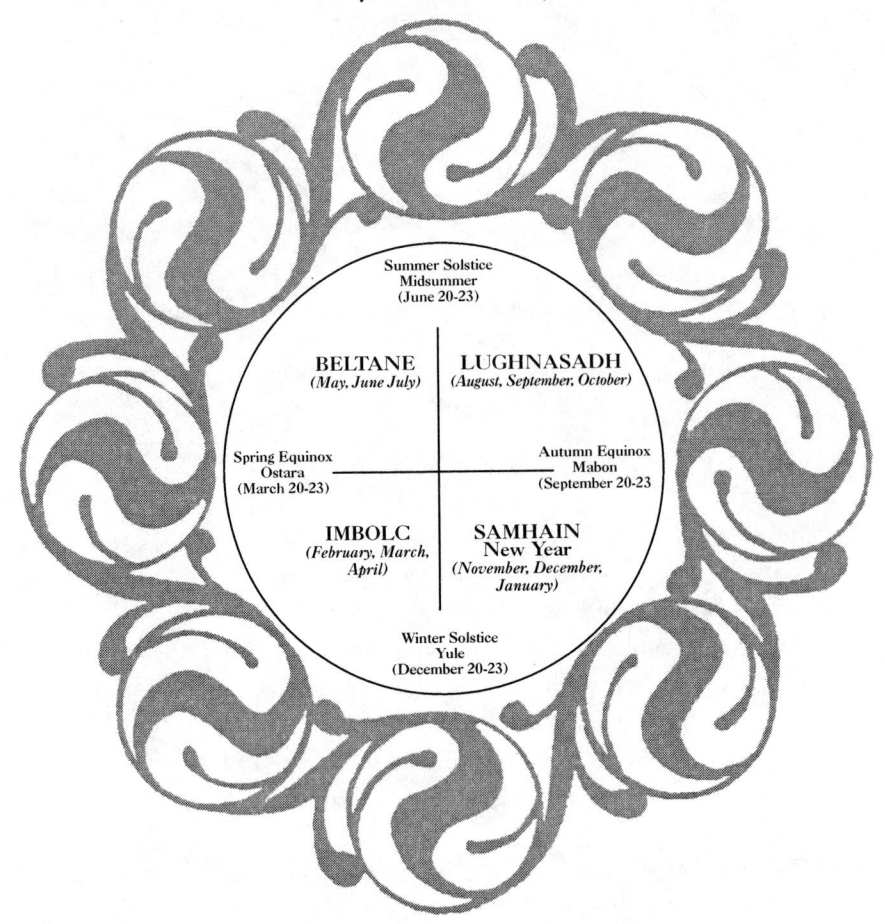

```
                    Summer Solstice
                      Midsummer
                     (June 20-23)

        BELTANE              LUGHNASADH
      (May, June July)    (August, September, October)

   Spring Equinox                    Autumn Equinox
       Ostara                            Mabon
    (March 20-23)                    (September 20-23)

        IMBOLC                  SAMHAIN
     (February, March,          New Year
          April)            (November, December,
                                 January)

                    Winter Solstice
                         Yule
                    (December 20-23)
```

Calendar of Celtic Ritual High Days. Most ancient peoples, including the Hebrews, tied their yearly calendars to the four seasons and the demands of planting and harvest.

TRADITIONS OF THE FOUR SEASONS

Samhain (*sow-inn*). The pagan New Year opened with Samhain, November 1. With "the dark [winter] half" of the year beginning, the harvest was complete, food stored, and animals brought in from the fields. Those needed for food had been slaughtered. Now the Earth could rest. Ritual fires blazed at dusk on the sacred hilltops to

Ceremonial Obligations

protect people and land. On the eve of Samhain (Christian "All-Hallows" or Hallowe'en) the Celts believed the barrier between the living and the dead, the physical and the spiritual, to be almost non-existent. For this one night, gods and humans, ancestors and fairies—all mingled freely in one another's realms.

Paradoxically, Samhain Eve was also a time of beginnings. The Celts respected the dead because, they believed, the ancestors would return to impart wisdom and remind the tribe of ancient customs. The occasion also offered a time of quiet reflection. Moreover, the growth cycle had already begun even as the Earth waited for returning light.[3] The days had been growing shorter, until the Yule season, which celebrated the rebirth of the sun god, after the longest night of the year. This time immediately preceded the "Christian" event of Christmas.

Imbolc ("to milk"). Even though Imbolc celebrated the approach of Spring and its lengthening days, Winter still reigned. Celts were expert at pasturing cattle, sheep and goats. For Gallic tribes milk was a favorite, health-giving beverage. During Imbolc, the Celtic goddess Brigit was the giver of healing and fertility, the muse of poetry, and the sponsor of fire and smith-craft. Christians called February 1 "Candlemas," for the blessing of church candles.[4]

Interestingly enough, the goddess Brigit so fired the Celtic imagination that she was transferred, almost entirely, into the Celtic St. Brigit of Ireland (Brigantia of Britain). Thus she created a major bridge between Celtic paganism and Christianity. St. Brigit (450-524 AD) created the first double monastery (men and women) at Kildare and became known as "Mary of Gael." Perpetual fire tended by nineteen nuns burned in her monastery for almost 1,000 years, up to the time of the Protestant Reformation.

Second only to Patrick in the roster of Celtic saints, Brigid took on a human, Christian form, keeping flocks and mentoring young people. She attained in the flesh what her pagan ancestors had only dreamed of.

Beltaine ("the fires of Bel[enus]"). This enthusiastic May 1 festival celebrated fertility and the union of the god and the goddess. The former was symbolized by the Maypole (masculine), hung with bright ribbons (feminine). Great "Beltaine Eve" fires were lit to honor "The Shining One," who had healing powers. Like Samhain, Beltaine led people outside of the boundaries of normal activities, into places where supernatural events occurred.

Nine druids took charge of each Beltaine gathering. Taking nine different woods, each made fire by friction. Then two separate bonfires were made from these flames. Next, all domestic animals and the people passed between the fires, to purge away winter diseases and evils. Each householder lit a brand at the Beltaine fires and carried it home to renew his domestic fires. By kindling his own "Paschal Fire" before the official Beltaine celebrations, St. Patrick once horrified the druids with his presumption.[5]

Lughnasadh. This August 1 harvest festival marked the end of the agricultural year. Celebrations called for ritual offerings, sun worship, dance, bull sacrifices and marriage. Weddings were more common after the harvest, when a man could decide whether or not he was affluent enough to take the step. Worship of Lugh[6] involved "trial marriages" (of nine months). The timing tended to emphasize the depth of the relationship between the land and its people.

As "the god of many gifts," Lugh served also as the sun god of the Insular (British) Celts. He lived in the golden fields and grew within the crops. He "speaks" this poetic summary of the calendar:

This has been our way:
Spring for ploughing and sowing
Summer for strengthening and encouraging the grain.
Autumn for ripening the corn and reaping it.
Winter for enjoying it.[7]

Sports, like swimming horses across lakes and contests of strength, were played to celebrate prosperity and good health. Mabon (Fall Equinox), however, ended the "chase of Lugh."

As to politics, people believed that Lugh also assisted worthy candidate-kings in their quest of kingship. Then, having given his all, he had to submit once more to the end of the cycle and the return of Samhain.

How devoted, then, did the Galatians have to be to their "special days and months," as the Apostle Paul put it? A look at the Celtic calendar will show heavy commitment. It went, in fact, beyond simple thanksgiving for a bountiful harvest to their involvement in rituals that seemed wholly at cross-purposes with the Christian faith. The Church could not condone the sexual initiations, the dancing, processions, singing, and the election of a May King and Queen. On top of all of this, villagers commonly added their own rituals to the traditional activities.

JUDEO-CHRISTIAN RITUALS

The word "ritual" generally refers to the established form of any ceremony or rite, according to the culture and custom. Broadly speaking, it describes activities, attitudes, and behavior in a sanctuary or place dedicated to God. Synonymous with every aspect of a reverent life, ritual embraces both piety and liturgy.

Throughout Scripture, a powerful vocabulary defines these ceremonies. They include arches for worship, altars for sacrifices, and other places for spon-

Ceremonial Obligations 33

taneous, freewill gifts. The book of Genesis provides early evidence of the beginnings of sacrifices (4:3-4) and worship (4:26). Thus, in the well-used sacrificial rites, Abraham received promises of land, rich with various Divine interventions (Gen 15:7-21). We also read of other rituals such as blessings, purifications, changes of garments, and offerings of drink and oil (Genesis 35).

Circumcision

The ceremony of circumcision was an important ritual in the Jewish family. When He was establishing His chosen people (Isa 43:20), God commanded all male infants to undergo this operation (Gen 17:4–14). He reaffirmed it with Moses (Lev 12:3), and Jewish families still practice it as a religious rite today. The day of circumcision calls for celebration as family and friends rejoice over the child's becoming part of God's covenant people (Jer 31:31–33).

Circumcision and dietary restrictions evolved into a bitter issue between the Galatian Christians and the Judaizers among them. Although the Celtic-influenced Galatians had a strong heritage of ritual observances, they were wholly unfamiliar with these Jewish laws. They might well have taken to human sacrifice with less aversion! The conflict over this ritual goes far in explaining why more women than men joined the early Christian church. The latter simply could not accept the painful and embarrassing after-effects (Gen 34:25).

Agricultural

Behind the Mosaic legislative narrative and Passover traditions are nomadic rituals of feasts and offerings of firstlings (Ex 12-13). During this dispensation, women danced and sang with timbrels, and men led in confession, sacrifice and sacred meals (Ex 19). By the time of David and Solomon, Israel practiced three basic agricultural rituals. First, the **Feast of Unleavened Bread** (Ex 23:15) called for the eating of unleavened cakes, the offering of first fruits and the waving of a sheaf of barley (Lev 23:10–18). Passover followed with its slain lamb, blood-sprinkled doorposts and lintels. Celebrative dance preceded this festival. Second, came **Pentecost** (Feast of Weeks, Num 28:26). A midsummer event between barley and wheat harvests, it involved the waving of two leavened loaves before God. Finally, the **Feast of Ingathering** (Tabernacles, Deut 16:16) was the greatest of the three. Illuminations and dancing (Isa 30:29) marked this harvest-thanksgiving occasion. The people lived in crudely constructed, temporary booths for seven days. They also celebrated the new year, poured out water as a libation (drink offering), and prayed for the coming of the former rains (Zech 14:16-17).

The chief source of information for Jewish rituals in the New Testament period is the *Mishna* (a codification of laws and regulations). In addition to the above-mentioned annual feasts, worship included the morning sacrifice accompanied by the recitation of Scripture and prayers. The Aaronic Benediction (Num. 6:24-27) was also pronounced over the multitude gathered in the temple courtyard. As part of their daily observances, the people also said grace before and after every meal (Mt 14:19; Mk 6:41; Rom 6:46).

Early Christian

Our knowledge of early Christian rituals is sketchy. The New Testament contains only one complete description, the record of the celebration of the Lord's Supper. Christianized, popular eucharistic prayers have their origin in the late lst-century *Didachae* (a prototype of the modern ministerial handbook). Early Christian rituals found their focus in baptism, preaching, and the Lord's Supper. All of these expressed faith in Jesus Christ, the Risen Messiah and the Living Lord. The Church, of course, acquired many inherited customs from Judaism. These have been re-interpreted and modified by Gentile practices.

Some Christian rituals have enjoyed a rich liturgical life: Public prayer, psalmody, Scripture reading, instruction by teachers/preachers, and private devotions. As the fledgling Church developed, special observances included ordinations, ministries to the needy, anointing of the sick, exorcisms, benedictions at weddings, funeral banquets, and days of fasting. In the form of the Christianized Passover festival, the annual Easter celebration is, perhaps, the oldest Christian ritual. Traceable to the early Jewish-Christian Church (1 Cor 11:20-21), it commemorated the death and resurrection of Christ at an evening "Lord's Supper."

REASONS FOR RITUAL

Why were the Celts and other ancient people so devoted to ritual? As we have demonstrated, the practices tied them to their land and to the cycle of the seasons. But, that is not all. The ancient mystery-initiations called for ceremonies relating tradition, culture and the occult. This concern led them to the rigid observance of "special days and months and seasons" (Gal 4:10). Thus, myths and symbols have been preserved in unique tribal histories. Mystery rites have also been described as "a special form of worship offered in the larger context of religious practice" that typified a variety of different cults in this period of early Christianity.[8]

Christianity has inherited the rituals of both Judaism and these mystery religions. Human interaction with an unknown or unseen God requires visual-

Ceremonial Obligations 35

ization through ceremony. Any generation faced with the challenges of superficiality and shallowness risks the loss of depth and meaning. This problem ultimately demands spiritual disciplines, forms that have been carefully and creatively hammered out over centuries of church experience. Ritual provides Christianity with just such a legacy. Rituals invite us "to explore the inner caverns of the spiritual realm. They urge us to be the answer to a hollow world."[9]

Paul addressed the Galatians' penchant for ritual practices, particularly those introduced by the Judaizers. He described these functions as "weak and worthless elemental things" (Gal 4:9).

3. Inalienable Rights and Restrictive Regulations

Those who rely on obedience to the law are under a curse (Gal 3:10).

At least one generalization can be made about the Celts. They thrived on competition. They still do. Our modern passion for sports—and violent ones, at that—arises out of this part of our Western heritage. When you are screaming in the bleachers for your football team, when you are glued to TV through the baseball season, when you are among the rowdies ring-side at a boxing event—at all these times (and many others) you are behaving very much like a Celt who lived more than 2000 years ago.

The matter, however, goes further. An even deeper, more far-reaching trait surfaces. The Celts seemed to be at their best in controversy. To this day, the Irish and their kin always seem to be running to court. Indeed, Gaelic people have always loved litigation, invigorating as a tonic and natural as instinct. Celtic piety, learning, and artistry truly inspired medieval Europe, bringing order to life through this detailed enunciation of law. Given their bold, fighting spirit, no wonder the druids and elders took care to create a great variety of protective laws. Thus they provided a measure against total self-destruction.

DRUIDS AND THEIR INFLUENCE

The druids fit into the top level of Gaelic society, among the chieftains, bards and seers. As philosophers, they maintained a social balance in the community. Their religious instruction provided a bridge between this and the "Otherworld." As scientists they served as practitioners of the healing arts. The druids were to the Celts as Levites to Hebrews, Brahmins to Hindus, and Brehons to the Irish.[1]

Druidism was an Indo-European institution, related to the Hittites, to pre-Greco-Roman civilizations and to Hinduism.[2] Although the druids have been idealized and made figments of imagination, they influenced their cultures profoundly. Druidic rites were practiced in oak groves. (The Celts never used temples until they came under Greek and Roman influence.)[3] The sanctuary at Drymeneton ("the sacred oak") in Galatia is recorded as having been used for a council of Celtic chieftains.[4]

Because the lands of the Mediterranean had long been denuded, the people naturally feared the strange activities of Celtic settlers. The passionate Gaelic love of nature astonished the locals. Their respect for the environment, rapport with birds and animals, and so forth, transferred into the portrayal of their pagan deities as natural forces. Not surprisingly, the Celts delayed for centuries before they experimented with urban living.

Love of learning, both religious and secular, was also a national Celtic characteristic. The druids believed their precepts too precious to be committed to writing. In fact, they banned writing. Since wisdom and laws had to be orally transmitted, it could take up to twenty years to train for the druidic priesthood. Without holy books or prophetic writings, all learning had to be immediate, in the here and now. The druidic refusal to have their teachings preserved in written form has, of course, left large gaps in our understanding of the Celts. Hence, most of what we know of them comes from their enemies. Those classical accounts, of course, are anything but unbiased.

Meanwhile, with the continuing contacts with the Greco-Roman world, the Celts used Greek letters for their trade transactions. With the coming of Christianity Latin letters prevailed.

The Honor Price

Along with other ancient cultures, every Celt had an "honor price" (Irish *eneclann*).[5] Detailed druidic laws determined everyone's legal rights and privileges. For instance, if one witness swears you stole his cow, and another witness swears otherwise, the person with the higher honor price prevails.

These regulations delineated every stage of life. Until age seven, boys and girls had the same honor price. The price for killing such a child was eight cumals or three milch cows. After seven, the children went to fosterage or education. As long as they were dependent children they received half the honor price of the father or foster-father.

Then came the "Age of Choice," that is, arrival at maturity and readiness for marriage—fourteen years for girls, seventeen for boys. Girls, however, could continue their education to seventeen if they wished. Surprisingly, fosterage for a girl cost more than for a boy. Each, however, had to be educated according to his/her rank, which the honor price measured precisely.

Judism system also had its honor price. For example, the injury of a pregnant woman had to be compensated according to her husband's demand (Ex 21:22).[6] Throughout Christian times, however, the death sentence has more often than not replaced the Celtic system of exacting.

Paul had great news for the Galatians. In Christ, everyone—no exceptions—had the same honor price (Gal 3:28). This idea would have come as a surprise to the Gauls, caught up as they were in their carefully stratified society.

HEALTH CARE AMONG THE CELTS

"Sick Maintenance"[7] was observed by regulations detailed enough to do credit to a modern American HMO (Health Maintanance Organization). Until the age of ten, a child had to be accompanied to the hospital by his/her mother. Depending on the type of marriage the chief wife could claim half her husband's honor price for her care. The second wife got one-third of his price and other wives got one-fourth. Concubines (and other unmarried people) had to get their honor prices from parents, partners, or kinfolk. In case of murder, men and women both had to pay the honor price of the victim. Fines for murder were twice that of manslaughter. Apparently there was no death penalty—as long as the fines were paid.

WOMEN'S RIGHTS

Under Celtic law, women enjoyed an amazing amount of protection. Actually, it recognized eight types of marriage,[8] and the laws for divorce were very carefully spelled out. In fact, a woman could regain her freedom for many causes: Verbal or physical abuse, abandonment for another woman (the wife would keep the house); the husband's telling lies about her; or his tricking her into marriage. Other husbandly failures included: Impotence, obesity, homosexuality, sterility, or religious celibacy. A man, on the other hand, could divorce his wife for unfaithfulness, persistent thieving, having an abortion (secretly), smothering her child, or "bringing shame to his honor."[9]

Inalienable Rights and Restrictive Regulations

The Romans criticized the Celtic liberation of women and the resulting polygamy. Empress Julia Augusta accused Celtic women of lack of morals because they were openly free to choose their husbands and lovers. Argentocoxos, wife of a Celtic chieftain had the last word: "We Celtic women obey the demands of Nature in a more moral way than the women of Rome. We consort openly with the best men, but you, of Rome, allow yourselves to be debauched in secret by the vilest."[10]

Within this rather generous framework, however, "immorality" could not be tolerated. For instance, a prostitute became a legal loser. That is, if she took more than seven sex-partners in one night! Such activity robbed her and any children born to such alliances of any rights before the law.[11]

In keeping with Christian principles, Scripture gives numerous instances of women taking prominent positions in the early Christian church. For example, Mary Magdalene and Mary (John Mark's mother) who hosted the first housechurch (Acts 12:12). Also, Martha (sister of Lazarus, Lk 11:38) and Lydia (business woman of Thyatira, (Acts 16:14). At first, this same situation prevailed in the founding of the Celtic Church. In due course, however, the Romanization of the Christian church and the tenor of Anglo-Saxon laws[11] worked together to restrict women.

At that point in time, Celtic Christians would have been especially drawn to the idea of the Mother Goddess.[12] When the Council of Ephesus (432 AD) proclaimed the Virgin Mary as a kind of "Mother Goddess," the idea would have been very familiar to Celtic believers.[13] Indeed, Paul went to great lengths to commend women for their leadership, as in the cases of Phoebe and Priscilla along with her husband Aquila (Rom 16:1-4).

A PAULINE PERSPECTIVE

The Jews of Paul's day had a totally different concept of the "law," than that of their contemporary readers and believers of Scripture. To them the law was not just ritual observances of a set of rigid rules. Rather, they believed and religiously clung to the perspective that a man could literally save himself by meticulously keeping the law. This "law" consisted of moral precepts (Ten Commandments), ceremonial rituals (eating, washing, etc.), and civil statutes (social conduct).

Paul's opponents insisted that the Galatians would attain salvation by total compliance with these codes. They taught that a meritorious life in which a surplus of good deeds was carefully catalogued would cancel out evil deeds, no matter how pernicious. In defense of the true Gospel which he taught the Galatians,

Paul was concerned only with the Judaizers' perversion of the moral and ceremonial codes. No evidence has been found to show that these false teachers enforced Jewish civil regulations.

In frustration, Paul retorted: "I shall ask you one simple question. Did you receive the Spirit by trying to keep the Law or by believing the message of the gospel. Surely you can't be so idiotic as to think that man begins his spiritual life in the Spirit and then completes it by reverting to outward observances?" (Gal 3:2-3 Phillips).

Although we cannot include the observance of these rules as part of the Judaizers' folly, Paul still reacted vehemently. He denounced the Judaizers' three grossest errors:

1. **Perfect Obedience to the Law.** The Judaizers taught that, in their own strength, people could give perfect obedience to the requirements of the moral and ceremonial laws. We stand amazed at the lengths to which people may go to acquire "good deeds." On the streets of Bangkok, for example, the Buddhists will purchase cages of wild birds (caught for the purpose). Then they set them free as a gesture of benevolence. The Hebrew custom of using "tear bottles" is another case in point. At a death, tears were to be shed ritually, at precisely the proper moment (Mal 2:13; Mt. 11:17; Lk 7:32). The professional mourners were usually women since they were considered most proficient at the art of wailing. Also, expecting friends to contribute to the grieving, the family supplied the guests with tear-bottles to catch the flow and thus certify the good intentions of all who came.[14]

   To this kind of artificial merit and "accounting" of good works, Paul responded with strong language when he said, "Those who rely on obedience to the law are under a curse (Gal 3:10). No "if," "but," or "maybe." Just an emphatic, "This is how it is."

2. **Jewish Living**. The Judizers demanded that non-Jewish believers adhere to their historic beliefs. By the time the message of salvation from God reached the heathen communities (including the Galatian churches), the Jews had already added a mass of man-made requirements to the law. These were commonly referred to as "tradition" (Mk 7:3). They were contained in an extensive body of literature known as the *Talmud* ("teachings"). The entire content of the *Talmud* was derived from oral tradition, encompassing several centuries of dogma.

By Paul's time, this material was codified into one basic portion called the *Mishna*, which spawned elaborate commentaries known as *Gemara*. The *Talmud* provided the structure of historic Judaism, but when it was being foisted on the Galatian believers, Paul rejected it, out of hand.

3. **Irrelevant Ceremonial Rituals**. The Judaizers attempted to enforce only certain features of the ceremonial rituals on the gullible Galatians. Clearly, however, these codes had expired and did not extend beyond the cross of Jesus. For example, the sacrifice of live animals was replaced by the presentation of the believer as a living sacrifice (Rom 12.1). More ritual irrelevancy appears in funeral customs worldwide.

Modern archaeologists continually turn up amazing mass burials among ancient peoples. Kings, emperors and even lesser nobility had to be accompanied to the next life. Not only with furniture, food, tools and stock animals, but also wives, concubines, servants and slaves. Evidence appears in the cultures of Egypt, China and other lands. In each society, apparently, a time came when these mass executions/sacrifices seemed to be wasteful. Live sacrifice, however, had to be replaced by something. In the case of the Egyptians, they painted people, gods and offerings on the tomb walls. In China, the Great One who died carried with him/her a collection of porcelain figurines (humans and horses) and "funeral furniture." Such provisions would be essential for anyone believing in the immortality of the soul and the afterlife. This idea the Celts also embraced with great enthusiasm!

AN ALTERNATIVE

Up to this point, Paul has been defending the doctrine of justification by faith—a staple doctrine he had presented to the Galatians. He firmly reminded them of the blessings they had already received. That is, the Holy Spirit. "Acceptance with God came by faith alone," he thundered. "No kind of legal observances had ever—or could ever—bring salvation."

Paul not only denounced the errors of his detractors, but he also provided important evidence as to why their teaching must be rejected and his Gospel retained. Upon accepting Christ as Lord and Savior, the convert had instant justification. No matter how well intended, works could have absolutely no part in this transaction. Indeed, the believer gained a "ruthless trust" in God,[15] who justified sinners and transformed them into saints through the daily experience of sanctification.

The Apostle reminded his readers that just before Moses died, he repeated the laws God had given him to ratify his covenant with the Hebrew people. They were accompanied by incredible promises of rich rewards and blessings for those who obediently adhered to every instruction (Dt 28:1-14). Moses also included some fearfully drastic curses for those who forgot, rejected, or ignored these precepts (Dt 27:15-26; 28:15-68). The Apostle insisted that the slightest deviation from the requirements of the law would incur these curses (Gal 3:10). Especially for those who deliberately perverted the faith of his beloved Galatians.

In a word, faith was obviously superior to the prescribed works of Judaism. Meeting the Judaizers on their own ground, Paul referred to the writings of Moses to prove his position and to demonstrate how they had attached exaggerated importance to some aspects of the law. By citing the experience of Abraham, Paul reasoned, that the patriarch, himself, had accepted the covenant by faith alone. Clearly, then, Abraham's spiritual descendants (Gal 3:15-29) must be entitled to the same inheritance.

The law requires perfect obedience. Therefore, if one is justified by faith, that transformation has to be accomplished on some principle other than a belief in the works of the law. This is how it happens. A just God accepts repentant sinners through His Son. Then, through immediate justification, they become the spiritual children of Abraham and heirs of righteousness. In contrast, those turning their backs on God's salvation-plan can never, by their own efforts, meet even the minimum requirements of the law.

Faith alone is the last word.

Part II

4. Breaking Down Barriers

"There is no such thing as Jew and Greek, slave and freeman, male and female; for you are all one person in Christ Jesus" (Gal 3:28).

Tall and muscular, with piercing blue eyes, the greatest of all Celtic warrior queens terrorized the Roman armies in Britain for almost two glorious years. Clad in a bright, flowing tartan cloak (fastened with an elaborate brooch) and wearing a great golden torc around her neck, she swept onto the battlefield. Thick red hair flying and her loud, harsh voice shouting curses, the Celtic queen gave her enemies cause to pause. Centuries of fighting the Gauls in Europe gave the Romans a healthy respect for and fear of such raw, untempered courage. Moreover, as one Roman writer observed: "The [Celtic] women are nearly as tall as the men—and equally fierce." Add to this, all of the drumming, the trumpets, and the screaming.

WOMEN, A SIGNIFICANT FORCE

So, meet Queen Boudicca (30-61 AD),[1] Britain's most celebrated heroine. Her story embodies much of what characterized Celtic womanhood. At age eighteen Boudicca married King Prasutagus of the Iceni. When Emperor Claudius had briefly visited Britain, he tried to re-establish Julius Caesar's control over the Province of Britannia. Things had slacked off, however, since Caesar's departure, more than a century earlier. The lightly ruled Celts, meanwhile, had been living pretty much as they pleased. In 43 AD, to confirm his holdings, Claudius designated several tribes in East Anglia as "clients" of Rome.[2]

Emperor Tiberius Claudius (10 BC– 54 AD)[3]

Although he spent only sixteen days in Britain, his negotiations managed to bring a good part of the southeastern portion of the island to heel.

When the generous and prosperous Client/King Prasutagus of the Iceni died eighteen years later, however, he left only half of his kingdom to Rome. With typical Gaelic regard for women, he left the remainder to support his wife and provide dowries for his two daughters.

Not surprisingly, the odious Emperor Nero now wanted all of the royal family's property. Certainly, he could not imagine why women would merit that much concern? The troops took the Queen hostage, stripped her, and publicly flogged her. This, while Roman soldiers raped her daughters. Iceni lands were then confiscated, and the women were sold into slavery.

HELL HATH NO FURY LIKE A WOMAN SCORNED

Infuriated, Queen Boudicca vowed revenge. She launched her massive revolt with at least 100,000 Britons behind her. Whipping her followers into a battle frenzy, she made a memorable and effective speech to rally her armies.

Breaking Down Barriers

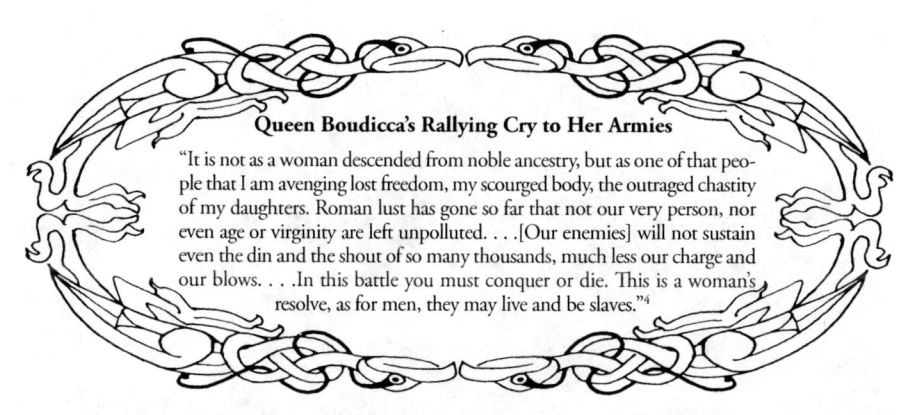

> **Queen Boudicca's Rallying Cry to Her Armies**
>
> "It is not as a woman descended from noble ancestry, but as one of that people that I am avenging lost freedom, my scourged body, the outraged chastity of my daughters. Roman lust has gone so far that not our very person, nor even age or virginity are left unpolluted.... [Our enemies] will not sustain even the din and the shout of so many thousands, much less our charge and our blows.... In this battle you must conquer or die. This is a woman's resolve, as for men, they may live and be slaves."[4]

Boudicca, indeed, may be regarded as a very early feminist. Celtic culture, as we have seen, favored many freedoms for women.

The Iceni Queen chose her time carefully. Three hundred miles away, the Roman legions had just conducted a massacre on the island of Mona (Anglessey), destroying the sanctuaries of the druids. No doubt it surprised everyone that even the Romans would dare to desecrate this most sacred center in all of Celtdom. Upon hearing of the Britons' rebellion, the invaders hastened back to East Anglia. Several Roman strongholds, however, had already been ravaged.

First, came the razing of Camulodunum (Colchester),[5] with its population of some 30,000. Next, the Queen's forces destroyed almost the entire Port of London. Lastly, Verulamium (St. Albans[6]) fell to Boudicca. A humiliating defeat for the Roman Procurator, Suetonius Paulinus! By now almost 200,000 Celts had rallied to the cause. The Iceni tribesmen, in particular, destroyed any person or property connected with things Roman. This included Roman citizens and even Britons who had Romanized themselves too obviously. Boudicca's rampage caused the death of at least 70,000 of these people. Her campaign featured torture, impaling, and beheading.

Actually, the furious Queen came very close to driving Rome out of Britain altogether. Why then do we come to the pathetic scenes of the final battle? Roman discipline and strategy prevailed. Suetonius chose a long incline, heavily forested on one side, and waited. Meanwhile, the exuberant, non-combatant Britons assembled behind the lines to watch the spectacle—grandfathers and babies, livestock and wagons loaded with loot. Sheer British ego made the defeat a certainty, the smaller forces of the Romans notwithstanding. Perhaps the Britons had brought their families and treasure to the battlefield to protect them from roving Roman bandits. In any case, the enemy drove the Celts back against the backdrop of their wagons and kinfolk, slaughtering 80,000 of them.

Left: Queen Boudicca and her two daughters ride in their war chariot directly toward the House of Parliament, London. This bronze sculpture is mounted on Westminister Bridge on the River Thames.[7] **Right:** Maps of Boudicca's campaign.

In the ancient tradition of Celtic leaders who chose suicide rather than defeat,[8] Boudicca poisoned herself.[9] She knew all too well the horrors she would suffer if Suetonius took her to Rome as part of his triumphal procession. As illustrated on the Triumphal Arch of Titus in Rome, prisoners followed the victor in disgrace and chains. At the end of the celebrations they would be executed. Chroniclers report, however, that the Iceni gave their proud Queen a costly burial, in an as-yet undiscovered tomb.

Powerful women were a long Celtic tradition. In 1954 the tomb of the "Princess of Vix" (6th - 5th c BC) was excavated and reconstructed.[10] Alone in her large burial vault and lying on a fully assembled wagon, she was surrounded by rich grave goods from all over the Greek world. The huge bronze *krater* (mixing bowl, complete with lid) buried with her is the largest ever found in Europe. Five feet high, it held 330 gallons. The Celtic elite, of course, could well afford to import Roman wine. The prospect of a single Celtic woman of this status and wealth, however, would certainly have terrorized the Romans.

THE PRIVILEGES OF CELTIC WOMEN

The world of the Celts offered its women a surprising number of freedoms. They had legal rights to own property. Marriage was flexible, and divorce came

Breaking Down Barriers

relatively easily. Women went to battle with their husbands, and the rebellion of Queen Boudicca was not an exception. A most alarming circumstance for the Roman forces! Her story has had much publicity, because her rebellion subjected the Romans to the fiercest fighting they ever faced in Britain.

Celtic women also served as ambassadors. Indeed, the word "ambassador" (messenger) is a Gaelic word. At the beginning of the Celtic Christian age (as is well documented in Irish literature), women took prominent positions in the rise of the new religion. Unfortunately, these privileges eroded away with the Romanization of Christianity, an attitude that has persisted until today.

The Romans were somewhat more tolerant than the Greeks, in that a wife could at least eat meals with her husband. The Hebrews also imposed heavy restrictions on women. None of these, however, came near to the generous laws of the Celts. One Cisalpine Gaul, Cornelius Pepos (100-25 BC), of the Vocontaii tribe remarked: "Many things which we consider proper are thought shocking in Greece."[11]

WOMEN, BOND AND FREE

Paul set out to explain to the Galatians the barriers the Judaizers had erected between their practices and those of the true Gospel. To do so, he introduced the story of Hagar and Sarah. He described the broad dimensions of freedom existing in the New Covenant. He realized that the Galatian churches had fought to retain their own culture and had given way to the Greco-Roman policies as little as possible. The new idea of tolerance for women would have struck them as reminiscent of the customs their ancestors had practiced from ancient times. The believers, of course, pressed forward to hear more about this Christian freedom.

"For it is written that Abraham had two sons," Paul reminded them, "one by the bondwoman [Hagar] and one by the free woman [Sarah]. . . . This is allegorically speaking" (Gal 4:22-26). He retold the story of Abraham's sojourn into Egypt and his wife's appeal for her maid, Hagar, to become a surrogate mother.

Now Hagar was not as pathetic as she later appeared. Indeed, she was the daughter of the Egyptian Pharaoh, by one of the concubines in his vast harem. Of all of the maidservants the king offered Abraham, Sarah probably picked Hagar because of her semi-royal status.[12] Despite his royal lineage, Hagar's son Ishmael could never be a true heir. He had been "born according to the flesh" (Gal 4:23). Sadly, his father tried to secure the promised blessing by the "fleshly expedient" of taking Hagar in marriage. This amounted to the "bondage of the law."[13] Therefore, Ishmael represented the Siniatic Covenant.

Under this covenant of works and unaware of their frailties, the Israelites cried: "All the words that the Lord has spoken *we will do!*" (Ex 24:3-7, emphasis added). On the other hand, Sarah's son Isaac represented the New Covenant, born entirely of faith. The Judaizers notwithstanding, salvation always depends not on what we do but on what God does. Upon receiving Paul's letter many (we hope most) of the Galatians rejoiced in the message of Paul's allegory.

They needed to reclaim the liberty they had forfeited. While Boudicca's British revolt was still some fifteen years in the future, the Celts' fiercely guarded independence was a matter of history. Nonetheless, the parallels are curious. The Queen's rebellion against Roman incursion and persecution championed the freedom of her people and the rights of women. Unfortunately, the results for Boudicca were as fruitless as Abraham's efforts to "help" God fulfill His promise.

THE JEWISH STRUGGLE FOR IDENTITY

In many ancient cultures social inequality and differentiation of the sexes created almost insurmountable barriers. The Jews were no exception. Both Paul and his Judaizing opponents knew all about segregation and prejudice.

As early as their entry into the Promised Land, the Israelites had been given at least three tokens of identification. First, each household had to place a small, parchment cylinder on their doorpost. It reminded them of God's commandments, statutes and judgments (Dt 6:1-9; 11:13-21). Second, they were instructed to wear arm or headbands (phylacteries, Ex 13:9). These recalled their divine deliverance out of Egypt and their pledge of obedience to the God who liberated them (Ex 13:9,16). Third, they were to attach a fringe or tassel of four cords to the corners of a specially designed outer cloak. Only men wore these to honor the Ten Commandments (Num 15:38-39) and to signify hope for the Gentiles whom they would later evangelize (Zech 8:23).

Jesus Himself wore this fringe (Mt 9:20; 14:26; Mk 6:56; Lk 8:44), as did Paul and his contemporaries. In time, however, the fringe or tassel[14] evolved into a mark which visited humiliation and even death upon Jewish men. Many were massacred in great numbers by marauding Gentile enemies—especially during the Roman invasion of 70 AD. Eventually, the fringe was attached to a kind of handkerchief to be worn in the pocket. Still later, prayer shawls had the tassels to be used only at home or in private gatherings.

A PROBLEM OF PREJUDICE

The Hellenistic world of Paul, by and large, regarded women as mere chat-

Breaking Down Barriers

tels. At the very bottom of the social ladder, only slightly above a slave. Indeed, a male newborn rated higher than his mother. Most pagan philosophers doubted that a woman could even have a soul. In some societies a man could kill anyone in his household, if he so wished.[15] While the Hebrew males did not carry their power *that* far, they felt their superiority keenly. Jewish men were wont to greet each new day piously with this prayer:

"Lord, I thank you that:
I am a Jew and not a Gentile,
Free-born and not a slave,
a man and not a woman."

The ancient Hebrews excluded women from almost every religious rite. The men decreed that when they appeared in the synagogue, the women's voices and appearance might arouse the men and distract them from worship. Hence, the women were secluded behind a barrier (*mechitza*). The *bimah* (the men's place to read the holy *Torah*) was kept at a safe distance.[16] No woman, no matter how intelligent, could ever be taught the *Torah*.[17] In practice, a Jewish father, husband or son could dispose of their women—for whatever whim they chose other than murder.

A minimum of ten adults (*minyan*) was required for public prayer. Even if present, women could not be counted, not even in a census of the population. Since public prayer was not necessary for them, they could not even participate in the *kaddish*, a memorial prayer for the dead. Nor could women bear witness before the law, because they were believed to be liars. Had not Sarah denied that she had laughed at the message of Abraham's divine visitors?[18] Centuries later, Jesus' resurrection became a case in point. In an attempt to change the behavior of His disciples, Jesus showed Himself to several women (more than the required two or three witnesses). He then instructed them to "go and take word to My brethren to leave for Galilee, and there they will see Me" (Mt 28:10). Yet when the women tried to share their testimony with the disciples "they refused to believe it" (Mark 16:11). Should we be surprised?

Women could not own property. Even the most distant male relatives would have the first rights. Although the law of Moses prescribed that only sons had the right to inherit the father's land, the case of the daughters of Zelophehad (temporarily) became an exception. When the women appealed to Moses, God instructed: "If a man dies and has no son, then you shall transfer his inheritance to his daughter" (Num 36:15). Moses, however, added a condition. The women could keep the property only as long as they married within their own tribe (Num 36:5-12).

Of course, there have been remarkable women in every place and generation. People with the confidence and stature of Martha of Bethany, for example. We read that "a woman named Martha welcomed Him [Jesus] into her [own] home" (Lk 10:38).[18] An exception to the rule! We must realize, however, that the sister of Lazarus actually owned the house from which the miracle of his resurrection took place. Probably she inherited the house from her marriage to Simon. Her name was found on the headstones in an old Bethany cemetery, alongside the names of Eleazar and Simon.

Scholars believe that it was at the home of Simon and Martha that Mary broke her alabaster box for Jesus (Mt 26:6). Commentators have suggested that Mary had been violated by her own brother-in-law, Simon! The home of these women had to have been exceptional. In the male-dominated society, for instance, an adulterous woman (like Mary) would have been stoned (Jn 8:3-4).

Naturally, Paul recognized gender differences. Men and women, necessarily, had different functions in the home and in the Church. The Apostle insisted, however, that he spoke of a person's—anyone's—relationship with God. One wholly dependent on faith in Christ. Indeed, human distinctions never have anything to do with the Christian life.[19]

PAUL'S CURE FOR PREJUDICE

Like every other Jew in the Roman province, Paul knew what it was to suffer prejudice. Yet, he was the one who persecuted the early Christians with zeal. (Acts 8:1-3; Phil. 3:6). One might hope that those who have suffered the indignities of such severe racial and religious prejudices would be the last to practice the same on other people. History confirms the contrary. Actually, those who are exposed to the harshest treatment in their early development often grow up to be the cruelest persecutors. Having suffered intense persecution, violated people often become tyrants at the first opportunity. (Moreover, persons who have been abused as children are likely to perpetuate the crime in their own homes.) Thus, the nation that had been divinely delivered out of Egyptian slavery succumbed to a veritable mountain of prejudices. Very prominently, against women.

The Apostle was, however, cured of his biases. After his unorthodox encounter with Christ on the Damascus road (Acts 9:1-31), he was forever delivered from his inborn hatreds. Later, he could humbly assert: "Though I am free from all men, I have made myself a slave to all . . . To the Jews I became as a Jew . . .to those under the Law, as under the Law" (1 Cor 9:19-20). Herein lay the only remedy: Being born again, "not of blood nor of the will of the flesh nor of

Breaking Down Barriers

the will of man, but of God (Jn 1:13). Having been propelled into the invisible Kingdom of God, this first generation of Christian believers (and all who would follow) was, as Peter said, "a chosen race, a royal priesthood, a holy nation, a people for God's own possession (1 Peter 2:9).

Although Paul had once unified the Galatian churches with the Gospel of grace, now the Judaizers had fractured those infant Christian communities. The pernicious specters of racism, along with social and gender distinctions, once more reared their ugly heads (Gal 5:15). The false teachers had managed to revive the old heritage of hatred and hostility.

Paul now responded with force. Sparing no words, he denounced their behavior. He used a threefold declaration that would assuredly have caught the attention of his Galatian audience. In Christ, all humanly constructed barriers must vanish: "Jew nor Greek [political] bond nor free [social differences] . . . male nor female [gender]" (Gal 3:28). The cross at Calvary leveled many divisive traditions. Reflecting the concern of Jesus, Paul stressed that salvation is given in the same manner and to the same degree to every believer, regardless of sex, race, or social standing."[20]

To be sure, no other Jew had ever yet gone where Paul went. He even went against his own traditional background: "A Hebrew of the Hebrews [and] as to the Law, a Pharisee" (Phil 3:5). Not only did he include women in his appeal, but he also elevated them to equality with men. Paul is the only New Testament writer who recognized women as "outstanding among the apostles who were in Christ before" (Rom 16:7). He included Priscilla, along with her husband, Aquila, as "my fellow workers in Christ Jesus" (Rom 16:3). "By justifying faith in Christ," Paul declared, "salvation is available to *all*!"

A FOLK MEMORY FOR GALATIANS

To Paul, prejudice, in any of its ugly forms, constitutes a lethal spiritual immaturity. Authentic sons and daughters of God simply had to grow up! The spiritually mature will, by faith, unite in Christ. The Judaizers, on the other hand, with all their busyness about salvation by works considered such an enormous, all-comprehensive teaching to be rank heresy. Such a relationship, Paul claimed, is not dependent on accidents or circumstances of birth but simply on faith in Christ. How radical is that?

Those pagan privileges for women would have been, at the least, a folk-memory to the Galatians, despite their Hellenization. Paul laid down a landmark statement. In his sermon on Mars Hill, Athens, he declared that

Christianity subordinates all differences: "He made from *one* every nation . . . to live on all the face of the earth. . . . They should seek God, in the hope that they might grasp after him and find him" (Acts 17:26). Fortunately, the old Apostle could not look down the centuries to see how the Romanization of the church would steadily erode women's rights. A loss perpetuated well into the 20th century in the Western world. Certainly, Paul would have grieved.

The loving Word and work of God erases all lines. The ones that divide the human family into despicable categories. The ones that demean women's high calling and undermine their worth. All people—especially the spiritual descendants of Abraham—have equal standing in Christ. Faith alone insures such a magnificent inheritance!

5. Face-off with the Judaizers

If anyone preaches at variance with the gospel which you received, let him be outcast (Gal 1:9).

Four hundred years after their first invasion of Britain, the Romans abandoned the islands (410 AD). Amid the ensuing chaos and the depredations of the Vikings (and other barbarian raiders), Celtic Christianity[1] lighted up what we call the "Dark Ages."

Meanwhile, the churches in Asia Minor also flourished. After the departure of the Apostle Paul, those believers turned to John for guidance. He lived among them until Emperor Domitian exiled him to Patmos, at age ninety.

A little more than a century after the time of Paul, a curious story links Galatia to the very early evangelizing of Gaul and Britain.[2] Two nameless men from Galatia headed west to preach the Gospel among their Gaulish kinsmen. On the road between Lyons and Auxerre in central Gaul (France), they encountered two Roman soldiers, Antonius and Marius. The latter were tending their horses and setting up camp for the night.

When questioned, the Galatians declared that they had sailed from Ephesus, in Asia, and were now seeking the house of Graeco, a Christian bronze merchant in Auxerre. Finding foot-travelers coming from such a great distance surprised the soldiers.

"No, we're not traders," the older missionary explained, in perfect Greek. "But we are, in a way, merchants. We would sell our wares to our brethren in Gaul and Britain."

"What wares? You have no wagons."

"Our merchandise is light, but it is very precious," the younger traveler replied. "What we sell is without money or price."

Bemused by the men's account of themselves, the Romans directed them on to Auxerre. There Graeco received them with utmost hospitality. He invited fellow-Christians to meet together at his villa. Everyone, of course, wanted to hear news of all the churches between Galatia and Auxerre.

In due course, Graeco dispatched the missionaries with a letter of introduction to his friend Lucian in Britain. Antonius recommended a safe ship for crossing the Channel, and they all (the Roman included) set off with Graeco's shipment of merchandise. The wooden-wheeled wagons, loaded with bronzeware and the two Galatians, rattled over the cobblestone roads from Londonium to Verulamium (St. Albans). Antonius, of course, had brought his horse with him.

Here, again, the ministers were received into warm Christian fellowship. They went out preaching the Gospel to the Romanized Britons[3] all over southern England. Other Celtic missionaries soon joined them. In the hands of these very early Gaelic Christians, the Gospel remained untainted. They adhered strictly to the teachings of Paul and the revelation of John.

How gratified Paul would have been to see how his beloved Galatians had carried Christianity back to their own people. How they blended evangelism with the practical business of everyday life. How satisfying it would have been for him to realize that the message of grace and freedom in Christ had won out over the machinations of the Judaizers with whom he had contended?

THE JUDAIZING OPPOSITION

Unlike those two Galatian missionaries, the non-evangelistic Judaizers never carried the Good News to anyone. Their persistent criticism and unrestrained opposition continually plagued Paul's efforts. In his wrath-filled epistle to the Galatians, he makes it clear that, for this very reason, he has broken completely with the Judaizing Christians. Why? Even while they claimed to follow Christ, they profaned His truth. Hostile to Paul's teaching, they denied that the work of Jesus on the cross was sufficient for salvation.

Describing the cross as the "signature of Jesus," Brennan Manning says that "hostility to the cross is the foremost characteristic of the world." Paul, on the other hand, he opiined "what stamps Christians most deeply is the fact that through Jesus' Cross the world is crucified to Him and He to the world."[4] The

Face-off With the Judaizers

Judaizers' legalistic practices and preaching contradicted these passionate insights. To them the cross seemed nothing more than a theological relic to be carefully preserved in their museum of religiosity. With them, Jewish rituals towered over this and other "antiquities" of their faith. They perpetually tore down the ministry of others.

As previously noted, the Greek word meaning "to Judaize" appears only in Galatians 2:14 where Paul rebuked Peter for refusing to eat with the Jewish believers in Antioch.[5] While we have no specific historical information on the origin of Judaizing, the preponderance of evidence points to two groups: the Gentile Judaizers and the Jewish Judaizers.

Gentile Judaizers distinguished themselves by being circumcised, not just to imitate the Jews but actually to live as Jews (Es 8:17). They changed their customs and observed every minute detail of Jewish ceremonial law. In fact, they often managed to out-Jew the Jews themselves.

We have several accounts of Gentile Judaizing. Plutarch wrote of a freed slave, Caecilius, who was said to be "guilty of Judaizing." Josephus tells of Metilius "who saved his life by promising that he would Judaize even to circumcision." Ignatius condemned professing Christians for "living until now according to Judaism" and for "professing Jesus Christ and then to Judaize." In the *Acts of Pilate*, Pilate tells the Jews: "You know that my wife is god-fearing and more than ever Judaizes with you."[6] In the light of her endearing comment about Jesus (Mt 27:19), Pilate had good reason to suspect she had converted to the Jewish faith.

Jewish Judaizers, an extreme group among Hebrew Christians, also demanded the full observance of all Jewish laws. Coming in the rich temple vestments, they well knew that this display would impress the vain Galatians. They hoped that the new believers would accept their word as final truth. In contrast, Paul, himself a Jew, had come to them in the plain garb of an itinerant preacher, and a physically handicapped one, at that (Gal 4:13). Moreover, from that unlikely position he dared to argue the case for his apostolic authority.

Although fewer in numbers, these over-zealous Jewish Christians out-distanced their Gentile counterparts in their

A Jewish high priest in his ceremonial dress (Lev 8:8). He served as a fashion model for the flamboyant Judaizers.

attempts to improve upon the teachings of Paul. Attempting to combine the Gospel of Christ with the observing of Jewish ceremonies, they traveled far. This, despite the fact that the Apostolic Council in Jerusalem had already rejected Judaizing (Acts 15:1-12). These misguided zealots, however, never gave up on trying to foist their interpretation of Christianity on their listeners.

Both parts of the opposition took the ritual of circumcision as their badge of honor, with the two factions literally tearing the Galatian churches to pieces. Both insisted that the new believers had to be circumcised in order to gain membership in the new church community. Therefore, both parties proved to be equally troublesome in the Galatian churches. Much given to ritualistic practice, the Celtic members in the congregation could not afford to ignore the issue. They fervently struggled to deal with both factions at once.

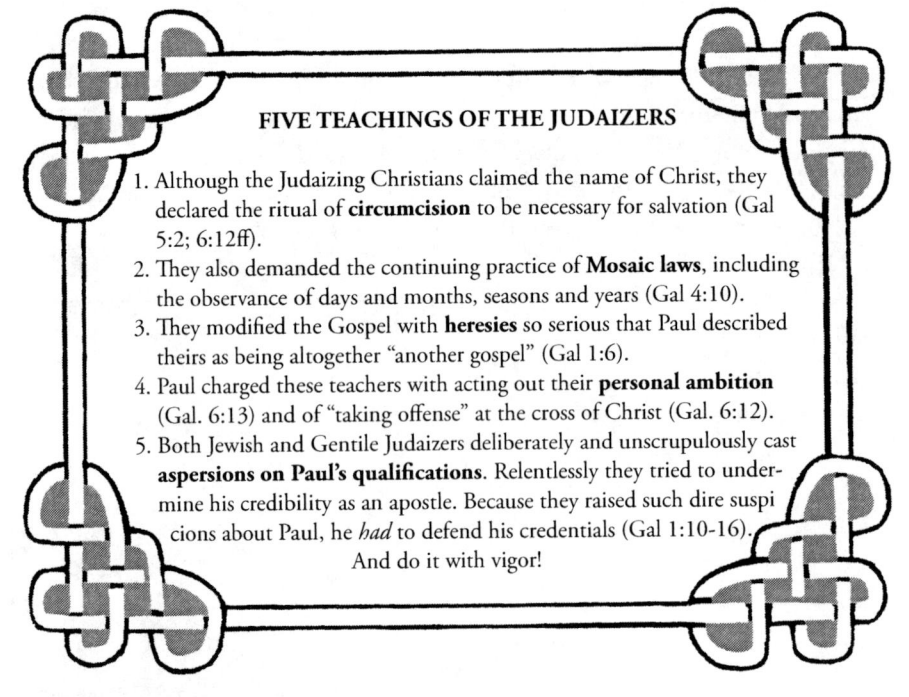

FIVE TEACHINGS OF THE JUDAIZERS

1. Although the Judaizing Christians claimed the name of Christ, they declared the ritual of **circumcision** to be necessary for salvation (Gal 5:2; 6:12ff).
2. They also demanded the continuing practice of **Mosaic laws**, including the observance of days and months, seasons and years (Gal 4:10).
3. They modified the Gospel with **heresies** so serious that Paul described theirs as being altogether "another gospel" (Gal 1:6).
4. Paul charged these teachers with acting out their **personal ambition** (Gal. 6:13) and of "taking offense" at the cross of Christ (Gal. 6:12).
5. Both Jewish and Gentile Judaizers deliberately and unscrupulously cast **aspersions on Paul's qualifications**. Relentlessly they tried to undermine his credibility as an apostle. Because they raised such dire suspicions about Paul, he *had* to defend his credentials (Gal 1:10-16). And do it with vigor!

ANOTHER MISUSE OF CIRCUMCISION

The rite of circumcision became an issue in the bloody dispute at Shechem. The ritual had its origin in the covenant between Jehovah and Abraham. God said:

> "This is how you shall keep the covenant between myself and you, and your descendants after you; circumcise yourselves, every male among

Face-off With the Judaizers

you. You shall circumcise the flesh of your foreskin and it shall be the sign of the covenant between us. Every male among you in every generation shall be circumcised on the eighth day, both those born in your house and any foreigner not of your blood" (Gen 17: 9-14 NEB).

Obviously, the ritual of circumcision set the Hebrews apart from other men. When Jews visited pagan prostitutes, no matter how well disguised they might be, they always betrayed themselves. Thus, the two spies sent secretly to Jericho almost "blew their cover" by going to the house of harlotry, managed by that ancient "Madam," known to us as Rahab (Jos 2:1-3).

The deception perpetrated by the sons of Jacob (Gen 34) might, at first, have inspired the Celts, formidable warriors given to hostage-taking. The Galatians, however, would have shown more integrity than Jacob's sons did in this situation. The story concerns their teenage sister Dinah.[7] Enthralled by the glamour of Shechem, the city near which her father had settled the family, she desperately wanted to join in the festivities with her Canaanite girlfriends.

One evening, therefore, she slipped quietly away from the supervision of her family to join the pagan party. Her stunning beauty—even at age thirteen—caught the attention of Crown Prince Shechem. As usual, he had been on the prowl at the party looking for beautiful women to bed. Taking Dinah hostage, he raped her. Then, in a gallant attempt to make a wrong right, he offered to marry her. Like many victims of hostile captivity, she became agreeable to the plan. Thus encouraged, the Prince and his father, Hamor, approached Father Jacob.

Dinah's outraged brothers now developed a plot to "permit" the marriage. They invited the men of Shechem to enter into a social, military, and commercial covenant with Jacob. The contract would be sealed by the rite of circumcision. Significantly, nothing was ever said of the religious importance of circumcision.

Clearly, it took much persuasion to convince the elders of Shechem to submit to the ordeal. King Hamor and Prince Shechem, however, declared a political coup. Now, they crowed, "We will not only be able to inter-marry with the Hebrews but also take their livestock and their property and all their animals" (Gen 34:23).

Adult circumcision—especially with the use of primitive instruments—entailed risk. Inflammation and fever usually set in on the third day. Therefore, the sly sons of Jacob bided their time until the third day to take advantage of the men's post-operative weakness. Like flames of fire in a dry thicket, they attacked and massacred all of the men of Shechem. They plundered the city, seizing all their cattle and goods and making captives of the wives and children.

Horrified, Jacob sternly rebuked his sons for their rash deception, "You have brought trouble on me, you have made my name to stink among the people of the country" (Gen 34:30 NEB). The sons easily vindicated themselves as avengers for the crimes of Prince Shechem, whom they had just murdered. It would appear that both father and sons were more concerned with the family's political power than with the welfare of the girl.

THE ORIGINAL INTENT OF CIRCUMCISION

The Jews accepted circumcision as an ordinance of divine origin, considering it to be an occasion for rejoicing. Many theories have been advanced about the purpose and significance of this rite. From the Biblical records and the history of ancient peoples, it appears that circumcision had at least five purposes:

1. A sign of God's Covenant of Grace (Gen 17:1-14). A deeply religious ritual, it could even "roll away" the reproach of enemies (Jos 5:1-9).
2. An act of initiation into manhood and citizenship. Today, Jews refer to the circumcision ceremony as the "Covenant" which guarantees membership into the tribe/nation of Israel. By the same token, the Judaizers intended circumcision to be the "gateway" into Christianity.
3. Useful physical reasons. These included: Prevention of disease, general cleanliness, the preparation for marriage, and the facilitation of sexual intercourse.
4. A form of sacrifice (in some cultures) of the reproductive powers to the gods of fertility. Some practitioners believed it to be a substitute for human sacrifice.
5. An act of purification to remove ritual impurity.

The post-operative pain, illness, and sometimes even death, caused the Roman Emperor Hadrian to issue an edict making circumcision, along with castration, a capital crime. Reaction to this decree was believed to be the cause of the Jewish revolt (132-135 AD) led by Bar Cocheba ("Son of the Star") who was highly regarded by his countryman as the Messiah. In the same connection, many men who would have accepted Christ refused to join the Church. Consequently, Gentile women made up a large proportion of the membership of the early Christian Church.

As Hellenistic influence increased in Palestine, the Jews became intimately involved with the Greeks and Romans in the gymnasium (Gr. *gymnasiun*, "to

Face-off With the Judaizers

exercise naked"). This situation led to difficult compensatory measures. Some tried to overcome the embarrassment of their circumcision by the painful practice of "epispasm."[8]

CIRCUMCISION AND THE GOSPEL

Paul's early work in Galatia had been very successful. With characteristic enthusiasm the now-Hellenized Gentile Celts had accepted Christ. Upon arrival, the Judaizers had received the same whole-hearted attention that the Apostle had. As a result, a veritable "epidemic of circumcision" had broken out. Paul addressed the situation head on.

He gave the act of circumcision a figurative and spiritual meaning: "For he is not a Jew who is one outwardly, nor is circumcision that which is outwardly in the flesh. But he is a Jew who is one inwardly: and circumcision is that which is of the heart, by the Spirit, not by the letter" (Rom 2:28, 29 NASB). Here Paul drew on an Old Testament injunction: "So circumcise your heart and stiffen your neck no longer" (Dt 10:16; 30:6). Paul believed, as did Moses, that the "circumcised heart" lies open and obedient to God's will and command. It does not close itself to the appeals of the Gospel or stubbornly strive against Him. Rather, it submits completely to the rulership of God.

Paul also taught that the true circumcision is not by hands, but by the "removal of the body of the flesh by the circumcision of Christ" (Col 2:11). He pointed out that for Gentiles neither circumcision nor un-circumcision had any value. Only "faith working through love" (Gal 5:6) in "a new creation" could succeed (Gal 6:15). Whereas this rite had been a necessary part of Jewish national life, it was *never* part of the Christian Gospel. And, above all, Paul declared, it could not be necessary to salvation.

In taking his stand on the circumcision issue the Apostle changed the course of Christianity. The Gentiles required only "circumcision of the heart." Although few of them could see it, the Jews also needed heart-circumcision. Ultimately they had to add this spiritual dimension to their strong "physical" tradition.

THE CRISIS IN GALATIA

The Galatian crisis that Paul faced was precipitated by the fact that Titus, a prominent leader in the Church, was himself not circumcised. His Gentile background excused him from the ordeal, and Paul argued passionately against it (Gal 2:3). At the same time, the Apostle insisted on the circumcision of Timothy (Acts 16:3). Now, the Judaizers denounced Paul for being two-faced.

One's "Jewishness" was transmitted through the mother's rather than the father's line. Timothy, however, had a Jewish mother, Eunice, and a Greek father (Acts 16:1-3). That made him legitimately a Jew, even though the family did not practice Judaism. Moreover, Paul also pointed out that Timothy's maternal grandmother, Lois, taught him the precepts of his heritage (2 Tim 1:5).

On the other hand, Titus, the son of Gentile parents, had been baptized as a Greek proselyte. He had incited the controversy by denying the necessity of physical circumcision. This public opposition, of course, deeply offended the Judaizers in Galatia. Because the powerful teaching of Paul gave the word "circumcision" a new and spiritual meaning (Rom 2:28-29), Titus never had to undergo the rite.

Having come to Christ through Judaism, the Judaizers now determined to sweep all the Gentile Christians into their camp (Acts 15). In turmoil, the Galatians found themselves torn between the two "Circumcision Parties" and Paul.

THE PROBLEM FOR PAUL

The Apostle's greatest concern seemed to be his new converts' infatuation with Jewish ways. They appeared to succumb very easily to the teachings of the Judaizers. Of course, Paul well understood the meaning of transferring allegiance, since he himself had moved from the culture of Judaism into the new community of Christ. Nonetheless, he proudly declared his Jewish heritage: "Circumcised the eighth day, Israelite by race, of the tribe of Benjamin, a Hebrew born and bred; in my attitude to the law a Pharisee; in pious zeal, a persecutor of the church; in legal rectitude faultless" (Phil 3:5). Indeed, he had the Jewish system ingrained into his very being.

Then he encountered Christ on the Damascus Road and later spent three-and-a-half years in the Arabian Desert under Divine tutelage. With little resistance, he simply accepted Christ. Later, he would explain, "To Jews I became like a Jew, to win Jews; as they are subject to the law of Moses. I put myself under that law to win them, although I am not myself subject to it" (1 Cor 9:20).

Today, we might expect the Apostle Paul to argue against the Christian concept of becoming "Spiritual Israel." He would think the idea a deceptively accommodating form of Judaizing. He felt Gentile converts could be genuine heirs to the promises of God to Israel, without becoming Jews. Indeed, he saw compelling Gentile Christians to "live as Jews" (either naturally or spiritually) as an abandonment of the Gospel.

Battling against the fanatical Gentile Judaizers, Paul responded passionately to their charges. He could tolerate no delay in delivering his message. He

Face-off With the Judaizers

would not allow them to obliterate the work he had done at great personal cost and exertion. Moreover, the issue went far beyond mere circumcision as such. The Judaizers challenged the sufficiency of Christ's work for salvation and prodded the Galatian converts to reject Paul's teachings. They identified the law as a permanent, valid prescription of Divine Orthodoxy. Therefore, they loudly announced that not one of the new Christians could join God's community without observing Jewish practices.

In a manner of speaking, Paul here appears as the first Christian "anti-Semite." This, despite his own personal Hebraic ties.

THE FAITH-AND-GRACE SOLUTION

Maintaining that no one can (authentically) keep the law, Paul preached a totally new way of salvation. God in Christ had provided a free way by grace. Therefore, asking the Gentiles to live as Jews as a condition of salvation had to be worse than useless.

Paul argued a further point. Prior to their conversion the Galatians were "the slaves of beings which in their nature" are no gods. How then could they "turn back to the mean and beggarly spirits of the elements? Why do [they] propose to enter their service all over again?" (Gal 4:8-9). Here the Apostle used the Greek word (*stoicheia*)— "weak and beggarly rudiments"—to describe the yoke of bondage being placed on these Galatians by hostile principalities and powers. No doubt, the Judaizers owed much of their success to the Gaelic affinity for religious ritual.

Paul pleaded with the churches not to build their lives around the rite of circumcision or any other ceremonial law. He identified these powers as the same "demonic powers that enslaved the Galatian Christians in their pagan past when they worshipped false gods."[9] From his rich reservoir of language, Paul employed harsh expressions in his polemic against the Judaizers. He *demanded* to be heard.

Also, given as they were to equitable law-keeping, the Celtic believers in the Galatian churches would have been particularly susceptible to the haranguing of the Judaizers. Probably equating circumcision with baptism for all proselytes hardly surprised the Gaelic converts. For this reason, Paul had to take great pains to clarify his position. So much so that he dared to announce: "If anyone preaches at variance with the gospel which you received [from me], let him be outcast" (Gal 1:9). In this time and place, the crisis required action—prompt and direct.

Having never been the one to back off from a confrontation, Paul exposed the Judaizers' greed, deceptions, and irrationality, for all time.

6. LIBERTY OR DEATH?

You, my friends, were called to be free men, only do not turn your freedom into license for your lower nature (Gal 3:13).

Some of the most significant Celtic gifts to humanity are the determination to be free, individualistic, and authentic. The constant Gaelic drive for liberty often turned out to be more important than life itself. Therefore, it must have been mind-boggling to the Apostle Paul to find that the Galatian Christians so quickly capitulated to the restraints imposed by the Judaizers. Immediately he appealed to their ethnic sense of freedom. They had to understand the difference between the ceremonial law and the Gospel of grace.

The Gaelic passion for freedom came through the teachings of their druids. It had been thoroughly embedded in their culture for at least a thousand years. No wonder the Romans feared and denounced those shapers of Gaelic society. One "super-druid" has entered both myth and literature for all time, Merlin.[1] He is connected to a variety of quasi-historical and legendary enchantments. Gifted with omniscient knowledge, he delivered his prophecies in complex poetry and was familiar with dragons and giants. Merlin crowned Arthur king, as a lad of only fifteen. Then he guided this Cornish/Celtic chieftain in his administration and in his battles against the Saxons. With the guidance of Merlin's marvelous intellect King Arthur became the very personification of the distinctive Celtic quest for freedom.

Liberty or Death?

THE CELTIC IDEAL OF FREEDOM

Queen Boudicca of Britain was a "feminist" champion of freedom. Over 100 years earlier, however, Vercingetorix (d 46 BC) of the Arverni, in Gaul, had set the pace for battling the Romans. The invaders invariably attempted to turn all Celtic lands into provinces in their own empire.[2]

While in Gaul, Julius Caesar had complained that only druids and knights were of any "social significance." Therefore, in 51 BC, he destroyed the Gaulish druid center at Remi, feeling duty-bound to raze this source of power held by the Gaelic elite. Upon hearing the news, Vercingetorix called his dependents together and, without difficulty, roused their passions against this insult to their basic freedoms. Indeed, all of central Gaul rose up against Rome.[3]

Having the ability to choose battle sites most favorable to his forces, Vercingetorix won a major victory with the fall of Gergovia. Then he retreated to his heavy, natural fortifications (*oppida*).[4] On the way, his troops burned the Gallic towns behind them so that the enemy had no provisions left to pillage. In the end, however, Roman discipline and superior strategy won the war.

The story, however, doesn't quite end there. The surrender of Vercingetorix reveals much about Celtic honor and determination for freedom. He was finally forced to withdraw to his hill-fort[6] of Alesia.

Julius Caesar subjugated almost all of Gaul when Vercingetorix of the 58 Averni rebelled in 52 BC.[5]

In the last stand, Vercingetorix controlled all of central Gaul and rallied 100,000 foot soldiers and 8,000 light cavalry. They came hell-bent on destroying the legions of Julius Caesar. Unfortunately, because of their busy preoccupation with building siege-works, this huge army could not win. Eventually, starvation faced the king and his troops within Alesia.

All of them well knew the murderous habits of the enemy. The Romans slaughtered non-combatants indiscriminately, just as they did men-at-arms. Attempting to secure freedom for his women and children as well as the elderly,[7] Vercingetorix sent these vulnerable people out of the fort. The Romans, however, turned them back, demanding nothing less than the surrender of Vercingetorix himself. (Caesar would not be robbed of any part of his victory.) Customarily, captive Celtic chieftains were humiliated and displayed in chains as part of the victor's ceremonial "triumph." Then they were executed.

Knowing what lay ahead of him in Rome, Vercingetorix might have considered his only option, suicide. Instead, he offered himself as a means of bargaining for the thousands of his tribesmen whom he had led in revolt. Having fought furiously for the freedom of Gaul, he tried to save all of those who would otherwise have been killed.

Calling his council together, Vercingetorix offered them two options: "Kill me and send my head to Caesar as appeasement. Or send me to him alive." His kinsmen chose the latter. Wearing his colorful best clothes and his golden torc and carrying his well-used weapons, the proud chieftain mounted his finest horse. He circled the ruins of the fort and then, with dignity, gave himself over to Julius Caesar, who waited for him amid the ruins of Alesia.

Caesar then took his distinguished prisoner to Rome in chains, loging in a dungeon under the Capitol. Six year later (46 BC), Caesar staged his official triumph. From the pit-prison he brought out the last and most famous of all the rulers of Gaul, Vercingetorix. Before cheering crowds, the captive bowed his proud head and was decapitated.[8]

Vercingetorix of the Arverni tribe in Gaul. The statue dominates the plateau of Alesis where the chieftian resisted Rome. After his defeat (52 BC), a small town developed on this hill, the site of that bitter Celtic tragedy.

THE GOSPEL OF FREEDOM

The book of Galatians has been called "the Magna Carta of Christian liberty." With their long tradition of the love of liberty, the zealous Galatian Christians should have been a ready audience for Paul's Gospel of freedom. They well understood the cost of it, and the sacrifices that were so often required. At first, they did. Then, the Judaizing interlopers began to seduce them back into spiritual slavery.

Paul, "The Apostle of the Heart Set Free,"[9] was distressed when he discovered the plight of the churches in Galatia. Having taken to heart the Gospel of Freedom, how could these beloved new Christians have traded the freedom of grace for the legalistic Jewish traditions advocated by the troublemakers?

Liberty or Death?

Paul might have approached the problem in a frontal attack. With the caustic vinegar of denunciation, he could have destroyed the heresy in a single stroke. After all, he had rebuked Peter for tolerating this very error into which the Galatians were now being drawn. (Gal 2:11-18). Instead, he chose to apply the sweet savor of grace. He drew on his own faith-experience to validate his teaching (Gal 3:11).

PAUL *VERSUS* THE JUDAIZERS

In terms of endearment, however, the often strident Apostle set before the sorely unsettled Galatians the issue of their freedom: "For *you, brethren*, have been *called into* liberty: only use not liberty for an occasion to the flesh, but *by love serve* one another" (Gal 5:13). The Apostle outlined a six-step argument against his opponents.

1. **You!** This emphatic you indicates that, had the Galatians been present in person, Paul would have pointed a friendly, bony finger at them and said: "This is about you. Not the Judaizers."
2. **Brethren** (Gr. *adelphoi*). The word denotes a blood brother—not only by biological birth to the same parents, but also through Christ. That is, rebirth and adoption. Paul wanted his hearers to recognize their role in a family, a "partnership of faith." Their identity derived from being "in Christ," not in keeping Jewish traditions.
3. **Called out**. This term comes from *kal* (called) and *ek* (out). That is, a strong, audible invitation to the Galatians, a call to leave their druidical paganism and to partake of Christian blessings. This growing fellowship of believers did not evolve by chance nor did it come with charismatic evangelists and orators. It came from God. The summons was to a greater-than-human appointment: "You did not choose Me, but I chose you, appointed you that you would go and bear fruit, and that your fruit would remain" (Jn 15:16).
4. **The Purpose of Freedom**. In their rapid slide into legalism, the Galatians must have been startled by the word "freedom" in this context. Few others knew so well the trials and triumphs attending the cause of freedom. No one could better appreciate the cost and passion of preserving liberty. Contrary to those who proclaimed salvation by works through the "keeping" of rigid rules, Paul extolled the liberty of salvation by faith. This liberty, however, was not a license to reject divine instructions (Lev 11:44). Nor did it release them from loyalty and obedience to God (Gal

5:6). Indeed, the Judizers had piled impossible restrictions on the people making a person "twice as much the son of hell" (Mt 23:15).
5. **Beware of False Liberty**. Paul warned against turning freedom into a self-indulgent "opportunity for the flesh." The Christians' great privilege had to be nurtured and not abused. It should shelter them from wickedness and not be a gateway into evil. Anyone thinking him/herself free from the moral law has accepted a lethal counterfeit.[10] At the other extreme, the reward of Judaizing is often a litany of legalistic restraints whereby the *adherents* hoped to avoid lawlessness. Liberty may easily be mistaken for license. Paul determined to make the Galatian Christians understand the difference between the two. Freedom is safe only with self-control.[11]
6. **By Love Serve**. To divert them from the false course on which the Judaizers had set them. Paul declared that most liberated Christians were bound to obey the law of love (Rom 13:8). To the Galatians he announced the basic principle: "For the whole Law is fulfilled in one word, in the statement, 'You shall love your neighbor as yourself'" (Gal 5:15).[12] What other rule of action could be more compelling, comprehensive, or divine in the Christian's life?

A DIVINE PARADOX

In summary, Paul introduced a wonderful paradox.

First, he argued for liberty. Now he insisted upon law. First, he championed Christian freedom. Then he declared that they must be slaves: "Through love be servants one to another." Herein lies the whole solution to the problem of law *versus* Gospel, works *versus* faith, legalism *versus* Christ-centered liberty. The list goes on: "The Gospel does not discredit moral law; it shows how this law can be fulfilled." "Faith" does not make "works" unnecessary; it produces works (Jas 2:17–18). "Christian liberty does not make one free to sin. It enables one to attain the righteousness that the law demands."[13]

As faith works through love, the one pardoned by grace learns to love the Lawgiver—and to do so with rejoicing. Often referring to himself as a servant (Rom 1:1; Titus 1:1), Paul declared that voluntary servitude to another is one of the very highest expressions of love.

The person who gives occasion to "the flesh," serves self, not others. Indeed, the only evidence that one is operating under the freedom of the Gospel is that he/she will not take advantage of other people. All of the "Fruits of the

Liberty or Death?

Spirit" will prevail (Gal 5:22-23; 6:10). In a marvelous way, Christian maturity ultimately fulfills the law (Rom 13:10).

In the early days of their conversion, the Galatians had been motivated, if not controlled, by this law of love. Yet, they had quickly turned to the legal requirements foisted upon them. Because they had taken their eyes off Christ, they fell under the spell of the Judaizers. So, they now spiraled downwards, out of control, acting like wild beasts toward one another (Gal 5:15). Having lost the power of vital faith, they allowed malice, hatred and bitterness to rule their hearts. Every form of feud and contention arose among them, as violent as in their pagan days (Gal 5:16).

Freedom of the Gospel comes only with the consistent exercise of love. In the universal conflict between good and evil, the Christian could win in just one way. Paul could only call the Galatians back to their first faith and to the model of their divine Master, Jesus Christ. His voice resounded with passion.

In a very un-druidic gesture, the Celtic wizard, Merlin, dictates his poems to a Christian scribe.[14]

III. Spiritual Practice

7. The Solitary Way

[After my conversion] I went off at once to Arabia [for three years]"
(Gal 1:17).

As St. Ailbe (d. 528 AD) observed in his ascetic teachings: "Two thirds of piety consists of being silent."[1] To be sure, the Skelligs (Irish "rock") off southwest Ireland have long provided such a retreat. "[It is] an incredible, impossible, mad place," Bernard Shaw wrote in 1910. "The thing does not belong to any world that you and I have lived and worked in; it is part of our dream world. . . . A magic . . . takes you out, far out, of this time and this world."[2] He was describing the Skelligs, three rocky islands, just eight miles off the coast of County Kerry, southwest Ireland.

On a flight from New York to Gatwick, London (if you sit on the left side of the plane), you can see the jagged pyramids jutting up out of the Atlantic. This, of course, pre-supposes that you have made your journey on a clear day.

On the largest rock, Skellig Michael, a little monastery with its six remaining beehive huts, perches on a narrow ledge, 600 feet above the water. The rugged sanctuary could accommodate just a dozen men and a few sheep and goats. (Cows and pigs tended to fall off the rocky cliffs into the churning ocean below.) This is our best-preserved example of early Christian architecture. Yet, none of the monks' writings could survive the harsh elements, to say nothing of the Viking invasions.[3]

The Solitary Way

Left: The Skellig Islands, Ireland. Right: The monk's private, domed beehive cells on Skellig Michael. Inside, each was furnished with a stone bed and shelves.

Little has changed in the last 1,400 years. The birds, the fish and the storms are still here. For only a few hours in the morning, a visitor can find a boat to make the pilgrimage to the sacred island. A penitential "stairway to heaven," composed of some 500 stone steps leads up to a narrow space between the two rock peaks, known as "Christ's Saddle."

At sunset, from the beach at Ballinskelligs Bay, County Kerry, one can see the islands, floating on a misty gray ocean. That view recaptures some of the mysticism of the Celts, both pagan and Christian. Established as a very remote retreat for Christian monks in the 7th century AD, this monastic complex shows just how far a Celt would go to secure silence, solitude and privacy for prayer and meditation. Interestingly enough, we find numerous solitary islands off Ireland's west coast. Since they do not face Scotland, Wales and England,[4] the Irish monks found them useful retreats.

CELTIC URBANIZATION

As their Celtic cousins had done in Ireland, the Galatian tribes settled into towns only in the Hellenized south of Anatolia. They preferred isolated farmsteads on the northern plateau, however, with houses scattered at a distance in fields and pastures. Much the same situation still prevails in rural Ireland today. Traditionally, the people went to market towns for fairs and trade. Also, they attended rituals at sacred centers where the king presided, if he had enough personal charisma. Then, whenever they came under attack, they could go to their walled forts for protection. Thus, each four-generation family lived according to their own rules.

Language and religion, not political unity, held Celtic culture together. Because Rome did not value an individual for his personal qualities, their society became a rigid structure of interlocked rules. Effective for discipline, of course. As the Celts gave way to Rome, however, they struggled long and hard to maintain relationships based on kinship. As the process of Hellenization went on, the Galatians became absorbed into the hierarchy, bureaucracy and pursuit of wealth—Rome's ideal of Empire. Paul, therefore, found the Galatians in the midst of the fracturing of their strong, ancestral society.[6]

Bamburgh Castle, Northumbria, became the stronghold of the Christian Saxon king Oswald. It lies directly across the bay from Holy Island (Lindisfarne), a source of religious inspiration from the time of Aidan onward.[5]

At the same time, several features in the Celtic character contributed to a deep need for solitude and even extreme asceticism. These include: (1) rural living, (2) basic Celtic wanderlust, (3) a fierce individuality, and (4) a love of learning, with all of its cerebral challenges. Therefore, Gaelic tribes turned instinctively to remote regions. For them, the result was an on-going political vulnerability that plagued the Celts everywhere and at all times.

CELTIC MONASTICISM

Monasticism (Gr *monos*, "alone") became an integral part of Christianity from the 3rd century forward. It came to the West from the great eastern tradition of asceticism (self-denial) and eremitism (the solitary life). It developed in a very complex lifestyle. Both austere living and a lively intellectual tradition characterized Celtic monasticism.

The Desert Fathers of Egypt and Syria greatly influenced Celtic Christianity. St. Anthony (250-350 AD) exiled himself to the mountain of Pispir by the

The Solitary Way

The Monk and His Cat

I and Pangur Ban my cat,
'Tis a like task we are at;
Hunting mice is his delight,
Hunting words, I sit all night.

Better far than praise of men
'Tis to sit with book and pen;
Pangur bears me no ill will,
He too plies his simple skill.

'Tis a merry thing to see
At our tasks how glad are we,
When at home we sit and find
Entertainment to our mind.

Oftentimes a mouse will stray
To the hero Pangur's way,
Oftentimes my keen thought set
Takes a meaning in its net.

'Gainst the wall he sets his eye
Fully and fierce and sharp and sly;
'Gainst the wall of knowledge I
All my little wisdom try.

When a mouse darts from its den
O how glad is Pangur then!
O what gladness to I prove
When I solve the doubts I love!

So in peace our tasks we ply,
Pangur Ban, my cat and I;
In our arts we find our bliss,
I have mine and he has his.

Practice every day has made
Pangur perfect in his trade,
I get wisdom day and night
Turning darkness into light.

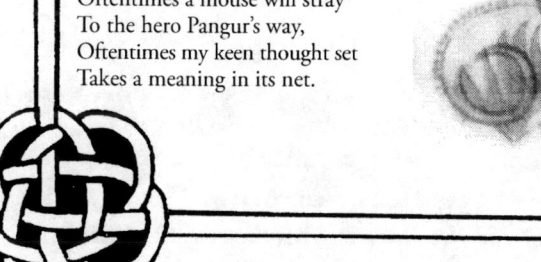

The fanciful poem, "The Monk and His Cat," describes the Celtic excitement over having emerged from a "bookless" society into the joys of extended learning. The earthy activities of the cat parallel the monk's quest for truth. This charming piece demonstrates the typical Gaelic talent for linking the commonplace with the spiritual.[7]

Nile River. This Egyptian hermit founded Christian monasticism and established "monastic rule." He spent years of solitude in search of the "immaculate austerity" of the early Christians. His was a natural reaction to the hedonism in contemporary churches.[8]

Many spiritual leaders today speculate that we run away from silence for fear of what we might discover in ourselves. Indeed, we are addicted to noise. Even the New Testament Gospels are full of action, noise and talk. Jesus debated in the synagogues, traveled with his disciples, and went to His death with a loud, angry mob. Consider, however, His private times of prayer and meditation, as well as His forty days in the wilderness.[9]

Celtic monks constantly sought silence. They embraced stillness. Instead of loneliness or emptiness, they found God. Well may we covet their sense of tran-

Left: The Irish High Crosses have been called "prayers in stone." They combined the circle of the sun and the seasons with the cross of Christ. The endless circle also symbolized eternity. A drawing of the 17-foot West Cross at Monasterboice (1857).[10] Right: The "Scripture Cross" at Clonmacnoise ("Meadow of the Son of Nos," c 900 AD). A picturesque abbey site on the banks of the Shannon River, Ireland. Its carvings tell Bible stories, including the crucifixion of Christ and His second coming at the end of time. The first scene above the base shows the resurrection of Christ with two soldiers seated on either side of the tomb.[11]

The Solitary Way

quility. Aware of this Celtic love for solitude, Paul told these believers (and none of the other churches) of his own self-isolation in the Arabian Desert. Living as they did on scattered estates, they would understand the benefit of "time out." Although historical evidence indicates that the Gospel filtered into Ireland earlier, the great Christian centers evolved in the 5th century AD, without bloodshed. Nonetheless, devout believers wished, as far as possible, to sacrifice themselves after the manner of Christ.[12] Their practices proved to be so ethnic that they might apply anywhere that we find the Gaelic tribes turning away from their paganism.

THREE GAELIC MARTYRDOMS

Irish Christians practiced three types of martyrdom.

1. The White Martyrdom

White martyrdom called for a follower to sacrifice "everything he loves in the world." He would give himself up to the ascetic life, fasting, manual labor, and contemplation in solitary places. White martyrs thrived on isolation. Only with effort did they serve as soul friends or establish monastic communities. This "divine restlessness" of self-imposed exile was often called "deep asceticism." Celtic mystics never hesitated to "crucify their bodies on the blue waves." St. Columban advised: "Let this principle abide with us, that on the road we . . . live as travelers, as pilgrims, as guests of the world."[13]

Some Celtic Christians, at this point, adopted celibacy. This choice, however, remained an option until the influence of the Roman church predominated. The founders of Celtic monasteries derived their learning from Rome, but when they returned to found their own religious houses, they organized them according to their own inclinations. With the strong influence of kinship and loyalty, many found no difficulty in allowing pious people to serve God as couples and family units.

A contemporary of St. Patrick, St. Kevin, descended from the royal house of the Kings of Leinster. From the age of seven, however, he showed unusual piety and had no interest in practicing his warrior heritage.[14] Seeking solitude, Kevin chose the lovely valley of Glendalough (Irish, *Gleann Da Locha*, "The Glen of the Two Lakes") in County Wicklow, Ireland. He lived as a hermit, sometimes sleeping in the hollow of a tree. He didn't plan for it, but his reputation spread far and wide. Students came from all over Ireland, England, and Europe, until his monastery grew into a great and holy city, as well as a famous school of learning.

It has been said that "saints who flee the world to find God in solitude often attract a crowd." Refugees from the world often follow them. Eventually,

Kevin had to come down from his rocky retreats on the Upper Lake. Hence, Glendalough became an ideal for the next three centuries. The monks there transformed solitude into a vibrant new form of Christian community.[15]

Today, thousands of people still visit this site. One must first pass the Glendalough hotel, restaurants, and the parking lot (with its large population of tour buses). Everyone leaves all at the gate leading down into the ruins of Kevin's monastery, the graveyard, round tower oratory, and cold stream. The ambitious then may spend several hours hiking up to the two lakes. In this quiet valley, dressed in Ireland's celebrated "forty shades of green," the spirit of Kevin lingers in a convincing way.

Left: The stream of Glendalough, Ireland, descends from the upper lake where St. Kevin lived as a hermit. Right: Because of his piety, St. Kevin attracted many followers. Here, "St. Kevin's Kitchen," became the center of a large monastic city. (Photos by Dorothy Minchin-Comm)

2. Green Martyrdom

Green Martyrdom took self-exile one step further. It involved travel, sometimes into uncharted seas. The Celts had a distinctive curiosity, fascination with new ideas and new settings, and an instinct to expand their boundaries. The green martyrdom, for the Irish, therefore, was more easily undertaken than for Christians from more urbanized and regulated societies.

In the case of St. Brendan the Navigator we have some difficulty separating history from hagiography (medieval saints' stories). What is fact and what

The Solitary Way

is fantasy? Where does mysticism end and maritime adventure begin?[16] The young Brendan heard a sermon based on Mt 19:29. It called for cutting all material ties and promised eternal life. Thus inspired, Brendan prayed to God for permission to cross the seas in search of the so-called Land of Promise—an Edenic Paradise believed to lie to the west of Ireland. Upon the voyage, Brendan said: "Is not God the pilot and sailor of our boat? Leave it to Him. He Himself guides our journey as He wills." His epic-tale of seafaring and faith became a medieval bestseller![17] Thus Brendan became a potent symbol of wanderlust.

Although they were attached to their land and kinfolk, the Celts, both pagan and Christian, developed a taste for voyaging to the ends of the earth and doing so in their tiny boats. Additionally the long journey often served as an act of penitence and repentance. Green martyrdom, therefore, had strong spiritual as well as material rewards. Today, we commonly speak of the spiritual life as a journey, and we have metaphors for life's long, winding road. In the following prayer of St. Brendan, note the intense "Celticness" of the possessions that he renounces.

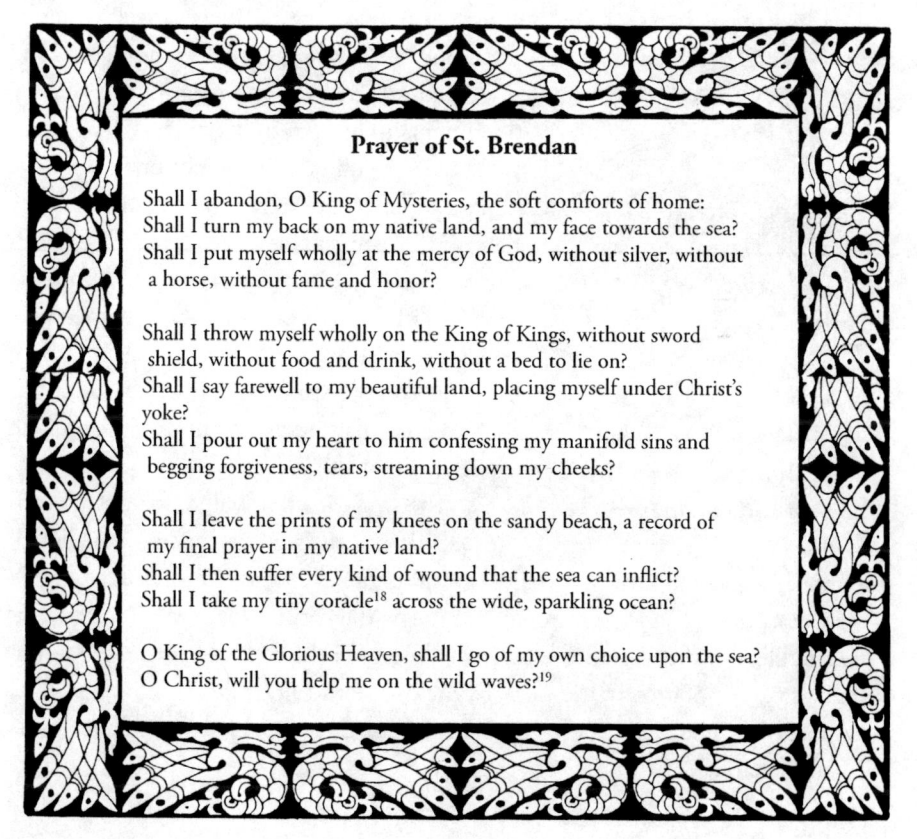

Prayer of St. Brendan

Shall I abandon, O King of Mysteries, the soft comforts of home:
Shall I turn my back on my native land, and my face towards the sea?
Shall I put myself wholly at the mercy of God, without silver, without
a horse, without fame and honor?

Shall I throw myself wholly on the King of Kings, without sword
shield, without food and drink, without a bed to lie on?
Shall I say farewell to my beautiful land, placing myself under Christ's yoke?
Shall I pour out my heart to him confessing my manifold sins and
begging forgiveness, tears, streaming down my cheeks?

Shall I leave the prints of my knees on the sandy beach, a record of
my final prayer in my native land?
Shall I then suffer every kind of wound that the sea can inflict?
Shall I take my tiny coracle[18] across the wide, sparkling ocean?

O King of the Glorious Heaven, shall I go of my own choice upon the sea?
O Christ, will you help me on the wild waves?[19]

Even the modern Celts in Ireland can be very ascetic. For instance, they like their pilgrimages harsh. On the last Sunday in July, they climb Croagh Patrick on bare, bleeding feet. Thousands return to this annual experience, apparently enjoying self-inflicted punishment as much as the old Celtic saints did.[20]

The story of Columba's self-exile and his founding of the monastery of Iona exhibit effects of both White and Green Martyrdom. On that tiny, three-mile island, he accomplished a trio of goals, his influence reaching all the way into the 7th century AD. First, the strong Gaelic love of studying and of copying manuscripts made it possible for the European heathen to be taught and nurtured into a uniquely mystical experience. Second, the monastery educated evangelist-monks to travel and re-Christianize many European lands. Finally, these monks of Iona preserved some of the most significant literary documents in our culture.[22]

St. Brenden, the Navigator of Clonfert (c 484–578 AD).[21]

Skeptics question the emotionalism of the "Dark Ages." Celtic religious enthusiasm, the heart of its spirituality, is embedded in both their mythology and their scriptural labors. To dismiss either of these would betray two basic beliefs. First, a personal God exists, along with angels and other spiritual entities. Second, humankind can have regular communication with these spiritual beings.[23]

St. Columba (521–597 AD) of Iona Scotland[24]

Therefore, when the tall, princely Columba neared his end, it is not surprising that he encountered angels and had a specific message about the time of his death. All Celts knew that "death had to be factored into the mathematics of daily life." The hope of the afterlife, however, made it just one more stage in the cycle of living.[25] We simply return to "Our Source." One week before his death (597 AD), Columba told his companions. "Look, an angel of the Lord is sent to recover a loan." All of them understood that life is a gift, not a possession or entitlement.[26]

The Solitary Way

3. The Red Martyrdom

Too lively and too stubborn to seek death deliberately at the hands of persecutors, the Celtic saints often chose to *fight* their way to victory. Nonetheless, they were intensely aware of the sacrifice of Christ and of the fate of so many martyrs in the Roman Empire. Whenever the call came, then, they faced death with unflinching courage.

Guided by the ascetic piety of the Desert Fathers, numbers of Irish monks traveled to the Continent where many suffered Red Martyrdom. At the same time, new Christian teachers arose among their Celtic cousins in Gaul and in other Gaelic colonies in Europe. We may briefly consider three of them.

- ***St. Martin** (316-397 AD) was a lowborn soldier from Pannonia (Hungary). Only reluctantly did he accept the bishopric of Tours, in Gaul. Much beloved throughout his long life, he established his monastery at Tours. It became a major training ground for Celtic missionaries.[27]
- ***St. Basil** (330-379 AD) came from Cappadocia, a kingdom neighboring Galatia. He inaugurated one new feature in the rapidly developing culture of monasticism—the establishment of religious communities. After years of self-exile and purification, he developed a spiritual retreat that became a social and scholarly center.[28]
- ***St. Honore** (c350-429 AD), unwillingly, became Bishop of Arles. After his conversion, he wanted to pursue the hermit-life. Coming from a noble Gallo-Roman family, he integrated his monastery with the lives of the people around him. A very successful outreach to the local villagers.[29]

These three Christians from Europe and Asia Minor pre-date St. Patrick and his mission to the Irish. Their monasteries exhibit several ingrained Celtic traits: A desperate need for the solitary life, a gregarious ministry to the monks under them and to visitors, and a compulsion to study.

PAUL'S TRIPLE MARTYRDOMS

Paul would not have, at first, recognized the Irish terms of "White," "Green," and "Red" Martyrdoms. He would, however, have realized that in his own life he had suffered—and eventually would suffer--all of them. These forms of piety had established themselves in the Christian Church, all quite un-Roman in nature. Paul's suffering may be seen as:

White: His retreat into Arabia? The Galatians being the only ones to whom he described his wilderness exile.

Green: His missionary journeys. After the resurrection, the twelve apostles and many of the early church fathers scattered. They carried the Gospel to the ends of the then-known world.

Red: His death in Rome, a victim of the tragic years of the persecution of Christians there.

Paul's Solitude

Paul was a gregarious person, not given to isolation and loss of companionship. His time in Arabia, however, set him apart from all of the other teachers who imposed themselves on the Galatians. It would have been of utmost importance to convey to them that he had endured several aspects of martyrdom. Paul's experience was both extraordinary and divine.

Scholars disagree on the exact location of Paul's "Arabian exile." Luke mentions that Paul preached in Damascus after his conversion (Acts 9:19-20). It is generally believed that Paul may have spent his time in the desert near Damascus, venturing into the city itself to preach from time to time. This area was the Syrian Desert, east of Damascus, not the Arabian Peninsula. By combining the time between Paul's conversion and his return to Jerusalem we get a three-year time line.

The Apostle Paul on a medallion in Siena, c 1320 AD.[30]

Paul related that he barely escaped arrest in this place, on the orders of the governor, the Nabatean King Aretas IV (2 Cor 11:32). His mention of Mt. Sinai in Arabia (Gal 4:25) is associated with the contemporary description of the region and is not in contradiction to his previous exile.

We may combine the information from incidental statements in Paul's writings with other sources such as Luke and Acts. "By now, withdrawing into Arabia, a thinly inhabited terrain, extending from the Euphrates in the West far to the north, he immediately turned away from all human influence in order to reflect in solitude on the matter of his calling, and on the turn which his life was now taking."[31]

The Solitary Way

Paul's Conversion

Paul gives the Galatians an account of events in his early conversion in order to explain his absence for such a substantial period of time. He did so for several reasons, including, but not limited to, the following:

1. To prevent the Judaizers from accusing him of having secretly visited the apostles in Jerusalem in order to receive instructions from them. He would remove their unjust censures by demonstrating that he owed no debt to anyone. Jesus Christ had been his only mentor. From Him came his knowledge of the Gospel, his qualifications, his call to the apostolic office, as well as his authority and power.
2. To emphasize that in his solitary retirement away from family, friends, and adherents to his new-found faith, he had received divine revelations to preach the Gospel.
3. To underscore the fact that his special appointment was to preach to the Gentiles (Acts 26:17-18; Gal 2:18). This task caused him not to turn to men for counsel. Thus he could remain fiercely independent, a trait admired by his Galatian audience.
4. To demonstrate that his main concern was not merely to provide biographical details, but also to establish the evidence of his solitary experience. The believers could relate personally to this kind of isolation.

The Galatians would understand that Paul had sacrificed every thing (Phil 3:1-6). Not only had he given up his position as the youngest member of the Sanhedrin, but he had also lost both marriage and family. Joachim Jeremias, a modern expert on the life and times of Jesus and Paul, said that Paul's wife left him when he became a Christian. This grief may explain Paul's poignant expression that he "suffered the loss of all things."[32] "Whatever things were gain to me, those things I have counted as loss for the sake of Christ. More than that, I count all things to be loss in view of the surpassing value of knowing Christ Jesus my Lord, for whom I have suffered the loss of all things and count them but rubbish so that I may gain Christ" (Phil 3:7-8). Thus, like the Celtic Irish Christians four centuries later, Paul took on the "White Martyrdom." The Galatians would have understood that kind of boldness.

Then, as a man of vision and action, Paul became a model of Green Martyrdom. According to Luke, he threw himself into his work as an apostle. He immediately embarked on a series of missionary journeys that would last for the next twenty-two years. His voyage took him and his companions to: Cyprus,

Perga, Pisidian Antioch, Iconium, Lystra, Derbe, and back to Antioch (Acts 12: 24-14:28). After dissension with Barnabas, Paul (and Silas) continued on a second journey: Cilicia, Lystra, Galatia, Asia, Macedonia, and parts of Europe (Philippi, Thessalonica, Berea, Athens, and Corinth). Again, he returned to Antioch (Acts 15:36-18:22). His third journey brought him once more to Galatia and Phrygia, Ephesus and Corinth, Macedonia and Greece, and finally, Jerusalem (Acts 23:1; 21:17).

Finally, history records that the Apostle Paul's life ended in Rome where he was executed. Tradition associates his experience of Red Martyrdom with Emperor Nero's reign of terror, a time of merciless persecution of Christians. The puzzled Roman biographer Suetonius wrote: "Punishment was inflicted on the Christians, a class of men addicted to a novel and mischievous superstition".[33]

Arrested and imprisoned on two separate occasions in Rome, Paul explained that he had been deserted by his companions and other Christians (2 Tim 4:16). He was, for a time, providentially protected from Nero's malice. Indeed, "rescued from the lion's mouth" (2 Tim 4:17). During his second incarceration, sometime shortly after the great fire in Rome (64 AD), Nero sentenced the aging champion of "the true Gospel" to death.

Paul addressed his last words to Timothy: "For I am already being poured out as a drink offering, and the time of my departure has come. I have fought the good fight, I have finished the course, I have kept the faith; in the future there is laid up for me the crown of righteousness, which the Lord, the righteous Judge, will award to me on that day; and not only to me, but also to all who have loved his appearing" (2 Tim 4:6-8).

8. THE JOURNEY-QUEST

I [Paul] went to the regions of Syria and Cilicia (Gal 1:21).

"The longest journey is the journey inward," Dag Hammarskhold once said. This former Secretary of the United Nations would have understood the case of Columba [Irish, *Columcille*] of Iona (521-597 AD).

Born a prince of the royal clan of Garton, Donegal, Ireland,[1] Columba renounced his claim to the high throne of Tara to become a monk. A handsome, ardent youth of extraordinary learning, he was also an ollam (master poet). His practical genius for organization and leadership, along with a proud martial spirit, placed him second only to St. Patrick in the annals of Celtic Christianity. His renunciation of his heritage and his single-minded dedication to God, caused Sir Winston Churchill to praise his "grace and fire." Through him the "light of Christianity burned and gleamed through the darkness," as the Gospel "was carried [back] across the stormy waters [from Ireland] to the North of Britain [and beyond]."

A COPYRIGHT DISPUTE

In the 6th century AD, history's first copyright case occurred in a very Celtic kind of dispute between the idealistic Irish monk, St. Columba, and his abbot, Finian of Molville (c 560). As a youthful scholar at the great Christian school at Clonard, he visited his former teacher. There he saw a copy of the Psalter, recently arrived from Italy—perhaps the first copy of St. Jerome's *Vulgate* to be seen in Ireland. Finian so treasured the beautiful manuscript that he forbade anyone to copy it.

In the high-handed manner of the young aristocrat that he was, Columba coveted and then secretly did copy the precious manuscript, toiling on, night after night. When Finian discovered Columba at work, he demanded that the book be returned, as well as its copy.

Because Columba angrily refused, the two monks went before King Diarmait High King at Tara, asking him to judge the case. He pronounced in favor of the old abbot: "To every cow her . . . calf, and to every book its copy." (A clever play on words here, since parchment was made out of calf hides.)

Enraged, Columba gave up his copy and stormed out of Tara. He called upon his princely kinfolk to avenge the injustice, appealing to "Christ my druid" to aid his cause.

A short time later, a princely kinsman of Columba disturbed the peace at a village fair by accidentally killing one of King Diarmait's servants. Spoiling for a fight, the two sides now faced off at the bloody Battle of Culdreimhne, County Sligo (561 AD). In a rage, Columba's clan defeated Diarmait, and 3,000 men (reportedly) died.

Then remorse and self-reproach filled Columba. Why had he allowed his warrior blood to overcome his Christian sense of duty? Conscience-stricken, he laid penance on himself for the carnage he had caused. Exiling himself to the Hebrides of Scotland (Alba), he founded a famous monastery on the island of Iona (563 AD). He vowed to convert at least as many Scots to Christianity as had died in the battle over the copied manuscript.[2]

With twelve companions he set sail from Derry, Ireland. Beaching their boats on the tiny island of Iona, they destroyed their little leather *curraghs*. No turning back. Standing atop a rocky cairn, Columba looked southwest, but he could see nothing except the empty ocean. "Here we will stop, for I can no longer see Ireland," he sighed. He never allowed himself to see his beloved Derry again, although it was only seventy-five miles distant. The monastery they founded became a very great Christian training center for missionaries.

Prayers for travelling mercies were an essential of every Celtic voyage.

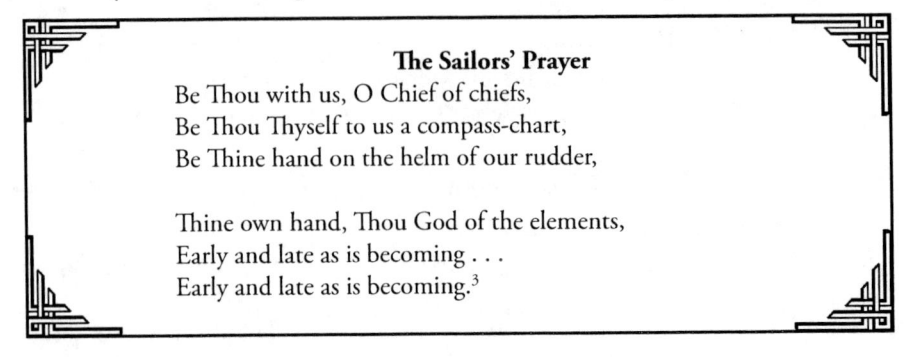

The Sailors' Prayer
Be Thou with us, O Chief of chiefs,
Be Thou Thyself to us a compass-chart,
Be Thine hand on the helm of our rudder,

Thine own hand, Thou God of the elements,
Early and late as is becoming . . .
Early and late as is becoming.[3]

The Journey-Quest

THE IONA MISSION OF SCOTLAND

The Iona monks went first to their emigrant Irish kinsmen who had established the Dalriada Kingdom in Northern Britain. Then they carried the Gospel to King Brude in the wilds of Pictland.[4] Next, the Celtic evangelists turned to the pagan Anglo-Saxons in Northumbria and then pressed on to Europe.[5]

Columba's song of praise for Iona shows that his love of nature is almost pagan in its effusiveness:

> Delightful I think it to be in the bosom of an isle
>   On the crest of a rock,
> That I may see often the calm of the sea.
>
> That I may see its heavy waves
>   Over the glittering ocean,
> As they chant a melody to their Father
>   On their eternal course.[6]

Iona lies one mile off the coast of Mull, Scotland. This tiny, treeless island in the Inner Hebrides is three-and-a-half miles long by one mile wide. St. Columba and his twelve companions arrived here from Ireland in 563 AD. Their self-exile produced one of the most important Christian schools in all of Europe.

THE MONASTIC RULES

An examination of general monastic rules may be helpful.

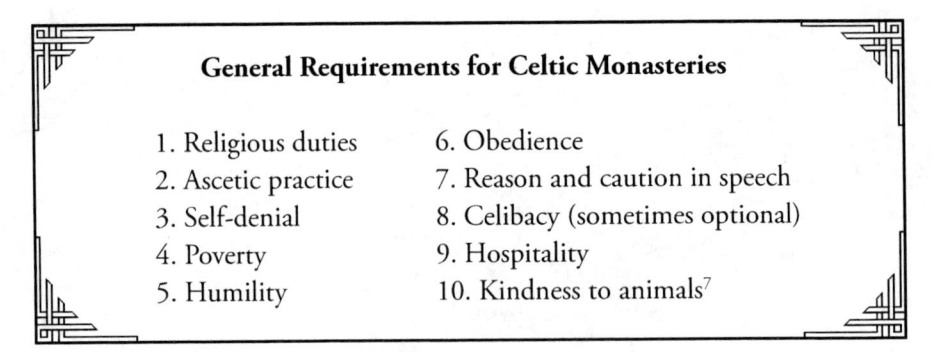

> **General Requirements for Celtic Monasteries**
>
> 1. Religious duties
> 2. Ascetic practice
> 3. Self-denial
> 4. Poverty
> 5. Humility
> 6. Obedience
> 7. Reason and caution in speech
> 8. Celibacy (sometimes optional)
> 9. Hospitality
> 10. Kindness to animals[7]

The specific Rule that Columba prepared for Iona reveals some additional details:

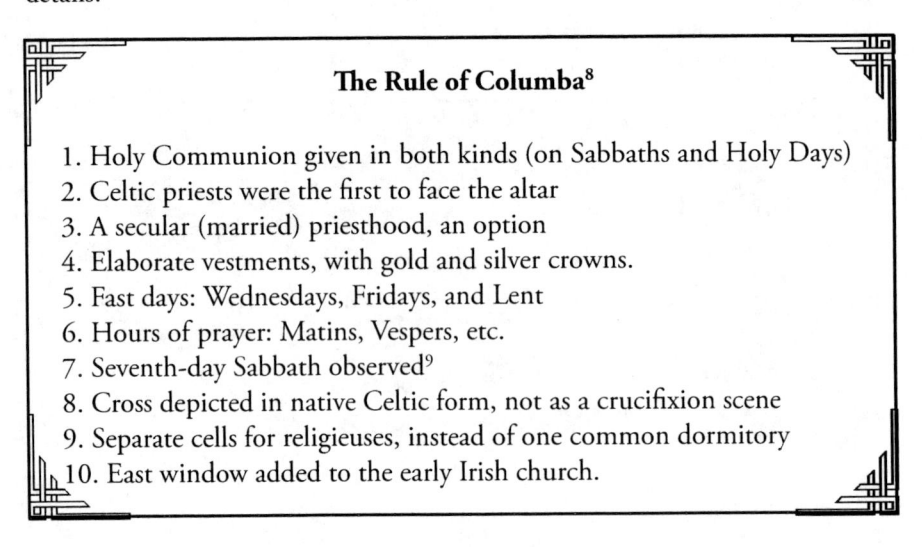

> **The Rule of Columba[8]**
>
> 1. Holy Communion given in both kinds (on Sabbaths and Holy Days)
> 2. Celtic priests were the first to face the altar
> 3. A secular (married) priesthood, an option
> 4. Elaborate vestments, with gold and silver crowns.
> 5. Fast days: Wednesdays, Fridays, and Lent
> 6. Hours of prayer: Matins, Vespers, etc.
> 7. Seventh-day Sabbath observed[9]
> 8. Cross depicted in native Celtic form, not as a crucifixion scene
> 9. Separate cells for religieuses, instead of one common dormitory
> 10. East window added to the early Irish church.

FOUR JOURNEY TYPES

A yearning to explore the unknown remains a heritage from our migratory Celtic ancestors. This tendency became a vehicle to spread Christianity, particularly in the case of the saints of the Insular (Irish) Church. The Celtic Church, east to west, held several characteristics in common, despite geographical distance and the pressures of Rome.[10]

The Galatians on the far-eastern edge of Celtdom were the first on record to hear the Gospel from the Apostle Paul. Some 500 years later, the Irish Chris-

The Journey-Quest

tians at the far-western side of the Celtic colonies, preached the Good News far and wide. The Anglo-Saxons, always fighting for their lives, had little inclination to evangelize their enemies. The Irish, on the other hand, not only welcomed foreigners into their monasteries but also went forth as missionaries into England and Gaul. For the first time in many centuries, they brought a vigorous Celtic presence back to the Continent.[11]

Because Celtic culture has been so enduring, we may examine the well-documented activities of the early Irish Christians. They had seamlessly blended together all of the basics of life. Spiritual fervor and artistic creativity followed them everywhere. Today we may read their prayers and learn from their faith, all the while savoring their practical ordinariness and their hard-working earthiness.[12]

The story of Columba reveals several things about Celtic attitudes toward journeys, both physical and spiritual. The Celts understood *peregrinatio* (Latin "voluntary journeying to exile") in a rich, multi-dimensional way. In it we find something basic, primal, fundamental, and universal. Unfragmented by doctrinal or class differences, it rises effortlessly above all artificial distinctions.[13]

The Journey could be an exile, an adventure, a wandering penance, or a quest. Or even all four at once.

1. The Voluntary Exile & Consecration *(Peregrinatio)*

Like Columba of Iona, Columbanus of Luxeuil (543-615 AD) was one of the greatest Irish exiles. A lonely, brooding child, he grew up to seek out melancholy, solitary surroundings. Describing Christians simply as "guests of the world," he was already middle-aged when he set out to wander over Europe. He founded monasteries, and finally came to die in Bobbio, Italy.[14] Ruthless regulation prevailed in his monasteries, including corporal punishment.[15] At the same time, high scholarship also prevailed. Indeed, Irish learning would preserve classical writings and inspire Christian Europe for the next 400 years.

2. The Adventure

Brendan the Navigator, of Clonfert, County Galway (484-578 AD), represented the older Irish order of monasticism and became one of the first "seekers abroad." Born on Tralee Bay, County Kerry, the child Brendan saw the Western ocean wherever he turned. The black fishing boats nibbling at the shore fascinated him. Here he learned the allure of the uncharted sea. Fostered out at age two, to St. Ita, a devout lady of Limerick, he dedicated himself to the religious life.

After Brendan saw a "Land of Promise" in a vision, he sailed westward with sixty monks. The story of his voyage, *Navigatio Sancti Brendan*, written in the 10th century, was translated into many languages. The manuscript exuberantly described their discovery. First came [an hour's] darkness," then "a great light shone around them. . . .They saw a land . . . thickly set with trees, laden with fruits . . . and for forty days they viewed the landing from various directions, they could not find the limits thereof."[16]

Of course, many fantastic, outlandish legends surround St. Brendan, involving whales, mermaids and preaching to birds. Enough authenticity remains, however, to convince us that authentic seamen's reports lie hidden here. The explorers not only reached volcanic Thule (Iceland[17]) and Greenland but also North America. This intrepid saint has been placed variously in Nova Scotia, Florida and Mexico.

Prayers of the Celtic Christians often went beyond the boundaries of time. The following grace for a meal would befit adventurers like Brendan. It speaks for all of those who lived precariously on the margin between time and eternity.

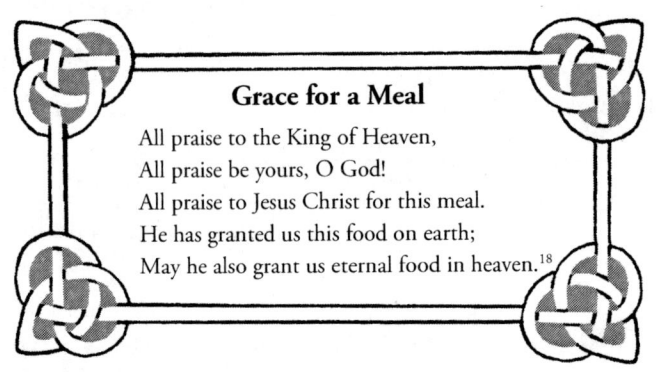

Grace for a Meal

All praise to the King of Heaven,
All praise be yours, O God!
All praise to Jesus Christ for this meal.
He has granted us this food on earth;
May he also grant us eternal food in heaven.[18]

3. The Wandering

Difficulties notwithstanding, the Celts had an inbred tendency to wanderlust. They migrated, as we have seen, all over Europe, driven by the need for more pasturelands and space for their vigorously plentiful population. We find there the restless energy, the burning curiosity, and the desire to expand both physical and mental boundaries. The Celtic monk traveled in the same character, with his leather water bottle, his crosier and his bell, and little else. Bent on spreading the Gospel, he coped with any kind of weather or privation. Although a kindly pilgrim on the road, wherever he was denied hospitality, the Celtic wanderer could bring a resoundingly efficient curse down upon the household.[19]

4. The Search/Quest

Celtic tales of initiatory voyages to the "Otherworld" set the stage for this journey. The hero, for example, is visited by a goddess bearing a perfect, jeweled apple branch. She comes from a place of eternal beauty beyond time, the Land of Apples. Fruit and flowers flourish there all winter. Peace and happiness prevail. Under the spell of a wild song, she invites the mortal to this quest of his heart's desire. The way is dangerous. Pitfalls and temptations beset him, and he sees the landscape with fearful clarity. Thus ran the Celtic myth of King Arthur and what developed into the quest for the Holy Grail. If it is not yet the pilgrim's turn to die, he must return to his earthly life. His vision will strengthen him, however, and he will be able to serve his tribe more fully.[20]

The quest for the Holy Grail[21] has become one of the most pervasive themes of Western culture. Not surprisingly, it has its pagan origins among Indo-European tribes, the Punjab of India and Persia. In the 12th century the journey to see the vision of the Grail consolidated into the romances of King Arthur in Spain and France. Eventually, in Lord Tennyson's "Idylls of the King," we find the knights of the Round Table pouring out of Camelot not only to fight the heathen, but also to go "a-grailing." A clear vision of the Grail insured perfection of Christian character and represented the ultimate mystical experience. Only the most pure in heart, however, could hope to catch a glimpse. This magnificent ideal grew directly out of its Celtic sources.

Gaelic people believed profoundly in the immortal. Their Otherworld was vividly real, a practical, business-like place. This idea never failed to surprise classical writers. They even discovered that a Celt would lend money on a promissory note to be repaid in the next world.[21]

THE OPENING OF THE CHRISTIAN WAY

The public outpouring of the Holy Spirit at Pentecost had profound effects on the 120 believers gathered in the Upper Room (Acts 1:15). Despite the diversity of languages among their listeners, they felt an urgency to bear personal witness to the life, death, resurrection and ascension of Jesus. Moreover, these first Christians would carry the Good News far beyond the borders of Jerusalem, winning thousands to the new faith. Thus, they inaugurated a marvelous "New Age" of blessings and forgiveness.

As the number of believers grew, they declared that they followed "the true Way." A "Way" of faith and life in Jesus Christ. As the Jesus-movement increased, the long names became inconvenient, so the people simply called themselves

"The Way." This name caught on rapidly. Soon, observers and opponents alike were referring to the early Christians as "The Way" (Acts 19:9).

"The Way" brought recognition to the Christians and opened up the opportunity to take the Gospel to all nations. Long before Christianity this expression is in the writings of the Qumran community, serving as a designation for that group's faith and life. Minority groups tend to abbreviate such expressions and make them part of their esoteric vocabulary. "The Way" is simply a shortened version of "the true way" or "the right way."[22]

PAUL'S MISSIONARY JOURNEYS

When we think of travel today, words like "cruise," "luxury coach," and "guided tours" readily come to mind. Or Business Class on an airplane. Or family vacation in a motor home. Or, at least, crossing the desert in our air-conditioned car. All of which effectively removes us from the realities of ancient times. Most people then never got more than twenty miles beyond the place where they were born. Certainly they could never have regarded travel as a pleasure.

Paul was not a person of great presence. By his own admission, he was not impressive in appearance or speech (2 Cor 10:10). (His humiliating disability will be discussed in a later chapter.) Yet, he possessed such profoundly deep qualities of mind and spirit that when God wanted a man who could face the challenges of life as a missionary to unknown (and often violently uncivilized) Gentile nations, He chose this little man.

Perhaps, Paul's zeal for ancestral traditions best qualified him for such a journey-quest. Some of his native and natural impetuosities appear in his letters and missionary experiences. "At times, the torrent of his [Paul's] thought rushes forward so swiftly that it outstrips the flow of his words, and his words have to leap over a gap, now and then, so as to catch up with his thought . . . . Time and again, Paul starts a sentence that never reaches a grammatical end, for before he is well launched on it, a new thought strikes him and he turns aside to deal with that. When he comes back onto the main track, the original start of the sentence has been forgotten. All this means that Paul is not the smoothest of authors or the easiest to follow, but it gives us an unmistakable impression of the man himself."[23] We find nothing artificial or merely conventional about this man Paul.

Therefore, nothing surpasses Paul's spontaneous expressions of tenderness toward his Galatian friends (Gal 4:9). His passion for the Gospel and his deep affection for his new converts explain his explosive indignation. Who would dare mislead his children in the faith?

The Journey-Quest

FINDING THE BALANCE

Despite his three-year retirement in the desert, Paul did not support monasticism as an ideal for the life of the practicing Christian. Rather, on his missionary journeys, he emphasized the importance of fellowship and togetherness. His great love and concern for his converts and companions fueled his sense of mission. He determined to help his listeners reproduce in their own lives the character of Christ, the fruit of the Spirit (Gal 5:22). Indeed, nurturing these godly qualities would require repeated visits, epistolary communications, and instructions carried by trustworthy messengers of the Gospel.

At the same time, Paul recognized a necessary balance. Like Christ, all believers would live "between the mountain (of solitude) and multitude (of social interaction). More than any other disciple/apostle, he understood the universal implications of the Person of Jesus Christ and the practical application of His life to spiritual growth. While many others participated in missions to the Gentiles, Paul's contribution was unique and far-reaching. For example, he emphasized that true religion was not a matter of rules and regulations. In Christ, men and women have "come of age" in a wholly new experience. People must matter more than laws and traditions. Therefore, discrimination on the grounds of race, religion, class, sex, custom or culture is an offense to God, a crime against His beloved creatures.

With his companion, Barnabas, Paul took this good news into the world of the Gentiles. His **First Missionary Journey** took him into Asia Minor, including South Galatia (Acts 12:24-14:28). There they achieved great success, in spite of the smoldering controversy over whether or not the Gospel should be shared with non-Jews. This virulent dispute threatened to divide the early church. In fact, the Jerusalem Council summoned Paul to make a defense of his ministry (Gal 1:11-24). When the Council released Paul to preach with still more freedom and vigor than ever, he departed with Barnabas for Antioch.

MORE MISSIONARY CHALLENGES

At Antioch, Paul and Barnabas were joined by John Mark.[24] A disagreement arose among the three, however, breaching the relationship. Barnabas and his cousin Mark sailed for Cyprus, leaving Paul to begin his **Second Missionary Journey** (Acts 15:36-18:22). Accompanied by Silas, he established churches in Philippi, Achaia (Greece), and Macedonia.

On his **Third Missionary Journey** Paul traveled through Galatia (again), Phrygia and Achaia to teach and encourage the believers (Acts 18:23-21:17). He also took a strong, commanding stance against his Judaizing opponents. He put them on notice that he was not going to allow them to ravage his converts like a pack of wolves among helpless lambs. During that time, he felt compelled to go to Jerusalem, even though Agabus, a local prophet, and others, warned him of impending danger.

After being arrested in the Jerusalem Temple, Paul was taken into the protective custody of the Roman commander, to be tried before the Sanhedrin, Governor Felix, Festus and Agrippa. In each instance, he gave a strong, clear witness to the ministry of Jesus (Acts 21:18-26:32).

Having appealed to Caesar in defense of his rights as a Roman citizen, Paul was sent to Rome for the final hearing and judgment of his case. A storm destroyed his ship on the way, and everyone had to swim to shore (the island of Malta). Even there, Paul seized the occasion to continue sharing his faith. Eventually, the journey continued to Rome, where Paul was held under house arrest until his trial and martyrdom, about 67 AD (Acts 27:1-28:31).

These exploits of Paul not only reveal the inherent excitement and impact of his journey-quest, but they also fill out his experience of triple martyrdom.

Gaelic Triads

Three people that are hardest to talk to:
  A king bent on conquest,
  A Viking in his armor,
  A lowborn man protected by patronage.

Three glories of a gathering [showing off]:
  A beautiful wife,
  A good horse,
  A swift hound.

Three things that come unbidden:
  Fear,
  Jealousy,
  Love.

Three absenses that make a house without cheer:
  A house without a dog,
  A house without a cat,
  A house without a baby.

Three candles that illumine every darkness:
  Truth,
  Nature,
  Knowledge.

May you have:
  Warm words on a cold evening,
  A full moon on a dark night,
  A guinea in your picket.

9. The Discipline of the Rule of Three

But when the proper time came, God sent His Son, born of a human mother and born under the jurisdiction of the law, that he might redeem those who are under the authority of the law, and lead us into becoming by adoption true sons of God. It is because you really are His sons that God has sent the Spirit of His Son into your hearts to cry, "Father! Dear Father" (Gal 4:4-6, Phillips).

Once a year, on St. Patrick's Day (March 17), we are told that the whole world becomes Irish. A harmless, fanciful idea, to be sure. But there is more.

A forest of tradition and legend has grown up around this man Patricus (c385-461 AD). Son of a Romanized British Celt, he was captured and sold into slavery when he was sixteen years old.[1] After six years working as a herdsman in County Antrim, Ireland, he managed to escape.[2] Following some education in Rome, he spent time at the Abbey of Marmoutier, Gaul (AD 431),[3] founded by St. Martin of Tours. Called of God in a dream, Patrick then carried his apostolic mission back to Ireland, twenty years after he had fled from slavery there. He founded more than 300 Christian churches.[4]

Shortly before he died, Patrick wrote his "Confession," one of the few written records we have from the early Celtic Church. It begins: "I, Patrick, a sinner, the most uncouth and the least of all the faithful."[5] Here he displays his Gaelic temperament in his impetuous anger against tyrants, his tenderness toward the weak, and his passion for saving souls.

THE ORIGIN OF THE CHRISTIAN TRINITY

Even at that early developmental stage, the doctrine of the Trinity appeared to have impacted the teaching of Christian truths to pagan Europeans. Both the Apostle Paul and St. Patrick employed the "Rule of Three" extant in Celtic culture, to make the case for Christianity. Patrick appealed to the idea of "threeness." Paul spoke to the majesty of the Trinity. Both of them recognized the pre-eminence of disciplined training among the Gaelic peoples.

The word "trinity" is not a Biblical term. Rather, it represents the crystallization of New Testament teachings about the co-existence of the Father, Son, and Holy Spirit in a unified Godhead. Theophilus of Antioch[6] first used the term. Later, Tertullian (c150-c230 AD), another of the early Church Fathers, popularized the word.[7]

Naturally, Old Testament concepts of Wisdom and the Holy Spirit (Pr 8:22 ff) have also influenced Christian theology. The most prominent idea to foreshadow the doctrine of the Trinity, however, is based on several Hebrew texts that refer to God in the plural form (Gen 1:26; 3:22; 11:7; Isa 6:8). That is, the impressive, majestic "we," reserved for royalty. Many theologians recognize them as the "Plural of Fullness," representing the three Persons of the Godhead.

MORE THAN SHAMROCKS

One popular legend tells us that St. Patrick used the local shamrock to explain the Trinity to his Irish audience, three leaves on a single stem. Actually, he needed no such demonstration. For millennia Celts had been aware of the significance of three, and threefold groupings appear everywhere among them. As we have already observed, their fundamental caste system consisted of three classes: warrior-aristocrats, farmers and serfs.[8]

The number three was lucky, and significant events were believed to "come in threes."[9] The druids taught that three characteristics marked the noble life: Generosity, hospitality, and bravery. Females outnumbered the males in the Celtic pantheon of gods. Indeed, all of society venerated the "Triple Mothers" (*Deae Matres*), who were usually depicted as carrying fruits, bread, and babies.

While the potency of the number "three" has appeared in other ancient cultures, the Celts carried it to a new level. Their poetry, prayers, announcements, and

The Discipline of the Rule of Three

all kinds of messages appeared in "triads" and/or triple repetitions. Through this basic language form, the druids conveyed their complex teachings and encapsulated Celtic wisdom. Their triads remain both astutely practical as well as profound.[10]

A frequent (though sometimes inaccurate) commentator on his enemies, Julius Caesar said that the Gauls all claimed to have descended from Dis Pater, the "All-Father." A visual demonstration of this druidic teaching lies in the Cerne-Abbas Giant. Spread over a green hillside in Dorset, England, he is 200 feet high, his figure delineated by chalk ditches two feet wide. His massive club in his right hand, his phallus, and the remains of a cauldron in his left hand together symbolize his three-part function. His ancient British worshippers honored him as Protector, Procreator, and Provider.[11]

In the" Breastplate of St. Patrick" (an address to the Christian Trinity) Patrick speaks first of his belief in "Threeness." Then he moves on to a "confession of Oneness." In customizing his teachings to his Celtic audience, Patrick reminded them that "threeness" in religion did not imply a coming together of three disparate elements. Instead, it expressed a great, unified potency, a concept well understood in the Celts' pagan traditions.[12]

Not surprisingly, Patrick framed his famous poem in a series of triads. Nothing in the content or form of this prayer would have been unfamiliar to the Irish Celts. Indeed, given their long history of "triadic thinking," it would have spoken wonderfully and familiarly to any other Celtic community as well.

> **Breastplate of St. Patrick**
>
> Christ be beside me,
> Christ be before me,
> Christ be behind me
>   King of my heart.
>
> Christ be within me,
> Christ be below me,
> Christ be above me
>   Never to part.
>
> Christ on my right hand,
> Christ on my left hand,
> Christ all around me
>   Shield in the strife.
>
> Christ in my sleeping,
> Christ in my sitting,
> Christ in my rising
>   Light of my life.
>
> I will arise today
> Through a mighty strength.

CELTIC INTELLECTUALISM

A powerful quest for learning is in-bred among the Celts. This, despite their belligerence and basic lack of cohesiveness. Who else would have been patient enough to spend more than half a lifetime to secure a druidic education? Or to face the challenge of severe training for the high courts of law? Or to present their wisdom and philosophy in cryptic verse and song?

As the earliest, strongest missionary movement in Northern European Christianity, the Celtic church challenged the Roman Church. The two parties came to the negotiating table at the Monastery of Whitby, England (664 AD). Overwhelmed by Roman organization, the Celtic Christians' submission caused the Church to decline over the next century. Ultimately Britain entered into the orbit of Roman Catholic influence.

Certain scholars have proposed a somewhat delicate idea here. The main arguments at the Synod of Whitby concerned two rather mundane issues: The proper date for Easter and the type of tonsure (haircut) that priests should wear. Did the Roman delegation wish to avoid debating the quick-witted Celts on more philosophical topics? Did they hope to win their case by arguing these safer, more concrete issues instead of abstractions?

Apparently these particular Celtic traits still prevail. Consider some of the most prominent people in academe and in the areas of politics, law, finance, arts and entertainment. If these highly gifted persons are not Jewish, chances are that a large number of them will be of Celtic heritage. How many of their names begin with O' or Mac, or are otherwise certifiably Gaelic?

Thus, the Apostle Paul, the learned Jew, preaches to the Galatians. What an appropriate matching of minds!

The Celts abhorred empy space and filled their designs with dense patterns. The endless spiral (left) and interwoven lines that had neither beginning nor end became a complex symbol. These represented eternity and human experience in time and space.

The Discipline of the Rule of Three

PAUL'S PRACTICE OF THE THREE-FOLD PATTERN

Obviously Paul was familiar with the Gaelic love of the "Rule of Three." In his celebrated love chapter (1 Cor 13:13), he concluded with a most memorable triad:

> In this life we have three great lasting qualities—
> Faith,
> Hope, and
> Love,
> But the greatest of these is love

Charles R. Erdman has observed that the Apostle formulated three-fold arguments for the Galatians, a structure not to be found so elaborately spelled out anywhere else in his writings.[13] Using their own Gaelic poetic structures, he created several groups of three-fold appeals. For example, Galatians 3:28 fell quite naturally into a poetic triad:

> There is neither Jew nor Greek
> There is neither slave nor free
> There is neither male nor female.
> For you are all one in Christ Jesus.

The Celtic scholar, Nigel Pennick, cites two more "bardic triads" in Pauline literature (Eph 2:1–22).[14]

The three marks of a godly man:	The three supports of a godly man:
To seek after truth,	God and His gift of grace,
To perform justice, and	Conscience itself, and
To exercise mercy.	The praise of every wise and good man.

Paul's convoluted patterns of argument (2 Pet 3:15–16) remind us of the fascinating Russian *matryoshka* or "nesting" dolls. A larger, outer figure may contain twenty or more smaller versions of itself inside, each one successively smaller. According to this model, Paul presented several didactic groupings.

A TRINITY OF HUMAN ATTITUDES

1. **Galatian Pride** (Gal 4:8-11). When the Galatians converted from their druidic paganism to Christianity, their new found faith set them free from the bondage of nature worship. Now, however, the Judaizers tempted them to give themselves over to the servitude of the Jewish law. Furthermore, they assured the believers that the observance of ancient

Hebrew rituals would make them more acceptable to God. Moreover, the enforced ceremonies attracted their superstitious tendencies. The flamboyant Judaizers promised them a superior kind of sanctification. They could even expect to occupy higher positions in the Church structure! Paul had to issue a severe warning that their vanity could cause them to backslide into their Celtic paganism.

2. **Galatian Affections** (Gal 4:12-20). Paul appealed to the Galatians' innate talent for affection and sympathy. Notably, this passage makes no statement of doctrine. In a warmly personal tone, he reminded them of their devotion to him when he first brought them the Good News.

"Those Judaizers," he cautioned, "are not seeking your good. Be sure of that. They're only zealous to pursue their own misguided ideals." In contrast, Paul committed himself wholly to the spiritual well-being of the Church. He entreated the members not to allow the practice of rituals to summon a spirit that would endanger their Christian liberty. He addressed them as "my little children,"(Gal 4:19) a phrase not found anywhere else in his letters. He had a very deep affection for these loving Gentile believers.

3. **Galatian Intellectual Capacity** (Gal 4:21-31). The Apostle spoke to their intelligence by drawing from the book of Genesis. Some scholars vilify Paul, accusing him of using a rabbinical argument to establish the doctrine of justification by faith. The allegory of Hagar and Sarah, however, shows that Paul appreciated the intellectual capacity of his Celtic audience. They could follow a complex line of reasoning. Truly, the Galatians did represent a sophisticated society. They were far more than savages roaming the wilderness in animal skins and terrorizing their enemies.

Indeed, the historian Sir Kenneth Clarke, in his early and definitive television series, "Civilization,"[15] showed how the scholar/saints of the Celtic Christian Church (4th to 7th centuries AD) affected us. Only through them, he declared, were we able to save our Western heritage, "by the skin of our teeth!"

THE TRINITY: A GLORIOUS MYSTERY

Paul found himself in a dilemma. First, he had to prove himself to the Galatians as an authorized representative of God. Second, he had to demonstrate that they themselves were also intimately related to God in a parent-child relationship. He accomplished these purposes by, again, relying on their affinity for "threeness." He produced proof that as God's people they had actually received the adoption of sons. He then pressed his point home with a strong demonstration

The Discipline of the Rule of Three

of the Trinity and its glorious mystery. In so doing, he underscored the triple mission of the Godhead (Gal 4:5-6).

1. **God-the-Father's Adoption: Slaves-to-Sons** (Gal 4:1–5[b]). In the Roman world two legal transactions existed whereby slaves could be liberated and have their status changed. One was by redemption, a process in which slaves were purchased and then set free by their generous owners. The other was by adoption, which enabled the owner to bring slaves into the family. Thus, their adoptive fathers could bequeath family property to them as sons. This arrangement included the issuance of a certificate of adoption. The Apostle used this familiar custom to show how believers were qualified as recipients of the divinely inspired "consciousness of sons."

2. **God-the-Son's Self-Sacrificing Gift of Redemption** (Gal 4:4–5[a]). The Son provided redemption of the lost children of God by purchasing them from the tyranny and curse of the law. In this passage Paul shows how the Son became their Kinsman/Redeemer," being born of a woman." He bought back God's property, His people whom Satan first seduced into sin (Gen 3). The Son could liberate them from enslavement to the law that the Judaizers had laid on them.

3. **God-the Holy Spirit's Certification of Sons** (Gal 4:6). Paul next enjoined the on-going work of the Holy Spirit, the same Spirit who had publicly anointed Christ for His mission (Mt 3:16). No longer did the Galatians have to submit to the corrupt suggestions of the Judaizers regarding the law. The Holy Spirit now certified that the filial relationship had already been established. Thus, the Apostle brings the three-fold truth of Adoption, Redemption and Certification to a striking conclusion.

MORE TRIPLE ARGUMENTS

Even within the listing of the gifts discussed above, another triune argument appears, as intricate as an unending Celtic spiral (Gal 4:4-6).

The sequence moves from:
- The design of the mission by **God-the-Father** to redeem Jews and Gentiles that were "under the law" (Gal 4:4), to
- The sovereign grace of **God-the-Son** through whom this plan proceeds (Gal 4:5), to
- **God-the Holy Spirit** whose regenerating work of sanctification is impressed into the hearts of the believers (Gal 4:6).

There are nine attributes or graces of the Fruit of the Spirit (Gal 5:22-23). These graces fall naturally into three groups:

*Our relationship with God.	"Love, Joy, Peace."
*Our relationship with others.	"Patience, Kindness, Goodness."
*Regulations for Christian Living.	"Faithfulness, Gentleness, Self-control.

THE GALATIANS' RESPONSE

Long enslaved to their pagan gods, how could these new believers relate to the mighty, all-powerful Godhead of Christianity? Paul had some specific recommendations for them, differentiating between their Christian and pre-Christian experience (Gal 4:1). Because of their preoccupation with pomp and patronage, he illustrated his point with the imagery of a landowning family. He showed how the heir would be marked for great wealth and destined to own the entire estate. At the same time, however, a guardian carefully managed his life (Gal 4:2). Treated as little more than a slave, the heir would continue until his father declared him old enough to handle adult responsibilities.

The Apostle's application is clear: "So also we, while we were children, were held in bondage under the elemental things of the world" (Gal 4:3). In other words, the Galatians' pre-Christian life resembled childhood when our ways are closely supervised.

In fact, the will of a guardian became the oppressive rulership of the "elemental spirits of the universe," like the religious superstitions of heathenism. Keeping people in bondage, the many gods denied them their full inheritance as creatures of the true God. Like their Celtic brethren elsewhere, the Galatians looked to magic spells, potions, and secret ceremonies to placate hostile, demanding spirits. They examined the stars to determine their daily destiny and consulted private charms and augury. Their enslavement to personal rituals left them no freedom whatsoever.

In responding to their superstitious, cringing fears, Paul presented yet another telescoped trinity of thought (Gal 4:4-5):

* But when the fullness of the time came,
    God sent forth his son,

The Discipline of the Rule of Three

> Born of a woman,
> Born under the law,
> - So that he might redeem those that were under the law,
> - So that we might receive the adoption of sons.

Paul ends his teaching by emphasizing the rewards of an intimate relationship with the Godhead. "As children," he said, "you no longer suffer under bondage." In a very Celtic sense of the word, the Galatian Christians had attained the "Age of Choice." They could now enjoy the maturity of son-ship. Indeed, God the Father Himself had declared the time to be right. It has "fully come."

A Celtic Prayer[16]

The Sacred Three be over me
With my working hands this day.

With the people on my way
With the labor and the toil
With the land and with the soil,

With the tools that I take
With the things that I make
With the thoughts of my mind

With the sharing with mankind
With the love of my heart
With each one that plays a part.

The Sacred Three be over me,
The blessing of the Trinity.

10. RAIDING AND WAR

"Grace and peace to you from God the Father and our Lord Jesus Christ"
(Gal 1:3).

The Celtic tribes, both east and west, challenged every move the Roman Empire made in an attempt to establish itself. What they faced in Asia Minor was a vivid preview of what Julius Caesar would later encounter in his effort to subdue Gaul and the British Isles.

AN ISLAND OF HOSTILITY

Rome tried, endlessly, to control the warring factions in the far eastern provinces of Asia Minor. Most troublesome of all, however, were the Galatians, living on an ethnic island of hostility in the central plateau of Anatolia.

The year was 189 BC, and the Romans had invaded the territory of Ortagion, King of the Galatian tribe of Tolistoboii.[1] The usual taking of prizes had occurred, and Chiomara, the wife of Ortagion, had been captured. One of the centurions then raped her. Belatedly, he discovered that she was the wife of the king they had been fighting. Prompted by ambition and overcome by greed, the Roman sent a ransom note to Ortagion.

The king agreed to the terms, and the exchange of gold-for-wife took place on a riverbank in neutral territory. The arrogant Roman, however, had not reckoned on the skill and high spirits of his outraged hostage. Never take a Celtic woman for granted!

The queen flung the ransom money at his feet. As he bent over to pick up his gold, Chiomara snatched a sword from one of the Galatian attendants sent to escort her back to her husband. In a single, calm stroke, she decapitated the Roman. Then she carried the grisly trophy back to her husband. In a fascinating defense of her virtue and in the genuine triadic Celtic idiom, she presented the head to him along with a cryptic triad:

"Woman, a fine thing [is] good faith.
[A] better thing [there is], only one man alive
who had intercourse with me."[2]

Polybius described Ortagion as "munificent, magnanimous, charming and intelligent" and his wife as a "woman of sensibility." The aristocratic couple named their son Paidopolites (Gr "son-citizen"), showing a feeling for Greek culture and city life.[3] At the same time, however, the basic Celtic impulses prevailed strongly, as the Roman centurion had learned to his destruction.

RAIDING: A GAELIC COMPULSION

Raiding and ravaging the countryside virtually kept Celtic society intact. It provided material gain and fed tribal superstitions. The Raid was a central, integral part of the Celtic social system, with each successful enterprise automatically leading to another. Thus the cycle fed itself. Young men aspiring to greatness would begin by raiding their neighbors. When the leader returned with prizes for distribution, his prestige would attract still more followers. As his expectations increased, long-distance raiding became a full-time occupation, requiring long months of absence from home. Eventually, long-term raids became permanent migrations.[4]

Each of the three tribes that settled Galatia had their own "hunting grounds," an apparently well-planned agreement among themselves. The Tolistoboii used the southwest coast of Anatolia, from Limyra to Ephesus. The Tectosages marauded further inland, from Laodicea to the south coast. The Trocmi confined their raiding to the northwest area of Ilium (ancient Troy) and the Hellespont.[5] To the east and southeast, however, the Galatians tended to leave the strong kingdoms of Pontus and Cappadocia alone.

THE CULT OF THE SEVERED HEAD

As an adjunct to their fighting, the Celts subscribed to the "Cult of the Severed Head." For them headhunting had symbolic meaning. As the Celtic hero continually preyed on his neighbors, headhunting supplied him with significant trophies. Greek and Roman writers alike remarked on the Celtic love for collecting heads.[6]

A classic anti-Celt, the Roman writer Diodorus Siculus expressed the usual disapproval of such barbarian excesses: "They cut off the heads of enemies slain in battle and attach them to the necks of their horses. These blood-stained spoils they hand over to their attendants and carry off as booty, while striking up a paean and singing a song of victory." After the battle, Siculus continued, "They nail up these first fruits upon their houses. . . . They embalm in cedar-oil the heads of the most distinguished enemies and preserve them carefully in a chest and display them with pride to strangers, saying that for this head, one of their ancestors, or his father or the man himself, refused the offer of a large sum of money."[7]

Because the Celts believed the head to be the seat of the soul, they took pride in owning and displaying it as an important exhibit. They venerated it both as war trophy and as a religious symbol. The victor could thus retain and control the influence of the dead person, deriving both his power and "sacred energy." Once lifted from the body, the head would be free to work for a man against his enemies.

Livy records how the Roman Consul Postumus was killed in a battle between the Romans and the Celtic tribe of Boii. After the consul was decapitated, his skull was cleaned and mounted in gold. This became a cup fit to present to the shrine of a god.[8]

A gable of heads, Clonfert Cathedral, Ireland, founded by St. Brendan (563 AD). The triangle contains rows of marigolds and human heads. While some argue that the heads represent saints, the façade is very much in the familiar pagan Celtic tradition of the "severed head."

Raiding and War

Archaeological findings in France[9] have uncovered a number of interesting artifacts, including a sculpture, showing four heads lying in a pile beneath columns with niches in which to set human heads. The Rhone Valley produced an image of a squatting beast clasping severed, bearded heads in his forepaws while he devours a body, with just an arm protruding from his jaws. These fearsome icons seem to have been widely scattered throughout Celtic lands. One constantly sees detached human (or other) faces peering out of Celtic artwork.[10]

As we have already noted, classical writers were naturally prejudiced against their enemies and elaborated extensively on the Celts' violent behavior. Before we accuse those historians of over-reacting to the distasteful Celtic habit of headhunting, however, we may as well admit that, on occasion, the Celts were cannibals too. For example, a current archaeological cave-site in south Gloucestershire, England, dates back some 2,000 years. It contains a grave of possibly fifty persons, ritualistically dismembered. Evidence suggests a great massacre followed by a great feast.[11]

Like so many old pagan customs, Celtic headhunting made its own way into church art. A doorway at the Abbey of Clonmacnoise, Ireland, for instance, is rimmed with severed heads. All of the heads of saints watching over us, we are told. Still, a strong, very ancient ethnic echo rings in our ears.

With Europeans, many Celtic traditions have survived into modern times. To be beheaded by a sword has always been the honorable way to be executed. This was the fate of royalty and the nobility. Hanging was reserved for common criminals and people of no account. Today the Celts would be nonplussed by our current arguments concerning the death penalty and finding humane modes of execution. For them the issue was simple and swift. They believed in life and death as a progression. Their expectation of an afterlife made it relatively easy to face death. While the Celts valued lusty and vigorous living, they cared little for life itself. More feasting and fighting always lay ahead.

JUDEO-CHRISTIAN CONCEPTS OF WAR

Paul was a Jew from the fighting tribe of Benjamin. The other eleven tribes easily recognized their warlike disposition and military accomplishments. When they went into battle, the banner of the Benjamites rode forth in the vanguard. The fight would begin with the shout: "For the cause of Benjamin!" Because of this background, we should examine the underlying agenda that the Apostle would be bringing to his dialogue with the Galatian churches.

In the Old Testament times, military engagements were considered to be holy wars rather than battles for political expediency. (The contemporary Islamic idea of the jihad or "holy war" is rooted in this same ancient Hebrew philosophy.) They believed in Jahweh as a warrior (Ex 15:3) who used the occasion of fighting to test discipline, ensure justice, and deliver His people out of danger. In fact, the Hebrew word for deliverer, *azar*, means "to rescue with military might."

Preparation for a holy war depended on the sanction and active participation of God Who declared the war (Num 31:3). He could be consulted by a variety of methods, such as dreams, the Urim and Thummim, or prophetic messages. The military commanders in these holy wars did not fight in their own names or by their genius, nor by the power of the State (2 Chron 20:7). He or she was prepared by a special gift of the Spirit of God, as in the case of Deborah and Gideon (Jud 4:6; 6:36). When the Spirit was withdrawn, the authority to command an army in battle also disappeared (Jud 6:11-14).

Because "Jahweh's War" (1 Sam 18:17) was engaged only by Divine approval, the number and stature of the combatants made no difference (Jud 7). Although an important part of their theology, Hebrews never represented a holy war as an end in itself or as a means of survival. They looked beyond the day of victory to the deliverance of God. They took the occasion to emphasize His sovereignty, His initiative and concern for their well-being, as their Preserver and Provider.[12]

In contrast to the Celts and other pagans who enslaved, tortured, exposed, and decapitated their prisoners, the Hebrews, under the direction of Jahweh, were usually forbidden to take either captives or booty in war.[13] Whenever they disobeyed, dire results followed (Jos 7; I Sam 15). On the other hand, their heathen opponents were generally so vicious that a Hebrew about to become a captive often found refuge in suicide (1 Sam 31:1-10).

In the New Testament, Jesus, Himself a Jew, said very little concerning war, holy or otherwise. He directed His mission toward creating and maintaining conditions of peace. Paul (Saul), on the other hand, demonstrated in his rabid persecution of the Church that he still had a strong attachment to his Benjamite heritage. Conversion to Christianity may have given him peace, but it did not necessarily make him docile. Therefore, it should come as no surprise that the early Christian Church (of which he was such a significant pillar) spiritualized the concept of "holy war." The believers lost none of their natural fervor or willingness to fight until death for their beliefs.

At the same time, they emphasized the fact that physical war belonged to the Province or the State, not the Church. The new Christians understood that physical war originated in greed and lust for power. In fact, it was one of Satan's

Raiding and War

implements to bring sin and death upon the world (Eph 6:12; Jas 4:1,2). They taught that the decisive battle of the Great Controversy between Good and Evil had been won through the death and resurrection of Christ. In this connection, they also envisioned a massive, physical Holy War called Armageddon (Rev 16:16). Finally, Evil would be destroyed and Good would triumph.

PEACE TO THE GALATIANS

Paul's greeting, "Grace and peace," was, of course, the standard, formal salutation that he used to open most of his letters to the churches.[14] This customary gesture was not a perfunctory thing with Paul. He used it here in spite of the many faults he had to attribute to the recipients of this letter. For the Galatians, however, the words did have special significance. Why? The Celts loved fighting.

When he wished that "grace and peace" be the lot of the Galatians, Paul was addressing the mixed group of Jews and Gentiles that made up these house-churches.

No matter how he deplored the defection of the Galatians to the Judaizers, he did not love them any less. He sincerely desired that they all receive the grace that comes from God to humankind.

Although the Judaizers had pitted one against the other (Gal 5:15), the Apostle did not take a page from their book. Instead, he drew from both cultures. For instance, the word "grace" (Gr *charis*) was usually a Gentile greeting, while "peace" (Heb *shalom*) was a distinctive Jewish salutation. In the common usage, grace referred to something that aroused a person's joy or desire. In the social setting it defined the favor and approbation that an elite person might extend to a member of the lower class. Peace, on the other hand, described a condition of wellbeing and wholeness, replete with "soul-rest."

Unfortunately, Paul's greeting did not describe what was actually happening in the Galatian community at the time. In addition to their own natural habits of contention, they had suffered severely from the destructive activities of the Judaizers among them. Of itself, the Apostle's salutation attempted to unite the divided churches. He could have adopted the style of his opponents and participated in a verbal "slug-fest." Such a measure would have titillated the deep-rooted belligerence of the Galatians.

Indeed, his loyal supporters would have been more than happy to take up arms against the enemy. He did not, however, draw on the natural fighting talents of the congregation or on his own former propensity for persecution. Instead, he appealed for harmony through the grace and peace from God. He also said this for the sake of the Jewish believers, those not yet comfortable with praying to "Our Lord Jesus Christ." His gentle greeting, however, gave no hint of the harsh denunciation of the "fighting words" he would ultimately apply to the Judaizers before the end of his letter.

Paul recognized that he himself, along with his Galatian converts, was truly energized by a certain native passion for battle. Nonetheless, in his greeting, he immediately established one point. The practice of the Christian life would not be motivated by belligerence. Instead, he pointed to the high authority of his call from God. He committed the infant churches to Christ's path, a way that would lead to a wiser, more compassionate fellowship.

Galatian Sensitivity

Although the Galatians had frequently attempted the conquest of Pergamum, the prize always lay just beyond their reach. King Attalus I, however, admired the nobility, the spirit, and the courage of his foes. In 201 BC he commissioned a bronze sculpture group to be placed in the temple of Athena. It commemorated the Pergamene victory twenty years earlier. To be sure, any Greek would have been proud to go to war with the Galatians, who were then at the height of their power. A marble copy of the now-lost original is in the Capitoline Museum in Rome.

"The Dying Gaul" is, rightly, one of the most celebrated portrayals of a Galatian in any art form and at any time. Every muscle in his body cries defeat. Every line in his finely chiseled face denotes intelligence and submission to the inevitable. Perhaps in this poignant moment of transition, his mind even glimpses the Otherworld that his druid had long ago described to him.

To such people as this the Apostle Paul brought the Gospel. For centuries the Galatians had lived their lives in a paradoxical mix of devotion and despair, passion and dignity, independence and tribal bonds, aggression and hospitality. These were the first Europeans to hear the good news of Jesus Christ. Paul very likely would have regarded his ministry in Galatia as unique among all of his other experiences of Christian evangelization.

11. Passion and the Virtues of Commitment

I am astonished to find you turning so quickly away from him who called you by grace.... Anyone can see the kind of behavior that belongs to the lower nature (Gal 1:6; 5:19, 20).

The ancient Irish records give us our most complete description of Celtic life and culture. Strong tribal bonds enabled traditions to hold wherever the Gaelic peoples settled. Profound emotionalism was a major Gaulish characteristic that usually baffled the staid Greek and Roman observers. Indeed, for them, passion and instability became part of the definition of a "barbarian."

While the Celts had enormous reserves of physical courage and irrational aggression the well-disciplined Romans, at the end of the day, overcame them. Their bravado usually spent itself quickly. Their drunkenness, recklessness, passion, and superstitions made them almost wholly unpredictable.

In 189 BC the Roman General Volso took command of a punitive expedition against Galatia. To prepare his soldiers for the encounter, he told them what to expect from their enemies:

> They sing as they advance into battle; they yell and leap in the air, clashing their weapons against their shields. The Greeks and Phrygians are scared of this display, but the Romans are used to such wildness. We have learned that if you can bear up to their first onslaught—that initial charge of blind passion—then their limbs will grow weary with the

effort and when their passion subsides they are overcome by sun, dust and thirst. And anyway, these Celts we face are of a mixed blood, part Greek. Not the Celts our forefathers fought.[1]

Judging from the artworks shown below, the Celts seem often to have bordered on what today we would call "manic-depressive."

While General Volso temporarily won some very bloody battles, the Celtic chieftain, Ortagion of the Tolistoboii, eventually achieved enough tribal unity to create a centralized state. He had sufficient security to survive several decades of independence from the surrounding kingdoms.[2] Despite the "diluted" bloodlines that Volso scorned, the Galatians, at least, made a good showing in that encounter. Unfortunately, even when they outnumbered the disciplined Romans, the Celts were usually defeated—all because of their uncontrolled passions. The Celtic capacity for making rash decisions and for succumbing to total despair shows us the other side of the ravening Gaelic warrior. This mix of uncontrolled valor and black despair became the foundation of Celtic instability.

This naked, leaping fighter embodies the fury of the Gauls. A terror on the battlefield, both Greeks and Romans had to respect him as a worthy adversary.

GALATIA AND PERGAMUM

In 232 BC, the Galatians had attempted a new conquest. They attacked Pergamum several times but were always defeated by Attalus I (241-197 BC). He made Pergamum a major religious center of the Hellenistic Period. For the Galatians, however, this rich city always remained just beyond their reach.

Nonetheless, their enemies memorialized the reckless Galatians in a surprisingly gracious way. Twenty years after Attalus' last decisive defeat of the Celts in 230 BC, the citizens of Pergamum erected a very striking sculpture-group to honor their foes.[3] With a sympathetic eye, the artists defined the character and power of the Galatian enemy with intense realism. Here we see a reluctant kind of admiration that the Pergamenes had for their proud, insanely courageous opponents.

Such a victory monument portrays a noble adversary that any army, even the Greeks, were proud to fight. They truly honored the dignity and courage of

Passion and the Virtues of Commitment 109

Reconstruction of a monument to the defeated Galatians in the Temple of Athena, Pergamun (210 BC). Commemorating 50 years of unceasing battle with the Galatians, this very realistic victory sculpture became the glory of the city. It portrayed a noble, courageous adversary that any army, (even the Greeks) were proud to fight. Finely carved marble copies of these Galatian figures were commissioned by Attalus I (240–200 BC) and taken to Italy.[4]

their Galatian foes. Finely-carved marble copies of the original are now to be seen in the Capitoline Museum, Rome. Below, the Dying Gaul sculpture dramatically portrays a warrior in his death throes.

Decades later, Eumenes II promoted Zeus-worship by building a great temple complex and library in Pergamum, second only to the library of Alexandria. He was determined to make the city a major Hellenistic religious center. He succeeded. As one of the Seven Churches of Revelation, this city accepted Christianity at an early date. In the third of his messages to the seven churches, the Apostle John commended the Christians at Pergamum for their faithfulness. This, despite the fact that their city was "where Satan lives." Indeed, the Apostle John declared that the very "seat of Satan" existed there among them (Rev 2:13 NIV).

When Attalus II (138-133 BC) died without an heir, he bequeathed his Kingdom of Pergamum to Rome. So, yet one more great city was bloodlessly absorbed into the Roman Empire.

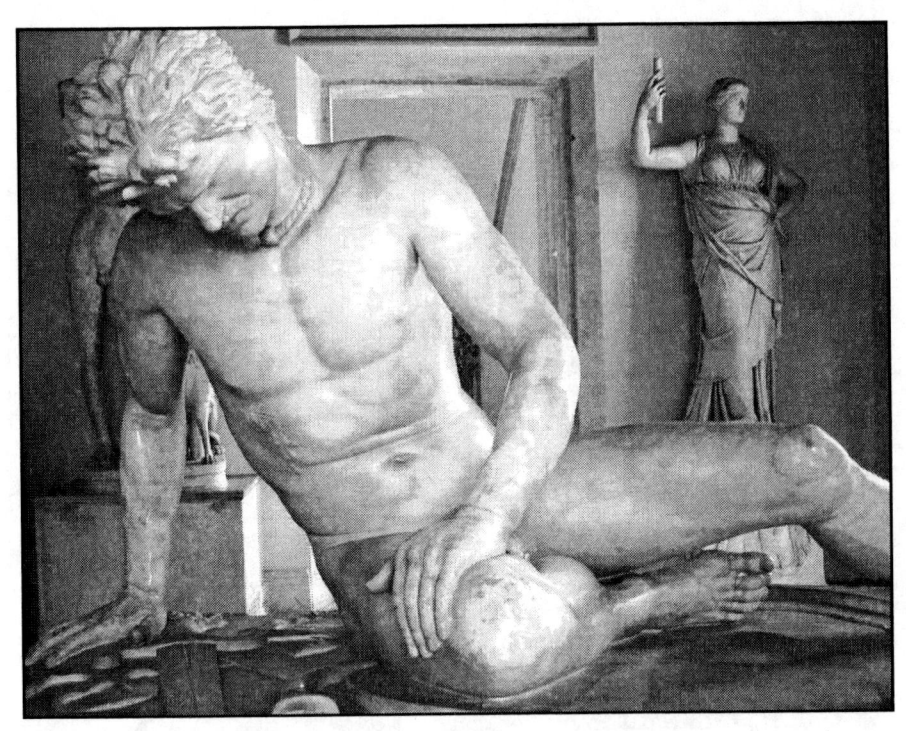

The Dying Gaul. The most celebrated figure in the Pergamene sculpture group is the "Dying Gaul." The naked, bleeding warrior rests on his shield, his trumpet beside him. His bowed head, tousled, greased hair and drooping moustache emphasize both the bitterness and the dignity of defeat. His gold torc marks him as one of the elite fighters. This tragic Galatian nobleman has thrown his trumpet and his sword aside and now waits for the end.[5]

THE ABYSS OF DESPAIR

No stranger to despair, the Apostle Paul identified himself fully with this strong Celtic trait. He wrote: "For we do not want you to be unaware, brethren, of our affliction which came to us in Asia, that we were burdened excessively, beyond our strength so that we despaired even of life" (2 Cor 1:8). He does not ex-

Passion and the Virtues of Commitment

plain these particular difficulties he experienced. Perhaps they related to the tumult raised by Demetrius the silversmith at Ephesus (Acts 19). Or maybe it referred to his "fighting with beasts" in that same city (1 Cor 15:32). Or was it some other unimaginably great tribulation (2 Cor 11:23-27)? In any case, pushed to extraordinary degrees, Paul and his companions feared for their lives and apparently fainted away in despair. He testified to this kind of situation, more than once.

Yet, at other times, the Apostle claimed victory. Paradoxically, he declared that he and his friends were "afflicted in every way but not crushed: perplexed but not despairing; persecuted but not forsaken; struck down but not destroyed; always carrying about in the body, the dying of Jesus, so that the life of Jesus may also be manifested in our body" (2 Cor 4:3-10).

In each case, both the victories and defeats, Paul used the Greek word *exaporeo*. It describes the case of being utterly without a way out, to be quite at a loss, to be robbed of all resources. He felt that the believers needed to know the sufferings, privations, and impact of these events on the early ministers of the Christian Church. He readily admitted that, like other humans, he and his companions fell victim to despondency. Then, on other occasions, their total reliance on the grace of God shone forth like a beacon of hope.

AN INVENTORY OF VICES

Freedom from passion is easier to lose than achieve. Although aware of the rivers of emotionalism that flowed through the culture of Galatia, Paul also understood the power of the Holy Spirit to work change and peace among these unique Christians. He methodically drew their attention to the deadly sins that were causing them despair. Actually, ancient peoples were fond of lists of virtues and vices.[6] Therefore, Paul used this sense of organization to present the deadly sins that were causing them such discouragement. We may classify his counsel in four groups.

1. Sensual Sins

In this category Paul includes vices like fornication/prostitution, harlotry and adultery. Also uncleanness (moral impurity), lasciviousness (wantonness), and all the other sexual perversions that prevailed in the surrounding heathen communities. Because of their strong bond with Nature in all of its aspects, the Celts were very free about their sexuality. Their rituals and fertility festivals permitted coupling without the least pretence of commitment.

Highly unstable kinds of marriages did exist in Celtdom, and the unions were renewable on an annual basis, allowing either partner to take a new mate.

The front of the Pergamon Altar of Zeus, as it is reconstructed in the Pergamon Museum in Berlin. The richly carved friezes depict one of the several victories the Pergamene Greeks had over the marauding Galatians. The Apostle John referred to this altar as the "Seat of Satan" (Rev 12:13).

Such prolific divorce and remarriage, of course, often produced a very messy, unpredictable society. Also, nature itself was always uncertain, and the threat of attack from neighboring clans never ended.[7] Moreover, the arbitrary and fickle dealings of their pagan deities disrupted Gaelic life. Given all of these confusing circumstances, the Celts could never see any reason for denying themselves the natural pleasures of sex. In many places, the average life expectancy was only thirty years. So, why wait?

Even the Celts-turned-Christian felt an innate spiritual urge to create, and procreate. Their new beliefs did not, at first, diminish their exuberant and immediate joy in physical life on earth.[8] Indeed, their ancient understanding of the thin veil of separation between "This World" and the Otherworld augmented their desires.

Paul faced this earth-centeredness in many of the churches he founded. The Galatians, however, seemed to have carried it a step further. Actually, the heathen Celts never could see themselves as "pagan." They had a sense that the world and everything in it (including themselves) was sacred. Mortimer Adler expressed the idea comprehensively: "The world is holy. Nature is holy. The body is holy. Sexuality is holy. The mind is holy. The imagination is holy. You are holy."[9]

2. Idolatry

Idolatry has always included witchcraft and the worship of idols. The former was a favorite practice of the Gaulish tribes. Our modern word "pharmacy"

Passion and the Virtues of Commitment

derives from the Greek word for "witchcraft" (*pharmakos*). This meaning indicates that more is involved here than just consulting a crystal ball. It includes the administering of drugs. The sorcerers of the day monopolized the word, because they used it to describe the potions required for their magical arts.

Irish records show that the pagan Celts were less concerned with idols than with natural, sacred locations. They encountered the gods in the forests, especially in the druidical oak groves. Goddesses, on the other hand, frequented the hills and rivers. At the holy junctions where water and land met, one might even hope to receive spiritual insight and poetic inspiration. Their mystical culture and their belief in the immanence of their deities prompted the Celts to observe daily rituals and seasonal celebrations to make contact with the Otherworld.[10]

3. Drunkenness

In drawing the Galatians' attention to the vice of drunkenness, Paul used a plural form of an old word *methe* ("habitual intoxication"). Thus he emphasized the excesses among them. It included reveling and drinking parties, but it also represented their propensity for completely losing control of themselves. By the same token, the Galatians drank deeply of the Judaizers' counterfeit teachings and quickly spun out into major delusions (Gal 1:6-10).

Today, who is having the most difficulty with alcohol? Westerners, as it appears, along with whoever has heavily absorbed their culture. While we find "strong drink" in virtually every society from the beginning of time, most people just drank until they were happy. Not until they became inebriated and went crazy! The Greeks' traditional devotion to Bacchus, their god of wine, has had an enormous influence over the Western world.

When Paul reached the Galatians, they were already thoroughly Hellenized. No Celt, however, needed a Greek to show him how to drink. Fifteen hundred years ago, both the Celts and the Germanic tribes highly prized their mead halls.[11] They were thoroughly addicted to the pleasures of feasting, storytelling, and, above all, drinking.

This fascination with alcohol remains very much with us today. Try downtown Dublin, Ireland, on a Saturday night. Be there at 4 a.m. when the pubs evict their patrons. Or sit in the bleachers at the Indy 500 or at a football game. Spectators will likely turn the event into a distracting "beer fest." Again, how many people do you know who are (or should be) in Alcoholics Anonymous?

The Galatians' drinking problem derived from their own Celtic legacy, plus the overlay of the Greek Bacchanalian orgies. No wonder Paul needed to include "drunkenness" on his vice list.

4. Personal Animosities

The vices that fall into this group manifest themselves in personal relationships. They include, but are not limited to, sins of the spirit—enmity, strife, rivalry, discord, and jealousies. The stirring of emotions that result in angry explosions created factions. These probably were the most destructive of all the classes of sin.

Even notable Christians have harbored these "sins of the disposition." They often busied themselves disciplining others for the more obvious and visible infractions. If, however, their own faults are pointed out, they become violently defensive. They may be permanently "bent out of shape." They may even terminate their religious relationships, unable to abide all of the "hypocrites" around them. Yet, their pride and anger will have lethal results. The Apostle counseled: "I have forewarned you, that those who practice[12] such things will not inherit the Kingdom of God" (Gal 5:21).

THE ELUSIVE VIRTUES OF COMMITMENT[13]

The Apostle summarized Celtic instability when he rebuked the Galatian converts: "I am astonished to find you turning so quickly away from Him who called you by grace" (Gal 1:6).

Unfortunately, the classical stereotype of the Celt is based on the (sometimes prejudicial) writings of Greek and Roman observers. They characterized them as fearless, cruel and barbarian, given to human sacrifices, even cannibalism. As we have seen, another problem for the carefully organized Romans was the fact that the Gaul could be irrationally brave in the first onslaught and then collapse in wild despair when the battle turned against him.[14] No one other than a fellow Celt could cope with such alien behavior.

Moreover, the Celts could be totally unpredictable, often too drunk and unruly or too paralyzed by superstition even to fight. Generations of the Celts served as mercenaries in the armies of surrounding nations (Seleucid and Ptolemaic rulers). One group of Galatians gave their Greek employers great difficulty because of an eclipse of the moon. Completely demoralized, they demanded that they (along with their wives and children), be returned together to the Hellespont. They insisted on being kept together, in case they might change sides! Indeed, they might even decide to leave Asia Minor altogether and return to Europe.[15]

Their wild legends and instability, notwithstanding, early Celtic Christians still saw themselves as created in the image of an all-powerful God, called "The Lord of the Elements."[16] Despite their reckless zeal for battle and their desire to become "Hellenized," their basic unreliability reduced too many of them to transient misfits.

Passion and the Virtues of Commitment

PAUL PREACHED THE GOSPEL

Time showed that the Celtic trait of instability had, indeed, surfaced among the Galatian churches. Like their ancestors, they had the reputation for being fickle and fond of change. When they first heard the Gospel from Paul, they precipitously renounced their mystical religion and druidical form of worship and followed the new teaching.

Now the pendulum had swung in the opposite direction. Repeatedly Paul would have cause to complain of the Galatians' instability that kept threatening their infant churches. The Judaizers came presenting letters, supposedly written by leaders of the Jerusalem church. They criticized Paul harshly, causing the Galatians to switch their allegiance suddenly.

No one in a public profession can escape criticism and rejection, not even a Paul. Probably he had not taken Galatian fickleness fully into account. He realized that such a disposition could impact any future commitments they might make. When he asked, "Am I therefore become your enemy because I tell you the truth?" (Gal 4:16), one cannot help but hear the angst and the pain that the aging Apostle feels upon being pushed aside.

Paul diligently contended that the Judaizers, in their attempt to silence his message, had caused the Galatians to lose their grip on the true Gospel. For the same reason, they denied him hospitality on his second visit. The meddling Judaizers banked on this reaction. Because Paul had been too far away, the Galatians could no longer feel his electrifying presence. The Judaizers, on the other hand, showed up every Sabbath. Paul did not. Just that simple!

The impostors painted Paul as a charlatan. Yet, they were the ones who dressed in flamboyant garments, who insisted on the best service from everyone, and who demanded the most money. Although they preached to the Gentile Galatians, they refused to mingle with them until they had been circumcised. Ecclesiastical bigotry in the extreme!

Indeed the Judaizers perpetuated the same abuses as the itinerant poets who still roamed Celtic lands. Always with a keen susceptibility to color and passion, the Galatians tended to forget what Paul had done for them. They found his travel-worn garments and physical disfigurement altogether non-memorable.

The proclamation and reputation of the Gospel of Jesus Christ was, however, at stake. Paul addressed the danger promptly and thoroughly. He did so by trying to draw the Galatians back to their early commitment and re-ignite their passion for the Gospel.

12. Boasting and Challenging

If you go on fighting one another, tooth and nail, all you can expect is mutual destruction . . . God forbid that I should boast of anything but the cross of our Lord Jesus Christ" (Gal 5:15; 6:14 NIV).

Anyone who has taken a basic college course in English Literature will, perhaps, remember that it all started with Beowulf.[1] He is the hero of a long, marvelous tale concerning the adventures of the Geats (a tribe in southern Sweden) and the Danes.[2] A mix of fact and fancy, paganism and Christianity, the story has a Scandinavian setting but is an Anglo-Saxon poem. Since the Celts and Germanic tribes held warrior-worship in common, we may look at Beowulf as an exemplar of Celtic culture as well as his own.

Our man Beowulf has listened to the bards and harping minstrels in the mead halls and has heard about the depredations of a monster. For twelve years, Grendel has preyed on the warriors in Herot, the mead hall of Hrothgar, King of the Danes. Nightly, the beast has carried men off. With fourteen companions Beowulf sails to Denmark. Mighty men all, but none as glorious as Beowulf, of course. The Danish king and queen shower the Geatish hero with gifts. More to follow if he can kill Grendel.

Is Beowulf able to deliver the Danish court from the monster? He steps forward and announces his qualifications for the task. Already famous for his superhuman strength and courage, he launches into an arrogant account of himself:

Boasting and Challenging

[Everyone knows] my strength.
They saw me come from battles, stained in the blood of my enemies, when I destroyed a family of giants, when I endured pain all night, killing water monsters, grinding them to bits to avenge for the Geats...
And now I shall, alone, fight Grendel, Lord of the Danes."

Beowulf fights honorably, without a sword--because the monster has no weapon![3]

This long poem is threaded through with the most extravagant boasting to be found in all literature. For example, Beowulf enters a swimming contest with his boyhood friend, Brecca. They "glide through the boiling waves of the winter's swell." They carry swords to "ward off whales." They contend in the sea for seven nights and days. On the eighth day Beowulf finally gets the edge over his companion. Meanwhile, on the side, he has killed nine sea-monsters.

Ancient heroic literature like this displays enormous arrogance. Indeed, excessive pride is a primary characteristic of all champions and would-be heroes. To be sure, Muhammed Ali was neither the first nor the last to proclaim: "I am the greatest." We hear the "Big Fish" story over and over again.

The psychological base for boasting lies in the fact that no one wants to "lose face." After you have publicly boasted about what you intend to do, you then have a powerful motivation to accomplish the task, at whatever cost. It promises you a shot of adrenalin. Exaggeration and vanity was a natural part of both Celtic and Anglo-Saxon raids. Exasperated, the Greek historian and geographer Strabo complained: "The Gauls have a propensity for empty-headed boasting."[4]

CELTIC PATHS OF PRIDE

The Gaelic tribes confronting one another with challenge after challenge certainly resulted in the performance of unbelievable acts of heroism. At the nightly feast, the greatest champion present cut off the "hero's portion" (of meat) for himself. Before that, no one else could approach the succulent roast boar. If, however, some other warrior believed himself to be more deserving of the prime cut, combat ensued. As often as not, one or more warriors died before supper even began.

Another long, much-admired English poem, "Sir Gawain and the Green Knight," also mixes the Celtic pagan and the Christian elements. On New Year's Eve, a Green Giant (Celtic element of Nature) crashes into King Arthur's feast at Camelot.

He flings down a challenge to the Christian knights at the Round Table: "Who is courageous enough to cut off my head?" he cries. Then he explains that a year later, the challenger must seek him out and allow his own head to be struck off.

Sir Gawain responds to this horrifying summons. After a series of temptations set up by the Green Giant, Gawain manages to score about a 90% victory. Hero that he was, he could not hold to the moral high ground perfectly. He did return to Camelot, however, bringing honor to the Round Table.

THE GLORY OF THE FIGHT

The old Gaelic sagas tell us about a mother who gave her male child his first solid food on the tip of her husband's sword, vowing that he should "find no death but in battle." The, Celts, in fact, had an insatiable desire to acquire personal honor in single-handed combat.

Diodorus Siculus described the terrifying appearance of a Celtic army. The warriors carried decorated, "man-sized shields" having "projecting bronze animals of fine workmanship" and horns "of one piece with the helmet." Some of them were naked and tattooed while others wore chain mail and gold or silver-plated belts.. Their trumpets of a "peculiar barbaric kind" blended with "the tumults of war." Their long swords were "as long as the javelins of other people."[6] Wherever the terrain proved to be flat enough, the Gauls (renowned horsemen) delivered the warriors to the battlefield in chariots.

In 55 BC, Julius Caesar encountered massed thousands of Celtic warriors atop the White Cliffs of Dover as he advanced on England. He described how they used their great war-chariots: "First of all, they drive in all directions and hurl javelins, and so by the mere terror that the teams inspire and by the noise of the wheels, they generally throw the ranks of soldiers into confusion. When they have worked their way in between the troops, they leap down from the chariots

A Celtic god/warrior, hauntingly depicted in bronze (3rd c BC). His one remaining eye (of blue and white glass) stares out over his torc. Somehow the dark of Celtic art is overlaid with the humanity of Greek art.[5]

Boasting and Challenging

and fight on foot. Meanwhile their charioteers retire gradually from the battle, and place the chariots in such a fashion that, if the warriors are hard pressed by the enemy, they may have a ready means of retreat to their own side."[7]

Of course, we have to settle for Caesar's own version of the Gallic Wars. What lay behind his conquests? Gold! More than 400 gold mining sites are said to have been available to him in the lands of the skilled craftsmen of the Celts. Above all, his achievements brought him political fame back in Rome. Thus his depredations were, supposedly, justified.[8]

THE BATTLE FRENZY OF CHAMPIONS

The "battle frenzy" of the Celtic champion terrified their enemies in war and threw them off guard. In the description of Cuchulain, the epic hero of Ireland, we must, of course, grant the bard some latitude for heroic exaggeration. Nevertheless, the overall portrait of the champion has enough reality in it to help us envision the battlefield uproar that the Celts so dearly loved.[9]

Cuchulain had fallen into his first battle-frenzy when he was only seven years old, horrifying his playmates. Now as an adult, confronted with the machinations of his arch-enemy, Queen Maeve, he has been sitting naked in the snow trying to control himself. Finally, however, he erupts, both physically and emotionally:

"Enflamed by his great courage, the slight youth became distended with contortions so terrible that once a hundred warriors dropped dead just at the sight of him.

"He quivered. His calves, heels, and buttocks shifted to the front of his body. His feet and knees switched to the rear of him. His muscles swelled until they looked like skulls. One eye protruded. His mouth stretched from ear to ear. Foam as thick as the wool on a sheep rolled from his open jaws. His heart pounded and roared like a lion's or a hound dog's heart. A halo played about his head, shooting sparks and rays above him. His hair stood up like red and tangled wires. As he grew hotter, torrents of blood spouted from him toward the four cardinal points of the horizon, and fell back to earth about him like red smoke, or red rain, or solar storm clouds."[10]

We can well understand that, imagining—much less meeting—such a warrior in the field would be devastating. An experience that would sear the mind of any soldier south of the Alps.

Exaggeration notwithstanding, however, we find some elements of this description uneasily familiar. Nor is all of this ancient history. How much of the "battle-frenzy" remains with us today? A large amount, if we really consider the matter. A professor of English Literature at the University of Virginia finds the American high school a fearful place, populated with big seventeen-year-old football players, spoiling for action. "Victory [is] achieved by the body over other bodies, the stripping of the armor, the taking of prizes, the humiliation of the foe—that is what the heart wants. Once you've had the feeling of total warrior triumph, nothing else exists."[11]

All is part of the Gaelic heritage. The Apostle quickly identified this passionate trait among the new Christians in Galatia.

In yet another triadic format Paul advises the Galatians against "biting" (Gr *daknote*), devouring (Gr *katesthio*), and consuming (Gr *analisko*) one another. The word "biting" (Gal 5:15) indicates a violent temper, resembling the snapping and snarling of dogs, cats, and wild animals. These phrases echo the theme of an ancient fable about two snakes that seized one another by the tail, each swallowing the other.[12] This tale vividly portrays the on-going friction among the Galatians and their neighbors.

COUNSEL TO THE BOASTING GALATIANS

Into this volatile and rather ridiculous society Paul had brought the Gospel. The confused, new Christians, belabored by the Judaizers, were past masters at boasting. Yet, to them, Paul stood up and declared: "Far be it for me to boast." Thus, he attracted their attention and allegiance, putting himself in vivid contrast with the Judaizing teachers. The latter gloated over their birth, their religious heritage, and the great influence they had among the churches of the early Christian world. Paul would not advertise his own glory nor need "as some, letters of commendation" (2 Cor 3:1).

Truth to tell, if anybody wanted to boast, Paul personally had much more occasion to do so than others. "If anyone else thinks he has reasons to put confidence in the flesh, I have more: circumcised on the eighth day, of the people of Israel, of the tribe of Benjamin, a Hebrew of Hebrews; in regard to the law, a Pharisee; as for zeal, persecuting the church, as for legalistic righteousness, faultless" (Phil 3:4-6).

Paul's claim to be a "Hebrew of Hebrews" indicated that he had remained pure in his language, the original Hebrew dialect. Indeed, he was one of the few Jews left in his world who could do so. He also spoke Greek. Indications are that he has also spoken Aramaic. As an ancient linguist, he could respond in whatever language his circumstances demanded. The Apostle was sufficiently cosmo-

Boasting and Challenging

politan to be able to "be all things to all men" (I Cor 9:22). The Judaizers made no concession to Celtic, or any other culture.

Paul could also relate to Galatian pugnacity because he himself came from the fierce, fighting tribe of Israel, Benjamin. Their battle cry encouraged every other tribe to do their best, and more. They fought well, and they won. Furthermore, the Apostle's original name "Saul" conjures up the military might of the first king of Israel, for whom he was named. Paul could instantly recognize the blustering Benjaminite heroics when he saw them.

Certainly, the Galatians' material wealth, eloquence, and love of fighting resembled Paul's heritage. What, then, had made the difference? "Whatever was to my profit," he wrote, "I now consider loss for the sake of Christ" (Phil. 3:7). He wanted the Galatians to understand that he gloried "in nothing but the cross of Jesus Christ" (Gal 6:14).

The Judaizers gloried in their conformity to the laws of Moses, in their zeal for the tainted gospel they preached, in their talents, learning and orthodoxy. The supreme boast of the Apostle, on the other hand, was in Jesus the crucified Messiah. He had laid aside his entire heritage of arrogance, warlike accomplishments and material benefits to take up a single challenge. Paul endured even when the cross of Jesus Christ had become a stumbling block to both pagans and Jews.

The Apostle had been born again into the culture of Christ. Thus, he could declare: "Though I am free and belong to no man, I make myself a slave to everyone to win as many as possible. To the Jews I became like a Jew to win the Jews" (1 Cor 9:19-20). Despite his very impressive qualifications, Paul had no confidence in himself. He simply labored to bring back the minds of the deluded Galatians to a straightforward dependence on Jesus Christ.

13. The Ties That Bind

> *God sent his own Son . . . to purchase freedom for the subjects of the law, in order that we might attain the status of sons (Gal 4:5).*

For his powerful stage play, King Lear, William Shakespeare dipped into Celtic mythology. In doing so, he made a statement about kinship and loyalty that leaves the reader/viewer stunned. The impact of this larger-than-life character coming to self-discovery overwhelms us.

Myth identifies King Lear (*Llyr*) and his son Manannan as Celtic ocean-gods. Later legend, however, remembers Lear as a pre-Christian warrior king, in Cornwall, southwest England. The aged king asked his three daughters how much they loved him. The two elder ones professed their devotion in highly extravagant terms. Succumbing to their flattery, Lear gave large land allotments to Goneril (wife of the Duke of Cornwall) and Regan (wife of the Duke of Albany). The youngest daughter Cordelia scorned her sisters' manipulative speeches. Instead, she simply said that she loved her father exactly as a daughter should, and no more. In a blind rage, Lear disinherited her.

A king of pagan Celtic Britain, Lear died in his attempt to test the bonds of kinship.[1]

122

The Ties That Bind

Unrealistically,[2] the foolish old man wanted to retain his retinue and his kingly honors. Instead, his retirement arrangements collapsed under the exploitation and abuse of his daughters and their households. Meanwhile, the dowerless Cordelia received suitors from across the English Channel.[3] The King of France claimed to love her and married her despite her lack of inheritance.

Storms physical, mental, and emotional engulfing him, King Lear fought for survival. Finally, his mind gave way. When Cordelia returned with the invading French forces, Lear anticipated reunion with his only honest daughter, the one he had so wronged. She, however, was arrested and hanged in prison.[4] Consumed in his madness, Lear tried piteously to believe that she still lived. Finally, falling beside her body, the King also died. In effect, as we shall see, Cordelia plays the role of kinsman-redeemer or *goel*.

Shakespeare's magnificent play, of course, has had numerous interpretations. For the present, we can simply appreciate the "Celticness" of the kinships that the tragedy reveals. Relationships defined, honored and betrayed, all against the complex backdrop of Gaelic culture.

The Celts honored four kinds of kinship: adoption and fosterage, clientage and hostagestaking.

A reconstructed rural home of the 4th century AD. On the grounds of Craggawnowen Castle, County Clare, Ireland, this Celtic farmer's house has been built, a Bronze Age-like dwelling.

KINSHIP—THE POWERFUL FOUNDATION OF CELTIC TRIBAL SOCIETY

Whether that of true blood or otherwise acquired, kinship was the only social cement in the Celtic world. Although a person owed allegiance only to his/her family, the tribe was one vast, extended family descended from a common ancestor. And that covered a great deal of ground.

Since most ancient societies were strictly hierarchical, one usually had scant hopes of escaping into a higher social rank. As noted earlier, these basic class lines prevailed in Celtic cultures where seven distinctive levels evolved. Gaelic tribes, however, built unique possibilities into their social system. Both men and women could actually aspire to higher callings.

Many Cinderella-type folk tales may appear to be the wishful thinking of the poverty-stricken looking for a way to climb the social ladder. Not so. They're more than that. Coming, as most of them do, from Celtic sources, they reveal an unusual kind of flexibility. Indeed, a person *could* cross class-lines. A woman might become a lawyer. A peasant might become a scholar. How amazing is that idea?

In Britain today, the now-expensive taste for thatched cottages remains as a quaint memory from the distant Gaelic past.

ADOPTION AND FOSTERAGE

The Celtic system allowed for kinship to be established through adoption. Thus bondsmen and those who were "kinless" could be adopted into the family. (That is, if they weren't criminals or otherwise undesirables.) Adoption might also be granted as a promotion for special talents like craftsmanship, military prowess, music, and so forth. This reliance on kinship instead of social institutions made it impossible for Celts ever to envision a centralized state.

To this more or less typical social pattern the Celts made one useful addition, fosterage. Fostering children in families unrelated to them created new kinship ties, not based on blood. In his *Gallic Wars*, Julius Caesar frequently referred to the bonds of obligation that the Gauls undertook at different levels. For instance, a king or chief might foster his children out from an early age, usually to humbler members of his own clan. Living with their foster-family, the sons learned the necessary skills of warfare, hunting, genealogy and horsemanship. The daughters practiced needlework, music and household tasks. The fosterage system not only cemented bonds of loyalty within the clan but also served as protection. If the king should be killed or his fortress raided, at least his sons would be safe.

Fosterage provided the best possible opportunities for all children, and the Celts practiced it regularly.[5] From Irish records we can learn the general outlines of the education of children in Celtic societies. Strong bonds existed among foster brothers and sisters. Foster parents became legally responsible for the youngsters' food, lodging, education, and protection. They even had to pay fines incurred by their foster-children.

Representations of triple mother-goddessess appear throughout Celtic lands. These domestic images celebrated the potency of the number Three and honored the mother-child relationship. For instance, from Cirencester, England, comes the figure of three women. Two hold vessels full of fruit and the third carries a tray of loaves and cakes. Another trio from Burgundy, Gaul, portray the first woman holding a baby, the second, a large napkin, and the third, a sponge for washing. All three bare one breast for nursing. The *Norns* represented Celtic intellectualism, the three goddesses being Past, Present, and Future. Their equivalent is found in the Greek *Fates* and the Saxon *Wyrdes*.

Although children were generally trained according to their own rank,[6] even girls were free to enter any profession. If they wished, they could become scholars in the bardic and ecclesiastical schools, earning all seven of the degrees available there. Leaders, judges, magistrates, poets, physicians—all professions stood open to anyone who could meet the standards. In pre-Christian times, women could (and did) fight as warriors alongside their men-folk.

When fosterage was undertaken simply for affection (*altramm serce*), no fee was charged. Otherwise, tuition had to be paid by the parents, higher for a girl than a boy. Basic education ended at the "Age of Choice," fourteen for a girl and seventeen for a boy. The legal contract of fosterage itself automatically ended with marriage, death, or the committing of a crime.

Fostering children in religious communities contributed measurably to the spread of the Christian faith. Many converted pagans went forth as missionaries for the Celtic Christian Church. Monasteries, in fact, resembled a new-formed tribe, a new version of tribal kinship. Since the innate heroism of the spiritual life attracted young warrior-aristocrats, early Celtic Christians were often of royal lineage.[6]

We find remnants of the customs of old Celtic fosterage in the medieval practice of apprenticeship. Likewise, the still-common English practice of sending very young children away to boarding school harks back to the same source.

CELTIC CLIENTS AND HOSTAGES

Retainers could bind themselves to individual members of the elite class in a relationship called "clientage," a bonding that implied obligations on both sides. In this way separate tribes could relate to one another in a mild, advantageous form of time-restricted kinship. Julius Caesar observed: "The [Gaulish] leaders do not allow their clients to be oppressed or defrauded, otherwise they lose their influence with their clients."[7]

Celtic hostages did not function in our modern sense of the word. Instead, hostage taking served as yet another benevolent bonding mechanism. Young men of noble families from one tribe sometimes lived and served with another tribe. This arrangement meant that warfare between these two tribes—for the safety of the hostages—would be relatively unlikely. A major step toward peace and one that was bound by a moral code!

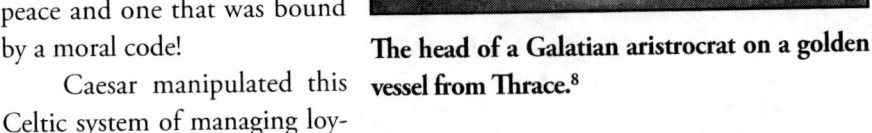

Caesar manipulated this Celtic system of managing loyalties to his own advantage.[9] The Romans, however, concluded the encounter with much less of a sense of honor than the Celts themselves would have practiced. Suspicious of Indutiomarus, a leader of the Treverit tribe in Gaul, Caesar ordered the chieftain to come to the Roman camp with 200 hostages (54 BC). He specified them by name, all of Indutiomarus' relatives, including the chief's own son.

The head of a Galatian aristrocrat on a golden vessel from Thrace.[8]

The Ties That Bind

Caesar surveyed the group with a practiced eye. Those Treverians whom he felt he could not trust, he set aside to take with him on his own campaign in Britain. He then dispersed the 4,000 Gaulish cavalry who had come to defend Indutiomarus.

Chief Dumnorix of the Aedui tribe, however, refused to cooperate and tried to escape with his horsemen. The Romans pursued, captured and executed the Gauls. Being rather off-hand about the demands of kinship themselves, the Romans secured their own position by violating the Gallic rights of hostage taking. Only thirty-four years earlier, Rome had betrayed a large group of chieftains from Galatia, massacring them in defiance of the sacred obligations of Celtic hospitality.

KINSHIP IN HEBREW CULTURE

The Apostle Paul boldly declared that he was "a Hebrew of Hebrews" (Phil 3:5). He certified that even though his Jewish heritage had been heavily influenced by Hellenism, he remained untainted. He took the occasion to demonstrate that although Christ had dramatically changed his heart, he was still integrally connected to his birth-culture.

One of the priorities in Paul's Jewish background had called for obedience to the laws of kinship. Hebrew heritage bound the community together by ties of family, marriage, and tribal connections. By payment of money, a kinsman was obligated to redeem a person or recover property for the original owner. In some cases, the transaction also involved the saving of a life that had been legally forfeited for a debt that the original owner had been unable to pay.

The Hebrew word *padha* is used in the Old Testament to describe the redemption of persons. Meaning "kinsman-redeemer," the word *goel* is closely associated with the solidarity of the family or tribal group. For example, if a man was forced to sell some portions of his property because he owed a debt he could not pay, his next of kin, the *goel* (if he had the means) had the legal obligation to repurchase it for the debtor (Lev 25:25). The kinsman was privileged to redeem a poor relative who sold himself into slavery because of a debt (Lev 25:47-49). Likewise, he had the duty of avenging murder (Num 35:19) and of recovering material property for the original owner (Lev 27:15, 19-20). The story of Ruth (Ruth 3:1-13) and a vignette in Jeremiah (32:6-12) are excellent illustrations of how the law of kinship operated in the practical lives of the Jews.

Naturally, this concept of redemption in Hebrew cultural practices would later apply to God's deliverance of individuals out of sin and all of the troubles that went with it. The most striking instance of the use of *goel* in describing God's redemption of humans appears in the experience of Job. He believed that God was his personal "Kinsman-Redeemer," and as such, must ultimately vindicate his integrity (Job 19:25).

In contrast, this Old Testament concept occurs only rarely in the New Testament. There the word "ransom" appears only three times (Mt 20:28; Mk 10:45; 1 Tim 2:6). Jesus, however, understood His own death as the work of a kinsman-redeemer. Repeatedly, He associated His suffering and death on the cross with the idea of a *goel*, a substitutionary sacrifice (Isaiah 53:5,6,10). Peter spoke of the blood of Christ as a ransom price for sinners (1 Pet 1:18-19). Paul emphasized the same thought (1 Tim 2:14. See also Ps 130:80).

With His own loud cry from the cross, "It is finished," Jesus Himself indicated that He was paying the price to redeem something forfeited. He deliberately used the word *tetelestai*, meaning "paid in full." This word derives from a story about an auction in the marketplace. As a child, He probably had heard this popular Jewish folktale.

Envision a busy Jewish marketplace, full of merchants and buyers bargaining for the slaves. One seller has a family of six. They must be sold for outstanding debts. At thirty pieces of silver each (the price of a common slave) the ticket runs very high. Many who would purchase turn away. Then from the back of the crowd, a shabbily dressed peasant steps forward. He identifies himself as a kinsman, willing to fulfill his obligation as a *goel*. Although at first the seller rejects him as a potential buyer, he insists. Pulling a bag out from the folds of his garment, he counts out the price—in gold, not silver. The merchant protests. "But these people aren't worth that much. Stop!"

Instead, the unlikely kinsman-redeemer continues until he has emptied the bag and shaken it out. By now, with pure gold, he has paid a sum far, far beyond the required 180 pieces of silver. Slamming his hands down on the gold, he shouts, "*Tetelestai!*" The transaction is complete. The property redeemed. And nothing owed!

After he (the *goel*) and his kinsman-slaves leave the market, he cries, "Go. You are all free."

REDEMPTION FOR THE GALATIANS

This image of the process used by the kinsman-redeemer prompted Paul to tell the Galatians: "But when the time arrived that was set by God the Father, God sent his Son, born among us of a woman, born under the conditions of the law so He might redeem those of us who have been kidnapped by the law. Thus, we have been set free to experience our rightful heritage. You can tell for sure that you are now fully adopted as His own children, because God sent the Spirit of His Son into our lives crying out, 'Papa! Father!' Doesn't that privilege of intimate

The Ties That Bind

conversation with God make it plain that you are not a slave, but a child? And if you are a child, you're also an heir with complete access to the inheritance" (Gal 4:4-7 *The Message*).

Redeemed and adopted! This idea brings into focus another significant Gentile understanding of family relations. Both Paul and the Galatians lived under Roman jurisprudence that did not allow for an adopted child being sold into slavery a second time. A certificate of adoption issued to ensure the bearer's freedom had to be carried always. Commenting on this Scripture passage, Charles R. Erdman underscored the fact that Paul was addressing "the universal sense of need, of moral helplessness, and of condemnation." The Apostle said that even the Jews devoted to law keeping and carrying a heavy sense of guilt could find the Savior.[9]

By this time, the Judaizers had restricted the application of Hebrew laws of kinship and imposed this servitude on the new Christians. Paul knew, however, that the Galatians had their own powerful kinship practices and would readily understand the concepts of adoption and redemption. Christ had released the new Christians from their spiritual infancy.

FOSTERAGE IN GOD'S FAMILY

By using the phrase "Abba! Father!" (Gal 4:6) as a figure of speech, Paul demonstrated that a great change takes place when Christ comes into the life of a believer. He combines both words to indicate the complete range of Divine Fosterage. Any person transported from a slave to a son or daughter is no longer subject to the law. Especially that which is enforced by human demands.

A familiar Aramaic term of endearment, the word *Abba* means "Daddy" or "Papa." It indicates a loving, trusting relationship. In New Testament times the child of a slave could not call his biological father *Abba*. Instead, he/she had to refer to him as *Pater*, a father who provides and protects. Only a *free-born child* could entreat his/her father with the intimate, passionate term, *Abba*.

Thus, Paul showed the Galatians that they had been born free in Christ with all of the privileges of inheritance. Therefore, they had to reject the Judaizers' efforts to bind them to obsolete laws! Indeed, "because you are born free and also adopted, you may use both terms, Abba! Father! Moreover, you can never be enslaved again."

Although we have been slaves to sin, Jesus invites us to a complete status change, adopting us as sons and daughters. As hostages, we are called by His name. Then, as clients, we choose to join His entourage and travel with Him.

Finally, Christ goes far beyond the self-serving methods of Caesar. Our Kinsman-Redeemer takes us all the way with Him. All the way into the heavenly inheritance He has guaranteed to us.

14. Help with the Heavy Load

If a man should do something wrong, my brothers, on a sudden impulse, you who are endowed with the Spirit must set him right again, very gently . . . . . Help one another carry these heavy loads" (Gal 6:1-2).

Second only to St. Patrick in the founding of Christianity in Ireland, Brigid of Kildare (452-523 AD) was ordained a bishop of the Celtic Church. She was the daughter of the poet Dubthach and his slave, Broiscech. A druid prophesied that the child the woman carried would be a "radiant daughter who will shine like the sun among the stars of heaven." Forthwith, the learned man purchased the mother and reared the infant Brigit as a foster-child in his own house.

In due course, Brigit founded her own "co-ed" Christian monastic city at Kildare, Ireland. There, she became widely celebrated as the humble, generous guardian of farm animals, pilgrims, healers, and midwives,

St. Brigit of Kildare (452–523 AD).[1]

Among her various foster-children was a youth from the community of Ferns. He came to her for counsel and often dined with her in her refectory. One

Help with the Heavy Load

day, at the end of communion, Brigit struck a bell. "Well, young cleric, there," she said. "Do you have a soul friend?"

"Of course, I do," the young man replied.

"But let us now sing his requiem," Brigit announced sadly, "for he has died. I saw when you had eaten half your portion of food that that portion was put in the trunk of your body, but that you were without any head. Or like the water of a polluted lake, neither good for drinking or washing. For your soul friend has died." This strange vision prompted her to continue. "Anyone without a soul friend is like a body without a head. Eat no more until you get a soul friend." This often-quoted story of St. Brigit[2] points to a need for a soul friend that takes on a sacramental quality: "Eat and drink no more until you find one."[3]

SOURCES AMONG THE PAGAN CELTS

The Celtic idea of the soul friend is an important consideration. Even the most self-sufficient among us sometimes feel the need for counsel, comfort and advice. From pre-historic times, the druid-type priests made themselves available as moral philosophers, legal advisors, and scientists. As an Indo-European institution, druidism pre-dated Greek and Roman civilizations and has been preserved in British as well as Indian cultures.[4] The Druid/Brahmin priest-type was exempted from taxes and other duties. Although he occasionally appeared as a terrible agent of human sacrifice, he was generally honored as a serious philosopher, a wise man, a healer, and a champion of liberty. Since his training could last up to twenty years, he accumulated vast stores of knowledge about the world, both human and natural.[5] Classical sources described druids for over 500 years (3rd c BC – 4th c AD).

With their additional skills in astronomy, magic and poetry, they embodied generations of gnomic (proverbial) wisdom. Among the Celts, this learned class also believed in a personal immortality. (The most familiar druid to Westerners today is the idealized, mythologized person of Merlin in the King Arthur cycle of stories.)[6] These druidic talents lived on in the Gaelic concept of the "soul-mate/friend."

Living as she did, at the beginnings of Christianity in Ireland, Brigit actually became a bridge from paganism to the Gospel. While she was not, by any means, the only saint to recommend the soul friend, she was perhaps the first in the Irish Church to emphasize the point.

Currently, we speak of our "soul-mates." That is, a deep, romantic ideal in the relationships between the sexes. To be sure, with the prevalence of divorce today, it is a wonderful thing when soul mates do find each other and marry. Then, at least, they can begin as friends. The spiritual soul friend of the Celts, however, went far beyond this stage and contributed much to the shaping of the Celtic Church.

ANAM-CHARA

Individualists that they were, the Celts always responded best to personal, private attention. The essential element of pagan Celtic spirituality, *anam-chara* (Irish, "soul friend") blended almost seamlessly into the practice of the early Celtic Christian saints[7]. Thus, the closely bonded Gaulish tribes took easily to the principle of the "soul-friend." Given their natural gifts of loyal kinship, compassion, hospitality, and fosterage, mentoring came naturally to the Celts. The custom extended from western Ireland to far-eastern Galatia. As a kind of chaplain and confidant within the religious communities, the *Anam-chara* tended to the "soul needs" of the monastery.

In contrast, the Roman branch of Christianity tended to foster "group functions," with monks usually living together in dormitories. Anonymous priests heard confession. Then people paid for indulgences, and so forth. Celtic religious communities, on the other hand, provided monks and nuns with private cells, or (where applicable) quarters for

A Welsh love spoon. This unique expression of devotion is something only a Celt might imagine. This hand-carved double spoon is designed for courtship. The man would labor to make his carving "one of a kind." When his lady accepted the spoon, she hung it by the door to indicate that she was "taken." Note the following symbols: A padlock (*I will look after you*); a keyhole (*My door is open*); a spade-shaped piece (*I will provide for you*); a single heart (*My heart is yours*); keys (*My house is yours*); a pair of commas (*Two souls*); bell (*We will live in harmony*); double bowls of the spoon (*We give generously*); double hearts in the bowls (*We feel the same about each other*).

Help with the Heavy Load

families to live together. This division of religious practice prevailed until the Roman party won the vote at the Synod of Whitby in 664 AD.[8]

Roman society was urban, organized from the top down. The Celts were hierarchical, but they were also strongly rural and retained their tribal life homogeneously across Europe. Flexible class lines led to familiarity and the enjoyment of common interests.

The *anam-chara* provided an intensely personal relationship. He/she could be a healer of body and soul, one who guided people in personal penance and who showed the way to forgiveness. These basic Gaelic social functions contributed to a distinctive kind of spirituality and mysticism. Nonetheless, despite their penchant for independence, the Celts still practiced real, corporate Christianity." That is, every believer had a moral obligation to every other person, both inside and outside of the Church.

Giving oneself as a soul friend has always called for constant patience and generosity, unconditional love and a great investment of time. Because we all need one another, soul-friending becomes a calling of the very highest order.

NEW TESTAMENT MODELS OF THE SOUL FRIEND

David and Jonathan became the Old Testament exemplars of deep friendship (1 Sam 18:1–5). The *Message* Bible literally defines them as "soul friends." The New Testament, however, broadens the concept more fully.

In this generation of antiquity, personal friendship lay at the heart of life. A soul friend in the New Testament had to be "close as your breath" (Gr *psuche*, "soul, breath") Such a person was best described by *philos* (Gr "friend, beloved, dearest"). Having no erotic suggestions, the word transcends our modern concepts of platonic relationships.[9]

Paul's instruction on church relationships included a broad base for soul-friending. In this context, his prose drifts effortlessly into poetry:

"Never be harsh with an elder;
    appeal to him as if he were your father.
Treat the younger men as brothers,
    the older women as mothers,
and the younger as your sisters,
    in all purity" (I Tim 5:1-2 NEB)

Because both Greek and Roman cultures extolled this ideal relationship, it became a theme among the writers of the day. The fact remains, however, that very few people have had the good fortune to experience a friendship of this quality, either then or now. Soul friends shared all things. Socially, materially, and spiritually. In good times and bad. Then, love, joy, and merrymaking further enhanced the connection (Lk 15:6, 9, 29).

The word *philos* occurs twenty-nine times in the New Testament and is almost wholly confined to the writings of Luke and John. The Hellenized Jews of that day actually taunted Jesus for being such a friend (Lk 7:34, cf Mt 11:19). Yet, even while they mocked Him, they came closer to the truth of His mission than any of them would have wished to admit. Jesus did, indeed, refer to the Master-disciple relationship he had with the Twelve as his *philoi* (friends). He invited them into this close personal relationship with Himself (Lk 12:4; Jn 15:14-15). This public designation also underscored His intention concerning their future tasks and destinies.

Philos means "service, concern and sacrifice" (Lk 11:5-8). In terms of hospitality and neighborliness, the soul friend can expect help from his or her counterpart, no matter how inconvenient the task. Indeed, sacrifice of oneself, even to the point of death, was the supreme duty of a soul friend

Sadly, at the Last Supper, Jesus shared His anguish over His imminent crucifixion, declaring that the soul friends dining with Him would violate their commitment: "You will all fall away because of Me this night" (Mt 26:31).

Aghast at Jesus' pronouncement, Peter cried: "Even though all will fall away because of You, I will never fall away" (Mt 26:33). He aimed to be the only faithful soul friend!

Jesus cautioned him about his arrogant claim, knowing that Peter would be among the first to fall. "Truly, I say to you that this very night, before the cock crows, you will deny Me three times" (Mt 26:34).

"Even if I have to die with You," Peter cried , "I will not deny You." With that, all of the rest of the disciples joined in declaring their soul friend roles (Mt 26:35). Peter's outburst substantiated the opinion of some of his friends that he too often spoke without knowing what he was saying.

A few hours later, Jesus invited His *philoi* to accompany Him to the Garden of Gethsemane. There, His soul "deeply grieved to the point of death," Jesus left eight of the disciples to watch the gate. Taking Peter, James and John with Him into the heart of the Garden, He begged them: "Watch and pray."

Then, alone, Jesus came face to face with the final, horrendous cost of man's salvation. As he wrestled with enormous agony, the ghastly illness called "*diapedesis*" overcame Him, and blood oozed from His skin.[10]

At this point, Jesus found His three closest friends asleep. "So, you men," He said, addressing Himself to Peter, "could you not watch with Me for even one hour?" (Mt 26:40).

Help with the Heavy Load

Next, came another disciple, Judas, with a posse to betray the Master. To him Jesus said, "Friend, do what you have come for." The Greek word *hetairos* used here for "friend" indicates one who was once a soul friend but has now betrayed that trust.

As we know, Peter publicly denied any knowledge of Jesus (Mt 26:69-75). Realizing what he had done, he separated himself from the other disciples. Jesus knew that poor Peter needed a special message. Therefore, the Resurrection Angel told the women at the tomb: "Tell His disciples and Peter that I have risen" (Mk 16:7 NASB). Afterwards, during breakfast on the beach in Galilee, Jesus reconstructed the scene of Peter's denial. Peter had triple opportunity to respond to the question: "Simon, do you love (*agapos*) Me more than these?"

Three times Peter replied: "I love You," thus eradicating his former, thrice-repeated claim: "I don't know the man" (Jn 21:15-17). This public testimony restored Peter into the full fellowship of a soul friend, a commitment that he never again betrayed.

AN APOSTOLIC MODEL

Not only was Paul familiar with the terms of the Greek philos, he also made it an important facet of a practical Gospel. In his classic statement to the Romans he challenged them to "be devoted (Gr. *philostorgoi*) to one another." (Rom 12:10). Here the Apostle combined the word *philos* with the word *storge* ("love of family, parents and children, a glue that holds all together"). In coining this new word, he declared soul friendship to be the duty of every believer.

Paul's hybrid word, *philostorgoi* is a *hapax legoumenon*. That is, a term used only once in the entire New Testament. It is translated as "devoted, kindly affectionate, tenderly loving," All of these terms capture the essential meaning of the soul friend. In other words, a "devoted." person must be a soul friend who never abandons the relationship, for any reason.

Paul admonished the Galatians: "If a man should do something wrong ...you who are endowed with the spirit must set him right again, very gently.... Help one another carry these heavy loads" (Gal 6:1-2). He referred here to the duties of "soul friending." From the Gospel of Jesus Christ he had learned that, although true soul friends may have disagreements, love, forgiveness and restoration always remain.

PAUL FINDS HIS SOUL FRIEND

As a newcomer to the young Christian community of faith, Paul required mentoring. A known persecutor, he also needed to be introduced to a potentially hostile group of believers. He stood between a rock and a very hard place. When he desperately needed a friend in Damascus, Ananias temporarily filled this role.

In Jerusalem Paul found the lasting model of a soul friend in one, Joseph. Not by chance, the man was nicknamed Barnabas, "son of encouragement" (Acts 4:36). Most people have thought that that was his given name, because he was so compassionate. Barnabas stood by the young Saul-turned-Paul at a difficult time. Paul's old friends would regard him as a traitor. Any new, Christian friends would naturally fear the one who had harried them so relentlessly.[11]

Author of the book of Acts, Dr. Luke was the first to mention Barnabas as a generous contributor to the Church. This alone might have qualified him for the perfect profile of a soul friend. Barnabas and Paul, however, had other affinities. Both came from the culture of the Hellenized Jews.[12] The rich authenticity of their relationship is confirmed still further. When Paul's popularity surpassed that of Barnabas, the latter, as genuine soul friend, showed neither jealousy nor envy. So strong was their bond, that Paul could even rebuke Barnabas to the Galatians. The Apostle accused Peter and other Jews in the matter of not eating with Gentiles, adding that "even Barnabas was carried away by their hypocrisy" (Gal 3:13).

We are not surprised, then, when Barnabas recommended to Paul a certain energetic, visionary youth who had passionately embraced the call to evangelism. The kind of evangelism that meant sharing the Good News where it had never been heard before. To this end, Barnabas had introduced his cousin, John Mark, to the Apostle. At first, as an apprentice, the young man accompanied Paul on his missionary journeys, and a soul-friendship grew between the two. In time, however, the situation became tense. Mark jeopardized the future of the mission by quarreling with his new soul friend and then abandoning his responsibility.

A few years later, we are glad to learn, Mark matured both spiritually and emotionally and became reconciled with his aged mentor. He attended Paul while the letter to Philemon was being written (v 2). So poignant was the restoration of this soul-friendship that on one occasion Paul appealed to Timothy to "pick up Mark and bring him with you, for he is useful for service" (2 Tim 4:11). For Paul, the word "service" surely included all of the facets of soul-friendship.

Knowing that the Galatians had spiritual mentoring as part of their ancient heritage, Paul warmly gave of himself as a concerned parent/soul friend. In effect, he said, "Try me! As I follow Christ, let me be a soul friend to you." Then,

Help with the Heavy Load

he went on to emphasize that they themselves possessed all the gifts necessary to serve one another in the same capacity.

SOUL FRIENDS TODAY

The "messed-up masses" today turn, with increasing desperation, to self-help resources. With religious commitment on the decline, we find psychiatric treatment, family counseling, and group therapy intensifying. Popular magazines are full of personal tests and advice. Television has recently offered a few common-sense talk shows. Meanwhile life escalates in pace and pressure by the hour. A kind of assembly line spirituality is evolving, and too much of it is rootless and faddish.

What, then, do we need to do? One popular publication surveyed the findings of a large number of scientific studies, which have examined the all-too-real medical effects of stress and isolation. These reports reveal four major benefits deriving from a person's maintaining a strong social network. In other words, soul-friending : (1) Increases the chance of surviving life-threatening illness; (2) creates a stronger, more resilient immune system; (3) improves mental health, decreases depression; and (4) extends life-expectancy measurably.

Some have spent a lifetime under heavy responsibility and subjected to stress-producing labor. With many lapses into workaholism, they have become "stress-junkies." The over-all conclusion is that friendships "play a far more important role in maintaining good health and having a long life" than most of us realize. Indeed, "social ties may be the cheapest medicine we've got."[13]

Furthermore, much data supports the idea that the soul-type of friendship not only helps us in crisis, but also encourages us to take better care of ourselves. The early 21st century has brought in a climate of distress, previously unknown. We face terrorism, serial kidnappings and killings, random sniper attacks, and a litany of other unspeakable tragedies. This kind of stress manifests itself in the breakdown of marriages, the escalation of terminal illnesses, and the explosion of senseless hostility. Why shouldn't our stress hormones go wild?

Where do we find our soul friends? In church and community groups. Or in very narrowly focused, single-friend interactions. The latter seems to be more evident among women than men. While men tend to do things together, women more often take time just to be together.

Jesus' pattern of soul-friending actually appears to reveal a feminine side to His personal friendship model. He called all of his disciples, including Judas and the women who followed and cared for Him, His *philoi* (Jn 15:15). Within this group He chose twelve close companions (Lk 9:1). Once again, from the Twelve, He selected three[14] (Peter, James and John) for special kinship and for support in the deepest crises (Mt 25:37). At this level, He became more open and vulnerable than He had been with any other human being. Finally, He arrived at just one. "There was reclining on Jesus' bosom, one of His disciples whom Jesus loved." (Jn 13:23). Thus the Beloved John humbly described himself as the Savior's ultimate, soul (bosom) friend.

Paul offered himself as a soul friend, knowing that we face the drudgery, the "dailyness" of our lives. The frustrations, the boredom, the disease, the despair. We each need—we *crave*—a soul friend. That precious person, who, in a single conversation, a telephone call, or an e-mail, becomes to us, as it were, "God with skin on."

Finally, the soul friend directs us to God Himself, the ultimate Soul Friend.

Jonathan and David–Soul Friends
(1 Sam 18:1-4)

By the time David had finished reporting to Saul, Jonathan was deeply impressed with David—an immediate bond was forged between them. He became totally committed to David. From that point on he would be David's number-one advocate and friend. Saul received David unto his own household that day, no more to return to his father.

Jonathan, out of his deep love for David, made a covenant with him. He formalized it wiht solemn gifts; his own royal robe and weapons—armor, sword, bow, and belt.

The Message

15. Love Never Fails

It was because of an illness that I first preached the gospel to you. Even though my illness was a trial to you, you did not treat me with contempt or scorn. . . .If you could have done so, you would have torn out your eyes and given them to me" (Gal 4:15-16).

ANCIENT CELTIC HOSPITALITY

A visit to Bunratty Castle, near Shannon, Ireland, enables one to experience today the very elemental nature of ancient Celtic hospitality. True, the medieval banquet is a made-for-tourists affair, but do not overlook its deeper implications. As you approach the entrance, two liveried servants stand in your way. They hold wooden platters full of broken pieces of bread surrounding a heap of salt in the middle. They require you to dip a morsel of bread in the salt and eat it before them. In so doing, you promise to abide by the rules of the Lord of the Castle. By accepting his hospitality, you agree not to betray him in any way and not to start a quarrel.

First, visitors are ushered into the Great Hall where they are offered a drink of mead (or other refreshment). Guests listen to the harp music and the singing of the ladies of this stately residence. Then they are led downstairs to the feast. More music and much food. The latter arrives at the table in large steaming cauldrons. A short dagger-like knife is the one piece of cutlery.

Just as the serving wenches complete their tasks, a cry goes up from the butler. He has seized a young (unknowing) guest by the collar: "We hereby arrest this man on charges of disturbing the peace of the ladies of the castle." Forthwith, the prisoner is thrust through a door leading down to the dungeon, his screams fading as he disappears into the nether regions of the stronghold. (He will later be "redeemed.")

Nightly, at Bunratty Castle, Ireland, a medieval feast is re-enacted to preserve the customs of Celtic hospitality. The serving wenches wait on a group of tourists trying to cope with the simpliticies of the banquet table. (Photo by D. M. Comm)

THE OBLIGATIONS OF HOSPITALITY

The whole process of Celtic hospitality is thus re-enacted. The presentation of a guest in need. The conditions of his/her acceptance. Above all, the dire results of betraying the lord's trust.

For this reason, fasting has long been a weapon of protest. Today modern Irish dissidents have practiced it as a means to their political ends. Mahatma Gandhi of India, coming from the same ancient Indo-European culture as the Celts, fasted as a means of political protest. To be sure, the shame of fasting also served his purposes, and he actually won his cause by embarrassing the British Raj.

"Well," we might say, "if someone wants to die by starvation, let 'em do it." Celtic heritage, however, forbade such irresponsibility. To have someone sitting at your door fasting was totally mortifying to a householder. The (Irish) Brehon laws demanded that you receive and feed anyone coming to your house. There-

Love Never Fails

fore, the "guilty" party would hasten to rectify the wrongs in question and thus remove the humiliation of such a breach of hospitality.

While Anglo-Saxon laws prescribed duties of hospitality for the elite, Celtic law covered everyone from the highborn down to the lowliest peasant awaiting a bowl of porridge and a cup of ale. Indeed, for the Celts, both pagan and Christian, whoever ate at your table actually became a "kinsman." Consequently, treachery toward one who has extended hospitality to you is the most despicable of crimes. Also a dominating principle among the Hebrews, Judas' breach of hospitality made his deed utterly despicable. He betrayed Jesus immediately after having been a guest at the Last Supper. Truly a deed of horror. The circumstances could not have been worse.

Based on a Celtic/Scots tale, Shakespeare's drama, "Macbeth" demonstrates the same kind of tragedy that comes with defying the laws of hospitality. Macbeth had entertained King Duncan of Scotland at his home, Glamis Castle (1040 AD). At the instigation of his ambitious wife, Macbeth murdered Duncan and assumed the kingship. Although Macbeth survived for another seventeen years, Malcolm, son of Duncan, eventually destroyed him. Celts would find it unthinkable that such a crime should go unpunished, or that such a one as Macbeth should simply die quietly in his bed. They regarded revenge as their only option.

Almost 1,400 years ago, a gentle Irish poet described the simple, homely act of hospitality at his monastery. Any Celt, in any time or place, might have said the same:

> I saw a stranger yestreen,
>
> I put food in the eating place,
> Drink in the drinking place,
> Music in the listening place,
>
> And in the sacred name of the Triune,
> He blessed myself and my house.
> My cattle and my dear ones,
> And the lark said in her song
> "Often, often, often, goes Christ
> In the stranger's guise."[1]

THE PRACTICE OF HOSPITALITY

Hospitality was a patriarchal practice and a sacred trust, widely understood throughout the ancient world. In fact, the Gaelic people adhered to this precept more stringently than even to their written laws. While the word does not appear in the Old Testament, the custom of hospitality is evident, particularly in patriarchal narratives. We trace it back to Abraham's entertaining the angels and to Lot's protecting his guests against the vile mob of Sodom (Gen 18:19).

The necessity of hospitality arose from the nomadic life of the patriarchs when public inns were a rarity, every stranger a potential enemy, and hospitals unknown. The ancient Hebrews, however, practiced hospitality more from fear and a need of protection than from generosity. They provided a guest with water for his feet, a place to rest, a tasty meal and provender for his animals. Even if he were an enemy, the visitor could enjoy these provisions for three days. He would be safe up to thirty-six hours after his last meal with his host. After that, he needed to be gone, or else![2] Under Celtic law, however, a man had to wait four days before he could even question the guest he had received into his home.

Like any other good thing, the practice of hospitality could be abused by pretenders, such as the Judaizers. Their presumption created much stress among the Galatian Christians who had to prove their commitment by entertaining church leaders. As a regular traveler, Paul often encountered aggressive interrogation and demands for his apostolic credentials. Potential hosts often became edgy, especially after the Judaizers had already passed through the community.

PAUL'S FIRST VISIT TO THE GALATIANS

The wandering diasporan Jews who had settled in Galatia had been influenced by the generosity of the local citizens (Gal 4:14). Having lost their own heritage of hospitality, they could only benefit from being assimilated into the Celto-Hellenistic culture. As Jews and Gentiles blended together in the Christian church, the Celtic members brought with them a liberality that sometimes embarrassed the cautious Jews. No doubt, the Galatians were widely known for their kindly reception of guests. Apparently the very mention of Galatia called up recollections of free, spontaneous fellowship.

The Apostle's first contact with the Galatians is believed to have come very early in his ministry, about 47-48 AD.[3] After his three years of spiritual retreat in Arabia, Paul savored the joyous welcome from the Galatians as a vivid memory, perhaps a highlight of his whole life. Never again would he be so generously received, *anywhere*.

Love Never Fails

When Paul arrived in Galatia, ill and disfigured by physical abuse and disease, he found nothing but unrestrained acceptance from the people there. We should recall that in his condition Paul could not have attended a synagogue, much less preached in one. On his first visit, however, the Galatians seem to have swept Paul away with loving care.

The Jews, however, found many other inhospitable reasons to reject Paul—some of which included Paul's propensity for sarcasm and irony. He could employ his razor-sharp wit and tongue in bitter denunciation of his opponents. Some of his remarks even included curses against those who attacked him and the Gospel. Still, the visible blemishes of his disease probably became the most significant cause.

PAUL'S ILLNESS

We have very little reliable evidence about Paul's physical appearance. The earliest extra-Biblical legend describes him as energetic despite his small stature. Bald-headed, his heavy eyebrows met above a slightly hooked nose. His legs were bowed. Paul himself wrote of a recurrent physical ailment that has been conjectured to include epilepsy, malaria, and an eye-malady (Gal 6:11). The further catalogue of his sufferings includes relentless persecution, with at least eight floggings and one stoning. To which may be added the stress of rejection by friends and supporters. He became *persona non grata* to his fellow Jews. Their rigid rules stated that no person with a blemish or a disease (especially of the eye). (Lev 21:16-21) could be the priest or spokesperson of a perfect God in their synagogues.

Until 70 AD Christianity was preached primarily in Jewish synagogues. This created a problem for Paul who openly described the repulsiveness of his affliction: "Though my condition was a trial to you, you did not scorn[4] and despise[5] me."[6] As healers, the Galatians took great pains in caring for their aged and sick. They even believed that a sick person could claim miraculous powers and perform astounding healings for others. The Apostle was an excellent candidate to benefit from their compassion and their medical skills.

Paul's success among the pagan Galatians pointed them to belief in Jesus Christ as the Son of God. Then a major problem arose. A group from Galatia had attended the Jerusalem Council and returned with their interpretation of Christianized Judaism, one which mingled the old legalism with the freshness of the new Gospel. These Judaizers, however, faced a hard task. Some Galatians found the rigid, inhospitable attitudes completely alien to their natural preferences, practices of many centuries' standing. Yet, their strong desire to please those in authority over them caused the Galatians to embrace these "off-color" teachings.

By the spring of 58 AD, Paul had received news that the Galatian churches had gone into reverse. "Where," he asked, "is the hospitality that was once attributed to you?"(Gal 4:14). He realized that if he should return to Galatia now, he would be received with utter coldness.

Whereas on his first visit the people had paid no attention to his physical disabilities, now the Judaizers were accusing Paul of outrageous conduct as well. Physically, he had collected money from them, to say nothing of the nursing care he had received. Spiritually, they claimed, he had not told them the truth. Pleasure and delight had disappeared. In a word, Paul had simply taken advantage of everyone for his own benefit.

More than Paul's pride was hurt. Fresh out of Arabia, he had brought them marvelous truths which they had now trivialized. Having defected from the Gospel he preached, the Galatians now received a hot letter from Paul. It went out, not just to one church but to the whole of Galatia. To some degree, the people still lived like Celts, in scattered communities rather than cities.

THE CELTIC HEALTH PLAN

Greeks, Romans and Jews viewed sickness and infirmity as a punishment from gods/God. Indeed, unwanted children were "exposed" to die in the wilderness (Ez 16). Inconvenient, elderly people were "put away." In contrast, the Celts were healers.

The centuries-old Brehon laws of the Celts humanely prescribed in minute detail the conditions for caring for the sick and the aged. The furnishings and supplies in the house of a dependent old person were described in detail: his food, his clothing, and his baths. Besides, his "head was to be washed every seventh day."[7]

Moreover, each tribal kingdom was required to maintain a fully-staffed hospital. The Celts derived many of their theories about healing from their connections with the Hittites (2400 BC or earlier). The doctor was required to provide plentiful ventilation for his patients, and a stream of fresh water had to run through the "hospital." If the physician blundered or mismanaged an operation, he was fined. If, through ignorance, he could not cure a patient, he could claim no fee.

If one person wounded another in a fight, after nine days he was obligated to bring his victim home and nurse him back to health. Strict regulations gov-

Love Never Fails

erned the operation of his home while the "guest" was being treated for his injuries. No music, no games, no arguments between husband and wife, and much else besides.

In reviewing these age-old Celtic laws in the 5th century AD, St. Patrick affirmed that the ancient lawgivers had been inspired by the Holy Spirit. The recommendations for diet, hot-and-cold water treatments, rest, fresh air, medicines and herbs produced an amazingly modern program for the maintenance of health.

THE ENTERTAINMENT OF THE POET OR PREACHER

Paul's wretched appearance notwithstanding, the Galatians received him without reservation. Moreover, he had something very much in his favor. He was a preacher. The Celts dearly loved the spoken word.

A sensitive response to The Word has always been a strong feature of Gaelic nations. Hearing it in poetry, song or story, was, for them, a nightly event. Thus, throughout Celtdom the service of speakers, poets and singers was highly prized. They might be "bards in residence" or itinerant entertainers. Irish law entitled a resident poet to receive a house and a stipend of twenty-one cows and their grass, two hounds and six horses. Everyone welcomed the touring poet and recompensed him even more handsomely.

Two thousand years ago, these Irish Celts first invented rhyme. Their love of wit and rhythm abounded. Sometimes, however, this kind of entertainment strained even Celtic hospitality to its outer limits. The story of Senchan Torpiest (6th century AD) is a case in point. He arrived in the court of Guaire the Hospitable, King of Connacht. The bard's entourage consisted of 150 student-poets, each with his "servant and dog." In addition, wives and horses also had to be accommodated. The King provided separate meals and beds for each of the multitude. The whole party stayed with the long-suffering Guaire for a year and a day! Violation of the sacred laws of hospitality must have tempted the king at times. Actually, despite the honors accorded them, more than once the Irish poets became such a burden to the land that the suffering people sought to exile or even to exterminate them.

The Celtic harp serves as the logo for the Bards and their music. As wandering singers, poets, and storytellers, the bards ranked near the druids in importance. Well paid, they could destroy a reputation with a song.[8]

No doubt Paul was grieved, finally, to realize that the Judaizers had persuaded at least some of the Galatians to regard him as an itinerant preacher who had far over-stayed his welcome. At the time of his visit, however, their willingness to hear the Word insured the excellence of their hospitality. They rejoiced in the Good News the Apostle brought, believing, even as they cared for their loathsome but blessed guest. Nowhere else could Paul have been so well received as by the Galatian believers. After all, hospitality had long been a primary Celtic virtue. For at least 1,000 years, they had regarded a guest as a sacred trust.

Conflicts such as those promoted by the Judaizers accounted for the fact that much of the Apostle's ministry to the young churches mainly involved "trouble-shooting." Nonetheless, Paul knew himself to be "made a minister" and called to be an apostle. He pressed on like one "born out of due time," for one purpose, to preach the Gospel (Eph 3:7; 1Cor 15:8). He must be heard. And, with all the force of a Celtic bard, he *was* heard.

ONE FINAL CELTIC CONNECTION FOR PAUL

Not unfittingly, Paul spent his final days among Celtic friends.[9] Having arrived in Rome for his appeal to Caesar in 58 AD, the Apostle became a guest of new Christians, many of whom would ultimately share martyrdom with him.

Among those who ministered to Paul before, during and after his execution (66 AD) was the British/Christian household of Rufus Pudens and Claudia (*Britannicum*).[10] Shortly before his death, Paul sent a message to Timothy: "Do your best to come before winter. Eubulus sends greetings to you, as do Pudens and Linus and Claudia and all the brethren" (2 Tim 4:21). The Apostle wrote from the heart of the Rufus Pudens family and the Christian-Gentile church that assembled in their home.[11]

A BLEND OF SCRIPTURE AND TRADITION

The account of these (Celtic) British Royals and the Apostle Paul is, however, not familiar. Apart from the scanty scriptural references, Roman historians[12] attested to the authenticity of the Roman senator, Rufus Pudens." Allusions are also to be found among the Early Church Fathers.[13] Since the mid-19th century, the interest in "British Israelitism" has continued to flourish.[14] They find the six years of "unaccounted time" for the Apostle Paul a time when he could have made his long desired journey to Spain (Rom 15:24, 28) and from there to Britain. Indeed, Celto-Saxon peoples have striven to find themselves both the spiritual and literal descendants of ancient Israel.[15] Modern DNA research has not

Love Never Fails

yet, however, found any genetic connection between Europeans/Britons and Israel.

Paul referenced a first Rufus in his letter to the Romans: "Salute Rufus chosen in the Lord, and his mother and mine" (Rom 16:13). F. F. Bruce identifies this Rufus with the father of Simon of Cyrene, bearer of Christ's cross (Mt 27:32), a person with whom Paul had developed a friendship.[16] At the same time, those who identify this man with "Rufus Pudens" claim that the two men were half-brothers.[17] Most scholars concede, however, that Paul regarded the mother of this Rufus' simply as his spiritual parent.

TRUE CELTIC HOSPITALITY

The second Rufus and his Gaelic wife, however, are of particular interest. Although based on fact, the story mixes many strands of history, tradition and myth. Here we shall attempt to put the "pseudo-historical" account together in a sequential way.

Rufus Pudens Pudentianus (d 96 AD) and his British wife **Claudia Britannicum** (37-97 AD) freely opened their home to all of those building the first Christian "Church of the Gentiles" in Rome.[18] This endless hospitality does not really reflect the graciousness of a Roman wife. Rather, it demonstrates the influence and power of the tall, blue-eyed Celtic woman who was the mistress of the lavish *Palatium Britannicum*.[19]

In his effort to exterminate both druids and Christians, **Emperor Claudius** ordered his Roman legions to invade Britain (42 AD). (They arrived with a troop of war elephants!) The General **Aulus Plautius** commanded the army, assisted by his aide/centurion, young **Rufus Pudens**. Their most formidable resistance came from **Caradoc**, King of Siluria, Wales.

The Emperior Tiberius Claudius (10 BC – 54 AD) was virtually a caricature of himself. Plagued with ill health and a total absence of social skills, he also lacked military and administrative experience.[20]

The Family of King Caradoc/Caractacus

King Lear (Welsh, *Llyr*) Sponsored by Augustus Caesar, Lear had been educated in Rome. Later he returned as a hostage for his grandson, Caradoc. Shakespeare created one of his greatest tragic heroes out of the story of Lear's foolishness. (The Welsh bards wisely said of him: "No folly but ends in misery.")

Bran (*Fendigaid*) **the Blessed** (20 BC-36 AD) resigned his crown to his son, Caradoc (36 AD) and became the Arch Druid of the College of Siluria (Wales). Several years later, he became a hostage for his son, traveling to Rome with Caradoc's family. He is said to have been baptized by the Apostle Paul.

Caradoc, the Pendragon of Britain[21] was born in Glamorgan (Siluria, Wales). An indomitable fighter, he had probably become a Christian before he was sent to Rome, along with some other members of his family.

Cyllin, First Son of Caradoc, returned to Britain where he was "sainted" by early British Church. He was martyred in 96 AD, and his wife died the next year.

Linus (*Lleyn*), **Second Son** was baptized and later ordained as the first Bishop of Rome by Paul (58 AD). Suffering much persecution, he was martyred with Rufus Pudens and his four children. Irenaeus wrote (80 AD): "The apostles having founded and built up the Church at Rome, committed the ministry to its supervision to Linus."

Cynon, Third Son was also baptized by Paul. He returned to Britain to help build the church there.

Eurgain, Caradoc's Elder Daughter. Her husband was Salog, Lord of Shropshire. They returned to Britain where she became the first Christian saint there.

Gwladys/Claudia, Caradoc's Younger Daughter. Upon her father's arrival in Rome, Emperor Claudius adopted her and named her "Claudia Britannica." At age 16 (53 AD) she married the Roman senator Rufus Pudens. Together, they helped establish the first Christian church in Rome. Although Claudia died a natural death, her husband and all four of her children died as martyrs.

Gwladys (Welsh, "Princess"), **Caradoc's Elder Sister.** Like the rest of the family, she was highly educated. She wrote prose and poetry in Latin, Greek, and her native Welsh tongue. In Rome she was called Pomponia Graecina, the latter name being an academic honor. Ironically, this very learned lady "married the enemy," Aulus Plautius.

The Family of King Caradoc/Caractacus

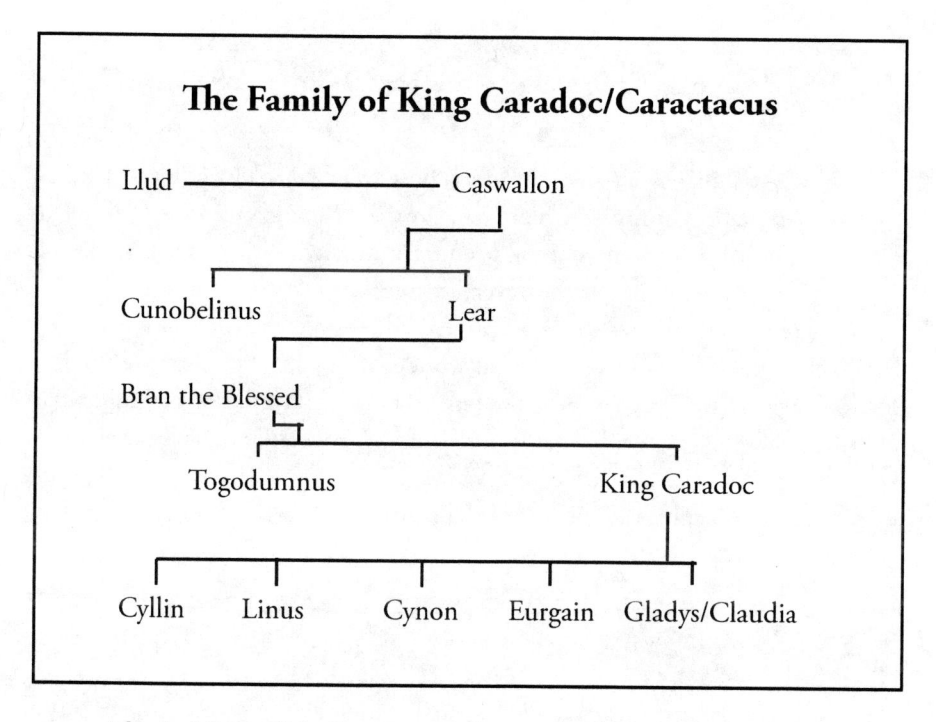

```
Llud ——————————— Caswallon
        |              |
    Cunobelinus      Lear
            |         |
        Bran the Blessed
                |
        Togodumnus         King Caradoc
                               |
    Cyllin   Linus   Cynon   Eurgain   Gladys/Claudia
```

After holding off the Roman invaders in almost nine years of guerilla warfare,[22] Caradoc faced his last battle at the head of 15,000 (Catuvellauni) troops. Seeking to escape, he sought protection from Queen Cartimandua (47-69 AD) of the neighboring Brigantes (now Yorkshire). Instead, she turned Caradoc over to the Romans.[23] As a result of this treachery, her "client kingdom" soon came under the direct rule of Rome.

Now, Caradoc and four generations of his family were taken to Rome in chains.(51 AD). These diplomatic hostages included: Himself and his queen, his father, Bran the Blessed, and his grandfather Lear. Also his five children and his sister Gladys.

When the British royal family arrived in Rome, they fully expected to be executed at the time of the Emperor's triumph—the usual Roman custom. Caradoc's younger daughter, Gladys, soon became the toast of Rome, and her keen intelligence was not lost upon the public. When her father went before the Roman Senate to plead for his life, she stood beside him. (Women were never to appear in the Senate.) The Romans both feared and respected this giant of a man with such a noble bearing. Caradoc calmly addressed the Senate in fluent Latin, explaining why he had resisted Rome for so long.

> **The Speech of King Caradoc Before the Roman Senate (52 AD)**
>
> "Had my government in Britain been directed solely with a view to the preservation of my hereditary domains, or the aggrandizement of my own family, I might long since have entered this city an ally, not a prisoner. . . .My present condition, [however], stript of its former majesty, is as adverse to myself as it is a cause of triumph to you.. What then? I was lord of men, horses, arms, wealth; what wonder if at your dictation I refused to resign them? . . . .I am now in your power—betrayed, not conquered. Had I, like others, yielded without resistance, where would have been the name of Caradoc? Where your glory? Oblivion would have buried both in the same tomb. Bid me live. I shall survive forever in history, one example, at least, of Roman clemency"[24]

THE EARLY CELTO-CHRISTIAN CHURCH IN ROME

Perhaps the eccentric Claudius spared Caradoc's life because the beautiful girl with the red-gold hair charmed him. He adopted her, changing her name from Gladys to "Claudia Britannicum." Amazingly, the captive Celts survived. Two conditions governed them: That Caradoc would remain a hostage for seven years[25] and that no member of his family would ever again take up arms against Rome.

Then, Emperor Claudius arranged for sixteen-year-old Claudia to marry into the popular senatorial family of Pudens. In 53 AD, a British pastor (Hermas), conducted the Christian ceremony at the Palatium Britannicum.[26]

Pudens' friend, the poet-satirist Martial (c40-c104 AD), celebrated the couple in several epigrams. Claudia had completely won the hearts of Rome:

> Since Claudia Rufina's eyes
> Report the blue of Britain's skies
> Why shows her bosom's classic face
> A peasant form of Latian race?
>
> Rufus, she your name who bears,
> Claudia, the foreign beauty,
> Now the veil of marriage wears,
> Vows my Pudens love and duty

Love Never Fails

In another verse, the poet remarked snidely: "The Celtic tail [that is, druidic power] wagged the Roman dog." Yet he respected this marriage that sealed the alliance between Rome and Britain—something that even Julius Caesar had failed to do a century earlier.

> Oh! Rufus Pudens, whom I own my friend
> Has ta'en the foreign Claudia for his wife;
> Propitious Hymen! Light thy torch and send
> Long years of bliss to their united life.[27]

At first, the British royal family had lived in apartments in the Imperial Palace. After the marriage, they all moved into the Pudens' Palatium Britannicum ("Palace of the British") where they literally fell into the lap of luxury. The palace, private thermal baths, and gardens were on a truly magnificent scale.[28]

CHRISTIANITY FINDS A PLEASANT SEAT IN ROME

We are told that as a young man, Senator Rufus Pudens had given lodging to Peter. When the Apostle baptized him, he was among Peter's earliest converts in Rome. Shortly after their marriage, Claudia was arraigned in the Roman senate for her Christian faith (47 AD). Her husband, Rufus, soon to become a believer himself, found her innocent!

Pudens residence, also known as *Titulus Pudentis*, became the meeting place for the Gentile Christians, with Hermas Pastor as the minister. The next name, *Hospitium Apostolorum* suggests that the Pudens home became a refuge for the apostles and other Christians, even as they went to their martyrdoms. Organized for a "house church," the building provided protection in times of persecution. Particularly when the Christians met in a "subterranean church" in the vaulted cellars. Whenever safety returned, they moved back into the vast senatorial palace above. Finally the site became the

The Church of Santa Pudenziana is somewhat off the beaten path in Rome. It is built upon the ancient two-story mansion of Rufus Pudens and Claudia.[29]

basilica of *Santa Pudenziana*.[30] A second-century inscription describes the church as the home of "Sanctus Pudens, the senator, and the home of the holy apostles."

Another member of the illustrious household was Seneca the Younger (4 BC-65 AD), a nephew of Pudens. While he always professed to be a Stoic, the early Christian Church in Rome favored him. (Some believe that Paul baptized him before his forced suicide in 65 AD.[31] Meanwhile, Claudia's children are said to have learned the Christian faith at Paul's knee. The Apostle probably spent his last two years living in Pudens house and receiving visitors there.

Some members of that family became martyrs shortly after the death of their beloved Paul.[32]

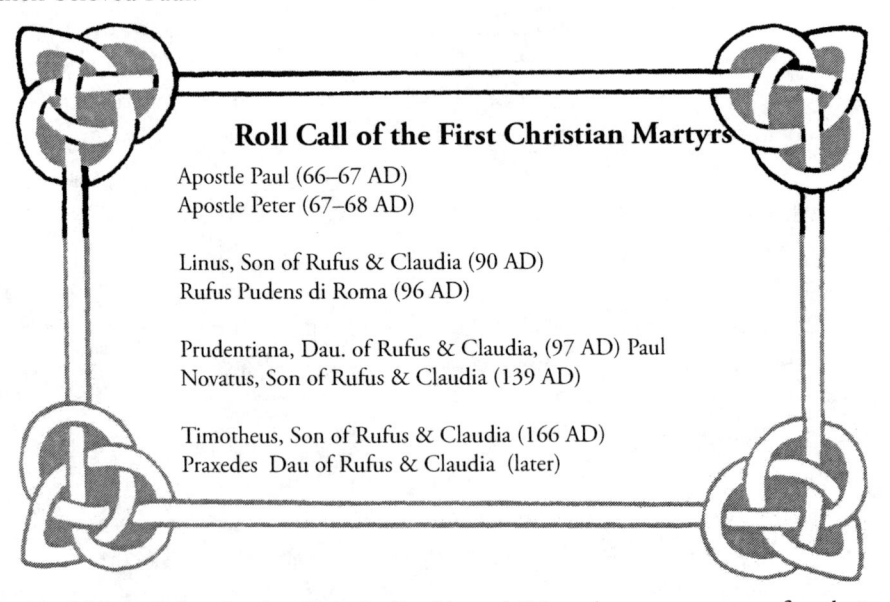

Roll Call of the First Christian Martyrs

Apostle Paul (66–67 AD)
Apostle Peter (67–68 AD)

Linus, Son of Rufus & Claudia (90 AD)
Rufus Pudens di Roma (96 AD)

Prudentiana, Dau. of Rufus & Claudia, (97 AD) Paul
Novatus, Son of Rufus & Claudia (139 AD)

Timotheus, Son of Rufus & Claudia (166 AD)
Praxedes Dau of Rufus & Claudia (later)

Although her husband and all of her children became martyrs for their faith, Claudia retired quietly to the family's Umbrian estate. She died there, a year after the death of her husband Rufus Pudens. She had long, long memories of the many Christians, great and small, who had found peace and love within her household. She embodied the best of Celtic womanhood and the power of the Christian faith.

Paul had witnessed the beginning of the Gospel in Claudia's family. He would have been so much encouraged to know that they had all remained faithful, to the doors of death itself. The Apostle began and ended his ministry among Gaelic believers—the Galatians in the East and the captive Britons in Rome.

16. A Flair for Design

Let us not become vainglorious and self-praising, calling forth and challenging each other to combat and envying" (Gal 5.26 HW)[1]

When we think of *haute couture*—the last word in classic elegance—we recall at least three contemporary fashion centers: Paris (of the Gauls); London (of the Britons); and Italy (of the Cisalpine Celts). In the New World the "transplanted Celts" of Boston and New York have continued their natural dedication to high fashion. In Istanbul, Turkey (formerly under Scythian and Galatian influence), little surpasses the Turkish swish of fine textured scarves and skirts, all in a blaze of color.

Therefore, almost daily, we may watch the models strut their stuff up and down the runways and compete in beauty pageants. Then, at the other end of the European spectrum, we have the dazzling "barbarian" extravagances of flamenco dancing (of the Celtiberians of Spain) and the French "Mardi Gras." In contrast, unless they have come under heavy Western influence, Asians are unlikely to display themselves in such a brazenly arrogant way, except, perhaps, for a *highly* festive occasion. Their everyday preferences are usually very plain.

Not accidentally, then, these tastes and talents have evolved out of ancient Celtic culture. The Celts, both then and now, have loved style, color, and ornamentation. Personal adornment and display have always mattered very much. Thus, through their mythology, their arts, and symbols, they have retained a highly visual link with mainstream Western history.

As already observed, the Celts lacked their own written history. Therefore, we must draw on classical writers and early Irish Christian literature to understand just how flamboyant the Celts could be. Strabo wrote: "[The Gauls] have a passion for personal ornamentation. They wear a lot of gold: they put golden collars [torcs] around their necks and bracelets on their arms and wrists, while dignitaries wear dyed or stained clothing that is spangled with gold. Their vanity therefore makes them unbearable in victory, while defeat plunges them into deepest despair."[2]

In all fairness, we must make one proviso here. As in all other cultures, of course, an inevitable drabness marked the Celtic peasants—a grayness which blended in all too well with the soil which they tilled. The Gaulish aristocrats and warlords, on the other hand, asserted their status in bursts of color and elegance, truly remarkable among these so-called barbarians.

METAL CRAFTING

As Europe's first and most skilled crafters of metal, the Celts perfected engraving, casting, punching, open-cut work, and "scorping" (grooving the metal with a stylus). They decorated bronze, gold, silver and even iron. These craftsmen, we are told, reached an amazing level of "exquisite sophistication" as they developed their tense, abstract designs.[3]

Their remarkable gifts for metal-crafting ensured their steady trade throughout the Greco-Roman world. Even after they came under Mediterranean influences, their unique Celtic designs survived. While the Gaelic craftsmen used Greek or Etruscan models, their own strong Celtic taste still prevailed. For instance, a flagon might be shaped according to the Etruscan style, but it would be decorated with Celtic designs.[4]

Not only is art a means of communication, but it also becomes the repository of ancient skills and beliefs.[5] Although most of the symbolic meanings have been lost to us now, we can still appreciate the geometric precision and vigor exhibited by the writhing, stylized birds and animals.

Naturally, these skills produced a wealth of personal jewelry, bracelets, arm-rings, and pins. Both men and women used elaborate brooches at the shoulder to hold their sweeping cloaks and mantles in place. To highlight this metalwork, the craftsmen embedded coral, glass, beads and precious stones in the brooches and necklaces. Cups and cauldrons, arm rings and bracelets were lavishly decorated with figures of humans and animals, as well as geometric motifs. Women used heavy gold hairpins in their long, thick hair.

A Flair for Design

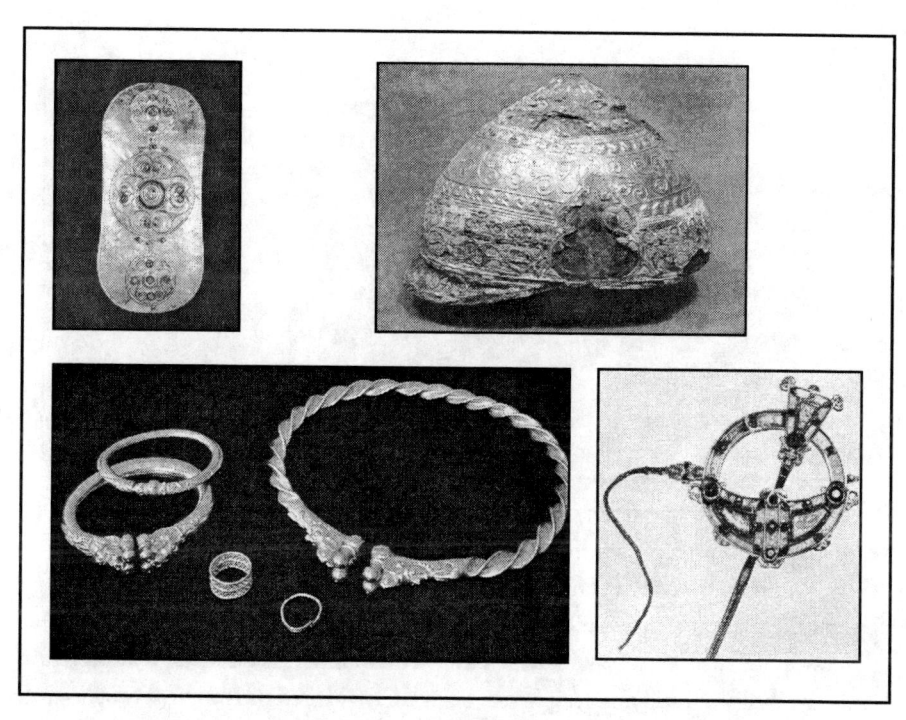

Top left: A gilded bronze shield, inlaid with red enamel (1st c. BC), retrieved from the River Thames at Battersea, London (1857). It had probably been deposited there as an offering to the river god. Top right: A bronze helmet (dating from the mid-4th c. BC) is embossed with tendrils and other patterns so dear to Gaelic artisans. Lower left: Pure gold treasures of a royal Celtic tomb discovered in the Saar in 1954. The rings, bracelets, and torc date from about 400 BC. Lower right: The Brooch of Tara (8th c AD). One of the most prized pieces of ancient Irish jewelry, it is richly decorated with a gold thread, enamel and amber. It was found in a wooden box near the mouth of the River Boyne. The attached chain indicates that it is one of a pair, intended to fasten a cloak.[6]

Funeral treasure also reveals the fine quality of the metal work. To be sure, the Celtic elite never departed to their Otherworld (heaven) impoverished. In 1954, the tomb of the "Princess of Vix" (6th-5th c BC) was opened.[7] Alone in her large burial vault, she lay on a wagon, surrounded by rich grave goods from all over the Greek world. An example of the Gaelic love for spectacle and excess. Moreover, the Romans never came to terms with the long Celtic tradition of such powerful women.

Left: The Gunderstrup Cauldron (1st c BC). It was made near the eastern fringe of the Celtic World, in the Middle Danube (Yugoslavia) region. Then, it turned up in a bog in Denmark. Decorated inside and out with Celtic deities, ritual scenes, and exotic animals, the enormous silver vessel certified the Celts' remarkable gifts for metal-crafting. Much of the symbolism is still not deciphered. Such talent insured their trade throughout the Graeco-Roman World and beyond. The cauldron measures 16.8 inches (42 cm) high, with a diameter of 27.6 inches (69 cm) Celtic cauldrons became the prototype of the legends of the Holy Grail. Right: One of a pair of bronze wine flagons (4th c BC), fancifully decorated. The little duck on the spout is threatened by two fierce animals on the lid, while a still larger animal with coral eyes joins the chase and forms the handle.[8]

The princely burial of a chieftain in Germany also yielded rich furnishings: much jewelry and cosmetic items, flagons, cauldrons and other feasting equipment imported from Greece. Another burial site contained a decorated bronze couch for the corpse to rest on, as well as a four-wheeled funerary wagon.[9]

CHRISTIAN MANUSCRIPT ILLUMINATION

In the Christian era, the western Celts lavishly incorporated their lively pagan pictures into the "illuminated" gospels and other sacred manuscripts (5th-12th c AD). These were painted on thick pages of parchment. With their love of learning and art, the scribes transcribed the Latin texts into elaborate Irish alphabets. They spent a lifetime on fine, close work which, of itself, was an act of worship for them.

A Flair for Design

On Holy Island, Northumbria, the Irish and English monks evolved a "cross-fertilization" of art traditions and produced the Lindisfarne Gospels. By combining Egyptian styles of knotwork, the Germanic love of color and the Celtic fascination with complex forms, they found a "powerful, abstract language" to express their mystic vision. This form of manuscript illumination, then, spread back to Ireland where it culminated in a masterpiece of Celtic genius, the *Book of Kells*.[10]

WEAPONS, DRESS AND HAIR: A STUNNING COMBO

The epic hero of Ireland, Cuchulain, cut a magnificent figure in his war chariot," made of crystal and yoked in gold. . . [with] its side plates of copper inlaid with silver." His enemies first observed the excellence of his two horses. Arriving in a swirling "long silken cloak of Persian blue," the hero stunned onlookers with his "flaming spear" which glowed "red and silver along its honed edge." In his girdle, "ready to hand, he carried a keen sword with . . . a short spear, plus thongs and rivets for use in hurling. Usually he carried [on his saddle] by the hair nine severed heads."[11]

Not to be outdone by her male counterpart, the Welsh Olwen became the ideal of Celtic feminine beauty: "She came wearing a flame-red silken tunic, and a great collar of red gold with precious pearls and rubies in it. Her hair was more yellow-gold than the flowers of the broom; her skin was whiter than the foam of the wave."[12]

Military custom required that certain of the warriors enter battle naked. These champions led the charge, clad in little more than their weapons. The large oval shields, spears, swords (with ornate scabbards), broad leather belts (with finely worked buckles), and war-paint made up their battle-dress. Blowing long circular trumpets, along with their singing and shouting, added fearful sound effects to the uproar on the field. In order to declare their superior rank and power, the naked aristocrats wore fancifully designed bronze or gold torcs (neck rings).

Taking another look at Cuchulain, we watch him set forth "when the day was fine." He wore "his fair-weather dress; fringed purple mantle which fell about him in five pleats, white breast-plate of pure silver inlaid with gold, war trousers of red, royal silk brocaded, body tunic of soft silk fringed with golden tassels. His purple buckler bore on it as escutcheon, five golden wheels, indicating the circling rays of the sun."[13]

Their vanity notwithstanding, the Celts made significant changes in European styles. They all loved color, even though it usually remained the privilege of the elite.[14] Being dedicated and expert horsemen, the Celts spared no pains to decorate the harnesses. They also invented breeches (trousers) for convenience in the saddle. Bright checkered tunics and pants, or jacket and kilt would ultimately become the symbol of both Ireland and Scotland. Women wore long robes and conical hats with veils. Using wool and linen, they brought the arts of dyeing and weaving to a high level. They produced distinctive cloaks and skirts in checks and stripes—what we now know as the clan "tartans."

The Celtic custom of bleaching their hair with lime fascinated the dark-haired Mediterranean people. Again, we look at Cuchulain who maintained a hair-do that would challenge our most *avant garde* hairdressers today: "His hair is three-colored: light brown near the scalp, red in its mid length, and golden blond on the ends. Thus, he seems to wear a golden crown. . . . Three braids were wrapped about his head, holding from his face the long, waving, golden mass of curls that blew lightly back from his shoulders. At his neck the brilliant golden coils of his torque collar and breast-plate flamed and gleamed before him. Suspended from the crown of his head were one hundred silken cords from which dangled one hundred garnets. On his cheeks were painted four balls: yellow, green, blue, and royal purple."[15]

Another surprising contribution to civilization was the Celts' invention of soap. They bathed nightly before the feasts. By introducing it to the Mediterranean Rim, they achieved a standard of cleanliness unmatched until modern times. Only the Romans came near caring this much for the bath, even though they did not acquire soap from the Celts until 50 AD.

Finally, all of these cosmetic achievements had to be exhibited in an

A bronze mirror from pre-Roman Northamptonshire, England. Such a beautiful, distinctive mirror reveals the high status of the lady who used it. Large and heavy, it would have been held up by a maid. The graceful design belies the fact that it is 2,000 years old! Their preoccupation with the Otherworld notwithstanding, the Celts lavished much care on their material treasures.[16]

A Flair for Design

appreciative arena. The Celtic hierarchy demanded that the elite, the druids and warriors, should travel with huge entourages. For example, Orgatorix of Helvetii (Switzerland) had a household of 10,000, not counting the dependents, debtors and clients who were attached to him.[17] Added to this, he would carry collections of finely wrought weapons and an abundance of heavy jewelry.

The magnificent material assets of the Celtic elite were enough to overwhelm their enemies, and the Greeks and Romans regarded them with both fear and fascination. Moreover, if the Celtic love of display is visible in our records from the green valleys of Western Europe, the Galatians, no doubt, had the same tastes as their relatives. Isolated in a dull, desert region, they had as much—maybe even more—reason to wear color and acquire beautiful possessions.

At the height of their power, the Celts laid siege to the city of Rome itself and, indeed, occupied it for seven months. During that time, they spared the proud city no indignity. Bent on rich spoils, they set a ransom of 1,000 pounds of gold and then used loaded weights to increase their gains.

"But this is unjust. It is too much," complained a Roman tribune.

Immediately, the conquering champion, Brennus, tossed his great sword onto the scales. "Woe to the defeated," he snarled in contempt.[18]

No wonder, then, that Paul had to address a rather bizarre situation in the Galatian churches. Quite apart from the depredations of the Judaizers, their communities were already riddled with feelings of discontent and ill will as they assessed one another's rich holdings. Such reckless displays of wealth created violent episodes of envy and revenge among the Celtic tribes themselves. Jealously led quite naturally to challenges, fighting, and even killing.

AN APPEAL FOR MODESTY

Paul's use of the word "vainglorious" (Gal 5:26) comprehends several Galatian characteristics. It means to be proud of one's birth, property, eloquence or learning. Vainglorious people swaggered or bragged about their social status and accomplishments in order to provoke envy and jealousy in others. The word "combat" (Gr *paroxysm*) connotes a violent temper, given to sudden outbursts and fits of rage—the inevitable result of self-exaltation and pride.

The Galatians had an inordinate love for dress and display. After experiencing conversion and hearing the good news about heaven, they, no doubt, felt assured that they would wear the brightest crowns, most gorgeous attire which art and skill could create. They dreamed of rich garments of royal purple and fine linen (Rev. 19:7-8). Their elegance on earth would be more than matched in heaven, surely. At least, so they supposed.

Christ's parable of the Good Samaritan (Luke 10:30-36) had exemplified this attitude and probed a deep, national problem. Paul carried the matter still further. In keeping with their cultural heritage, the Galatians would have been prone to antagonize everyone because of their haughty airs of superiority over their inferiors. At the same time, both Jews and Judaizers were equally capable of disdaining—even abusing—those they considered disadvantaged. Altogether these elements produced a really volatile mix.

The Jews also prided themselves on their birth. As descendants of Abraham, they would claim admission to the nearest places around God's throne. For example, James and John, the sons of Zebedee made a bid for the closest seats, at the left and right of Christ in His Kingdom (Mk 10:35-37). Boasting their valor and their wealth, the Galatians would have seen nothing wrong with such a request.

Furthermore, both the Galatians and the Judaizers placed too much value on their supposed advantages of learning. In a word, the churches had become a turbulent cauldron of hard feelings and hatred. Both sides were ready to quarrel and take revenge at a moment's notice. These distinctions created such controversy that discussions often ended in physical combat, even in the church (Gal 5:15). The Judaizers took advantage of this weakness in the Galatian church. They used the natural Celtic tendency to combativeness to their advantage in order to defame Paul. They hoped not only to turn the believers' hearts from the Apostle but also to instigate a fight, should he attempt a return to the churches he had founded.

When Paul said, "Let us not become vainglorious," he was not simply making a request, as we might understand it today. He voiced a strong, though courteous, command to stop this destructive behavior. He knew that it had the potential for annihilating these isolated little churches he had established just seven years earlier. This "vainglorious" attitude, of course, had no basis in reality. Like a bubble that bursts and is seen no more, it would leave behind a long trail of death and destruction, both physically and spiritually.

The Apostle recognized how vulnerable the highly decorated Galatians could be under the pressures surrounding them. Since self-love, self-exaltation and pride utterly destroy, Paul set himself completely at variance with the gaudy Judaizers. Instead, he just recommended simplicity of character and the practice of charity (Gal 5:20–26).

A Flair for Design

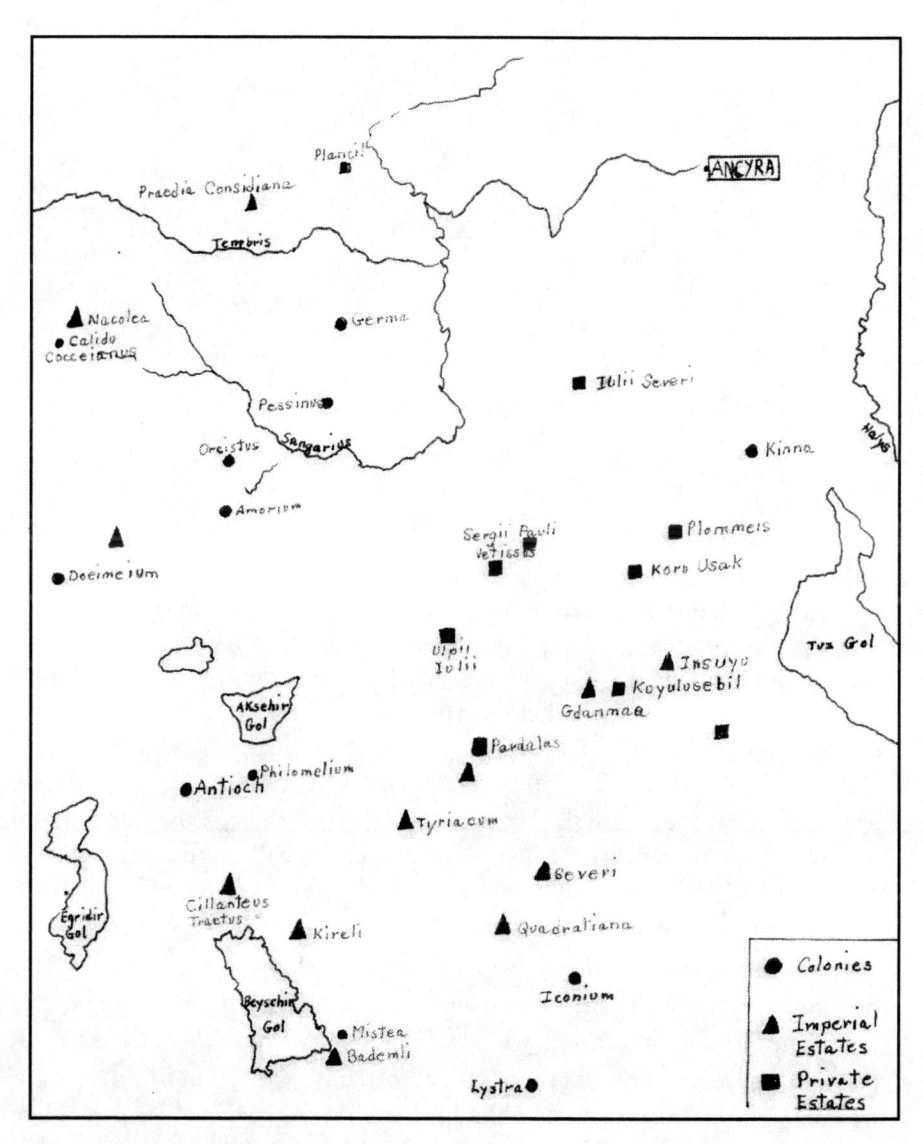

Map of Imperial and Private Galatian Estates in the time of the Apostle Paul. Drawing by Eileen Minchin-Davis.

17. Bewitched

You stupid Galatians! You must have been bewitched (Gal 3:1).

High-level literacy and modern technology have conspired to make us lose sight of the importance of the spoken word. Indeed, we now treat it very casually. "Oops! I misspoke!" "Forget it. I didn't mean what I said." Almost the only place where it matters any more is the "I do's" in the wedding ceremony. (Even then, if we're to factor in the divorce rate, we have to conclude that—for more than 50% of the time—it means little even there.) Therefore, we try to create security for ourselves by having all the forms signed in triplicate, at the very least. Try buying a house. You will spend at least an hour signing all the legal documents, and then you'll need a very large box to carry away all the paper work.

Ancient societies did otherwise. The blind, aging Isaac fell victim to the deception of his wife and son Jacob when he bestowed the all-important birthright blessing on him. Esau's arrival threw Isaac into a panic. He had already eaten Jacob's venison and pronounced the blessing. "Your brother came treacherously and took away your blessing," the old man groaned. "I blessed him and the blessing will stand" (Gen 28:33-37). The words had gone out into the air and nothing could change them or bring them back. Words spoken ritually take on a life of their own. As one wise writer has said in a Celt-like triad:

> These things can never be recovered:
>
> a spoken word
>
> a spent arrow, and
>
> a lost opportunity.

Bewitched

The spoken "word" (Heb *devar*; Gr *rhema*) was very important to the Jews. So significant was it that the "Ten Commandments" were referred to as the *devarim*, "The Ten Words." Jesus Himself declared that man shall not "live by bread alone" but by every spoken word (Gr *rhema*) that proceeds out of the mouth of God (Mt 4:4) Paul declared that "faith comes from hearing, and hearing by the [spoken] word of Christ" (Rom 10:17).

THE PRACTICE OF MAGIC

Reverence for the potency of the spoken word is also part of the larger practice of magic. The purpose of magic is to acquire knowledge, power, love, healing or wealth. This result may be achieved in many ways: Divination; augury (study of sacrificial animals); bird flight; astrology (knowledge of the future); alchemy (turning base metals to gold); sorcery; spirit mediation; and necromancy (communication with the dead). While our Western tradition carefully separates magic from religious or scientific practices, elsewhere the distinction becomes much less clear.

Magic is sometimes divided into two classes. The **High Magic** of the intellectual elite bordered on science. The word "magic" derives from the *magi* (priests of Chaldea and Medea). Classical authors revered the magi for their comprehensive wisdom and their power over demons. In the Persian Empire the priestly caste of the magi was divided into two groups. The Medo-Persians claimed to have extraordinarily profound religious knowledge based on the monotheistic teachings of Zoroaster. Certain classes of Babylonians functioned as magicians and soothsayers and were sometimes imposters.[1] **Low Magic** referred to common folk practices and superstitions. These practitioners provided a variety of charms. To heal or ward off illness and danger. To guarantee success in an endeavor. To trick an enemy and create illusions. To entertain (conjuring and sleight of hand).

Another distinction lies between **White Magic** and **Black Magic**. The former was ostensibly used for beneficial purposes, medicine, healing and blessings. The latter worked evil, like voodoo, obeah and pocomania in the Caribbean. Also "bone pointing" among the aboriginals of Australia. Shamanism, sorcery, witchcraft, and cursing have been found in almost every culture. This mix of magical practices is as pervasive as the air and as old as the history of humankind.

The Wise Men of the East who brought gifts to the Christ Child appear to be of the Persian tradition (Mt 2). Summoned by the King of Moab to curse Israel (Num. 22-24), the Seer Balaam, on the other hand, exhibited more Babylonish traits. Nonetheless, it was Balaam's prophecy, "A star shall come forth out of Jacob, a comet arise from Israel" (Num 24:17), that led the magi to Bethlehem. King Balak of Moab suffered the frustration of the patriarch Isaac on a royal scale. Exasperated by Balaam's uncontrolled blessing of Israel, the king finally clapped his hands together in utter despair. He said, in effect, "Just shut up and go home!" King Balak and Balaam, however, both knew that the Word had gone out, far beyond recall.

THE CELTIC DRUIDS

The wise men of the Celts drew their skills from the same Indo-European sources as the Babylonians, Persians, and Hindus of India. Probably no other group of people in world history have revered "The Word" more than the Celts. Three great, enduring bonds held them together culturally (if not politically): (1) A system of law, (2) Language, and (3) Religion.

Though basically unsympathetic to their enemies, classical writers described a three-fold hierarchy of privileged, professional classes among the Gaelic people. Along with the bards and seers, the druids ("knowing the oak tree") belonged

A 19th century drawing of a druid in the sacred oak grove, with his sickle, under the mistletoe. At the right is Stonehenge that pre-dated the druids by many centuries.[2] A shrine in Galatia called "Drynemeton" indicates that the druids had a council/worship center there also.

to this class. They conducted worship in the forest sanctuaries and did not use temples[2]. Nor did they participate in war or manual labor. They paid no taxes.

The druids had great political influence, forecast the future and fixed auspicious times for enterprises. Considered intermediaries to the spirit world, they also used powerful spells. They could throw up a magical *aire druad* ("druid's fence") to safeguard a whole army. Or they could destroy anyone with a hex.

Celtic custom required that members of the royal family should pronounce formal curses on their enemies. Legend has it that Queen Macha once caused the men of Ulster to feel the severe pangs of childbirth so that they could not go forth in battle to defend their province.

The druid's most important function, however, was as a highly influential teacher. Only they were equipped to educate the young nobility. Their office required up to twenty years of training to memorize all their verses and incantations. Since the Celts prized learning and intelligence, they dreaded the druid's power to produce insanity by sorcery. He could prepare a "madman's wisp" (straw or grass), into which he would pour evil incantations. When he tossed the grass into the face of the victim, that person either turned into an idiot or became wholly insane.[3]

Druidism prospered throughout the Gaelic tribes because of their zest for learning and their ethnic love of "The Word." The bards produced poetic sagas and songs for the pleasure and instruction of their proud, warlike aristocracy. The Gaelic tribes valued all of the skills of divination very highly. Since the Celts considered it wrong to commit their own learning to writing, they eventually came to use the Greek alphabet for the mundane needs of life.

Although we can know little historically of Galatian ritual, we realize that, as Celts, they would not deviate easily from their culture. An important sacred site in Galatia was "*Drynemeton*" (Gaelic, "a sacred grove of oak trees"). Despite strong Hellenistic influences, the Galatians apparently still preserved druidic practices here. The tribal administrators assembled regularly at this wilderness sanctuary in the Drynemetos.[4] They long preserved these traditions, until they finally hybridized their beliefs with Roman religion. Then, for the first time, the Galatians began to build temples.

As Christianity replaced druidism, St. Martin, Bishop of Tours (371 AD), is given much credit for evangelizing the Gauls.[5] The *first* Celts to hear the Gospel, however, had received it directly from the Apostle Paul more than 300 years earlier.

Unfortunately, it was a short step from druidism to the machinations of an imposter like Simon Magus.

SIMON MAGUS

Not surprisingly, the widespread practice of magic posed a problem very early in the experience of the Christian church. As a result of Saul/Paul's persecution, the Christians scattered throughout the countryside. They did not, however, go silently. The evangelist Philip created a great sensation among the "mongrel" Samaritans whom the Jews thoroughly despised. In addition to his preaching, Philip caused "great joy" by exorcising evil spirits and healing debilitating diseases. One observer in his audience paid professional attention, realizing that the apostle's "magic show" was more spectacular than his own. This episode took place in the 1st century AD, between the stoning of Stephen and the conversion of Paul (Acts 8:9-24).

Simon Magus, a Syrian Jew and a practitioner of magic, came from the Samaritan village of Gitta. His name indicates that he had trained in the Persian schools of the magi. Revered throughout northern Palestine for his vast supernatural powers, Simon was entranced by the miraculous evangelization of the Christians.

After Philip the Deacon baptized him, Simon immediately sought to improve his own skills. He offered to purchase from Peter and John the divine power to transmit the Holy Spirit to others.[6] Roundly rebuked by Peter, Simon, according to the account in Acts, was reconciled to Christianity. The 2nd century theologian, Justin Martyr, wrote that Simon visited Rome in the time of the Emperor Claudius (41-54 AD), where his followers deified him for his miracle-working powers.

A further 3rd century Christian legend[7] asserts that, in his claim to messiahship, Simon had further confrontations with Peter in Rome. He challenged the Apostle before Emperor Nero (54-68 AD), claiming to be able to fly.[8] Jumping from the top of the Roman Forum, he fell and broke both of his legs. Then he invited his friends to bury him, assuring them that he would arise in three days.

No one ever heard of Simon Magus again.

THE GNOSTIC HERESY

The eloquent Bishop of Lyons, Irenaeus (125-202 AD), ascribed the founding of gnosticism to Simon Magus. He suggested that Simon regarded himself as the entire Trinity (Father, Son and Holy Spirit). He taught his followers that they were saved by grace, and not by works of law. He claimed that his descent from above (through several heavens) affirmed him as the redeemer sent by the unknown god. This teaching, of course, closely paralleled that of the Christians' faith in Jesus.[9]

A modern term used to describe this system of 1st century belief, Gnosticism derives from the Greek *ginosko* ("to take in knowledge, recognize, or to understand completely"). It indicates a constellation of religious phenomena that reached its zenith in later centuries. This philosophy included beliefs in the innate immortality of the divine spark that differentiated the body from the soul. Gnosticism taught the necessity for the escape of this divine element back to its source, an unknown god who controls the visible universe by evil spirits. It viewed the world as God's body. At its center lay the idea that this divine power sent knowledge (*gnosis*) to earth by means of a redeemer. Because Simon Magus claimed to have no beginning, he could therefore fulfill this redeemer role. In turn, he imparted this knowledge to his disciples who "by origin" were related to him.

Necessarily, the Gnostics needed extensive rituals to prepare both the living and the dying for ascent to the realms above where their Unknown God lived. Paul encountered this Unknown God of the Gnostics when he preached to the Athenians on Mars Hill (Acts 17:22-23).

In Antioch, Menander, a closely connected disciple of Simon Magus, provided another Gnostic alternative to Christian doctrines. He insisted that he, not Simon, was the real savior who had been sent to earth from above as the redeemer. Irenaeus said he also claimed a magical baptism that provided him with perpetual youth. Indeed, immortality. Still, just as death proved Simon's final defeat, so time carried away Menander as well.[10]

A Summary of Gnostic Beliefs[11]

1. Belief in a magical baptism that provided perpetual youth
2. Antinomianism (against law)
3. Libertarianism (absolute free will)
4. Denial of Christ's incarnation and physical resurrection
5. The essential evil of matter
6. The female principle ("Wisdom of God").

Gnosticism proved to be one of the earliest heresies embraced by groups of people professing to be Christians. They mingled much gnosticism with the Pauline letters and the Gospel of John. So much so, that many scholars (particularly in Germany) came to the conclusion that both Paul and John had given themselves over to this devious teaching. British and American scholars, however, stepped up to bat, denying this theory. They further argued that another strain of gnosticism had appeared in the 2nd century, strongly influenced by heterodox Judaism and Christianity.

A strong consensus held that a Jewish Gnosticism had developed, not only because Simon Magus was a Jew, but also because of the interference of the Judaizers. They feared demons and had "a long-lasting tendency within Judaism to invoke angels for protection." They also tended to assimilate local pagan beliefs in the realm of magic and folk lore."[12]

BEWITCHED BY THE JUDAIZERS

The Gnostic philosophy progressed rapidly from Syria to Antioch, through Galatia and into the rest of Asia Minor. Indeed, wherever the evangelistic efforts of the apostles introduced Christianity, gnosticism reared its ugly head. Fully aware of its popularity among pagan worshippers, Paul feared its potential influence on the fledging churches he had established in Galatia. He clearly alluded to its resurgence when he asked the Galatians: "Now that you have come to know God, or rather to be known by God, how is it that you turn back again to *the weak and worthless elemental things*?" (Galatians 4:9, emphasis added). The "weak and worthless elemental things" referred to the ranks of evil spirits that Gnostics claimed to be instruments of God. He might also have asked, "Having known the True God, how can you return to an Unknown God to whom you were previously enslaved?" (Acts 17: 23)

The Judaizers seemed to have been impressed by the seductive power of Gnosticism. To be sure, their lack of integrity permitted them to use Gnostic methods to foist their legalistic views onto the vulnerable new Christians in Galatia. Paul's poignant plea proves how well (like magic) the trick had worked: "You stupid Galatians! You must have been bewitched!" (3:1). Using the Greek *baskaino* ("bewitched"), he chose a word meaning "to harm by magic; to bring evil on a person by feigned praise or to mislead by an evil eye and charm by words." The Judaizers, of course, were experts in this type of communication.

"To bewitch" also connoted the more sinister system of witchcraft that was the basis of many Gnostic rituals. On these occasions, the Gnostic priests leaped about, contorting their faces, shouting threats, and altogether frightening their listeners. Much like our modern, high-pressure salesmen, the Gnostics won over their audiences without allowing anyone time for reflection or investigation.

Paul was not exaggerating or being impudent when he used strong language to address the Galatians. If this had been merely sleight-of-hand or the

Bewitched

simple "pulling of rabbits out of a hat," the Apostle would not have exhibited such passion against his opponents (Gal 4:9). The Galatians faced disaster because of their willingness to yield to the hybridized influences of the Judaizing magicians. Their susceptibility to theatrical performance blinded them to the evil nature of the powers to which they were surrendering. Appalled by the real harm the Judaizers were working in the minds of the Galatian converts, Paul rose to a stunningly vigorous defense of the true Gospel.

"YOU DEAR IDIOTS OF GALATIA!"

The use of spells, incantations, or charms, obviously, indicated the magician's strong desire for control and power. With supernaturally channeled words, such a master could easily influence events. Spiritual agencies, magic words and symbolic numbers were thought to have an innate power of their own. A skilled practitioner could achieve strong material transformations, both good or evil. Whoever had a secret knowledge of spells and numbers was either greatly honored or greatly feared.[13] Our current preoccupation with dispelling fear and doubt indicates that we have been threatened. Indeed, they have cast a spell over us. A spell that must be broken!

Paul's harsh address to the Galatians shows that their Celtic susceptibility to magic, spells and eloquent words was a matter of deep concern to him. "O you stupid/foolish Galatians, you must have been bewitched" (3:1). Other translations help to show that the enchantment they had fallen under was, indeed, a verbal one. "Who has put a hex on you?" (The *Message*).

In his lively translation of this text, J. B. Phillips adds yet another dimension: "O you dear idiots of Galatia, . . . does God, who gives you his Spirit and works miracles among you, do these things because you have obeyed the Law or because you have believed the Gospel?" (Gal 3:3, 10). Here we get a sense of the frustration of a reasonable but loving father counseling a vulnerable, headstrong teenager. "Don't be so dumb. You need to grow up!"

18. THE PAINTED PEOPLE

For I bear on my body the brand-marks of Jesus (Gal 6:17).

Of the many attractions of Edinburgh, Scotland, the annual Military Tattoo has to be the most spectacular. Bagpipes, swinging kilts, ranks of rolling drums and prancing horses. These military exercises are performed at night before the walls of Edinburgh Castle. The evening ends with a lone piper high on a parapet playing "Amazing Grace," the final act in a series of colorful, thrilling events.

This is the way the entertainment is *supposed* to be. Twice, Dorothy Comm made careful travel plans to get herself to Edinburgh at the right time to see the Tattoo. Twice, her party sat in the bleachers under a merciless downpour of rain. On the first occasion, the woolen blankets the concierge had lent them for warmth became so waterlogged and heavy that they could scarcely haul them back to the hotel. The second time, the floods almost washed them down the steep approach to the castle gate. At both events, with traditional Celtic stubbornness and endurance, the performers carried the show through to its finale.

Why such dogged determination to see the Tattoo? Herein lie the colorful remnants of Gaelic war maneuvers, horsemanship, and glittering pageantry. A stimulating feast for the senses and well worth the effort, rain notwithstanding. Dorothy never did, however, have a clear view of this ancient celebration. She had to make do with a video of an earlier parade. So much for Scottish weather!

The Painted People

TATTOOING AND BODY PAINT

The other meaning of "tattoo" is equally Celtic. It refers to the custom of marking and puncturing the skin and then applying permanent dye. Along with body painting, this kind of art has always had significance.

The Egyptians practiced tattooing as early as 2000 BC, and some say that the custom is as old as the story of man himself. Traces of red ochre at various primitive sites in Europe suggest that early pre-Celtic people might have decorated their bodies for hunting or celebration."[1] Several Roman writers noted the Britons' love of paint. Julius Caesar wrote: "All of the Britanni paint themselves with woad which produced a bluish coloring."[2]

The Picts, a very early Celtic group, flourished in northern Scotland for almost 600 years (300-843 AD).[3] In contempt, the Romans called them the

Left: A tattooed Celtic warrior in his nakedness, replete with long hair, neck torc and a severed head. Right: Tattooed druid priestesses.[4]

"painted people." The Irish named them *Cruithni* ("people of the designs"). The Picts carried body art one step further to permanent tattooing. In addition to their natural heritage of body modification, the Celts of Galatia would also have had the model of their Anatolian neighbors, the Scythians, who also practiced tattooing.

WHY BODY MODIFICATION?

Today, body modification is no longer the exclusive privilege of primitive tribes or the "bad guys" in society. We have various ways to "make a statement," some (fortunately) are reversible. For example, you can color or bleach your hair. You can curl it, straighten it, spike it, or, like a Gaul, grease it. You can shave it off or let it grow long and frowzy. As for dress, you have an endless spectrum ranging from the classic to the bizarre, from dignity to seduction. These features are changeable by the day, if not the hour.

As for our bodies themselves, by now we must have enough skin preparations and lotions to float several ocean liners. Considering that we so much admire smooth, flawless skin, one might wonder why anyone would deliberately choose frightful painting or painful tattooing.[5]

Tattooing, however, has deeper meanings. It expresses individuality and freedom. In doing so, you have asserted yourself and broken a (Biblical) taboo. Sharing tattooed symbols strengthens relationships and helps the police track gang members. Tattoos actually indicate a kind of ownership, whether it be romantic or commercial. Through this bloody rite you can also memorialize a loved one or declare your undying love. (If you change your mind, however, you had better find another girlfriend with the same name!)

Anthropologists assure us that tattoos are a statement of uniquely human freedom! To that, we may add pride. Significantly, animals make almost no conscious effort to alter their appearance. In expressing individuality with body-modification, one, no doubt, feels stimulated for having broken a taboo. For some people this would be an invigorating experience. Still others, who find protection and mystical empowerment in skin deisgn, will defend tattoos as a beautifully expressive art form.

Then, beyond tattooing itself, lies the flamboyant practice of body piercing and scarification. That is, the practice of slashing the skin and filling the wounds with irritants to prevent smooth healing.

Above all, these body-marks are permanent. You have to earn them through many hours of excruciating pain. Then, if ever you change your mind and want them off, you must endure more pain and more time for the laser procedure required to get your skin cleared up again. Tattoo removal is not only expensive but is said to be even more painful than the original application.

Supposedly, with all the pain and expense involved, one might have some kind of a "spiritual experience," whether the tattoo is being put on or taken off. The point, however, is debatable.

THE CELTIC USE OF SKIN DESIGN

A hierarchical, highly efficient military machine, the Roman army eventually took over most of Europe from the Celtic tribes. Long before that, however, the Romans recognized the fighting skills of their huge, passionate foes to the north.[6] The Punic Wars (3rd century BC) constituted Rome's first success as an international power. To this end, they recruited a large number of Celtic adventurers as mercenaries.[7]

Facing the Gauls as enemies produced some very chastening and humiliating chapters in Roman history. Bands of flamboyant *gesatae* (L *spearmen*) stood at the forefront of the battle, naked, tattooed or painted with blue (woad) dye.[8] They wore only a belt and dagger. Then, brandishing shield and spear, they bore down on their enemies, blasting great trumpets and screaming oaths. Their elaborate golden torcs (neck rings) marked their social rank. Derived from earliest history, these Celtic customs were surely enough to give pause to any Roman hero, however disciplined.

Writing of the crushing Celtic defeat at the Battle of Telamon (225 BC), the Greek historian, Polybius (202-120 BC), described the "very terrifying . . . appearance and gestures of the naked warriors in front, all in the prime of life and finely built men, and all in leading companies richly adorned with gold torcs and armlets." He suggests that the Gauls discarded their clothes for convenience in the fight. More likely, this habit had ritual significance and implied the oneness of the fighting body with the "surrounding forces of nature." Also, as gifted healers, the Gauls knew that wounds, open to the air, could heal quickly and without infection.[9]

Some sixty years later, another historian described a much less magnificent defeat at the Battle of Ancyra. At first, the Galatians unsettled the Romans by removing their clothes. Perhaps they had no time for the paint or the trumpets. In any case, they seemed to have become too soft and "Hellenized" and were not in good form. The soldiers cut them to pieces, the blood from their wounds gushing "out from their podgy white bodies."[10]

THE BRAND-MARKS OF CHRIST

The Israelites associated tattooing with pagan cults. Their neighbors practiced rituals of self-inflicted laceration in their worship (1 Kgs 18:28) and in the mourning for their dead (Lev 19:28). These customs included the drawing of patterns on the skin by making punctures and inserting pigments.[11] God found these acts so pernicious and destructive that He prohibited all such "writing of incision" (Heb *seret/saretet*) among the Israelites. "You shall not make any cuts in your body for the dead nor make any tattoo marks on yourselves: I am the Lord" (Lev 19:28; Lev 21:5). In other words, such practices diverted humankind from experiencing the fullness of Divine presence.

The Greek word *stigmati* denotes a mark on the flesh by puncture with a hot, sharp instrument (such as a needle). It also referred to hot irons that left a permanent indentation (brand) to certify the ownership of horses or cattle. Similar branding marks were also used as a security measure for soldiers and runaway slaves as well as for the punishment of criminals and scoundrels. Then again, *stigmati* constituted a simple mark of consecration in idol-worship. Why then did Paul declare that he bore the brand-marks of Jesus in His body?

As a "Hebrew of the Hebrews" (Phil 3:5), Paul obviously would never have disfigured his body in any way, not even to win over his beloved Galatians. Paul's declaration shows that he referred to the marks which accompanied extraordinarily severe abuse.

The term *stigmati* also describes a person made infamous and repulsive to public view by brand-marks put on his body through corporal torture (2 Cor 11:23). Certainly, he would never commend tattooing to the Galatians whose culture had already steeped itself in war-mongering and violent nature-worship rituals. Neither was it a piteous appeal to the hospitable Galatians for sympathy. Like a man priding himself, however, on a hard-won trophy or wreath of victory given by a king, Paul challenged his audience. He asked them to reject the Judaizers' notions, even if it led to the kind of suffering he himself had been experiencing.

Possibly Paul wrote this letter to the Galatians while he still suffered from open wounds. No doubt, many scars remained from the imprisonments, beatings, and stonings he had endured, to say nothing of the shipwreck (2 Cor 11:23-27). Yet, all of the pain could not obscure one powerful idea. He knew that he had received those brand-marks in the service of Jesus Christ.

No doubt, the ever-recurring hardships and ill treatment left ulcers and sores that remained unhealed for a long time. As the Galatians tenderly cared for him, they could not help but realize his terrible physical condition. The Apostle saw the marks as a potent, visible evidence of his confidence in Christ, and he wore them as a badge of honor (Rom 8:18).

We also find a subtle grammatical structure apparent in the Greek, although it is lost in the English translation. It reveals a much deeper meaning than just the painful, repulsive scars on Paul's body. In the original manuscript, the "gen-

The Painted People

itive case of ownership" is used in the Greek phrase, "the brand-marks of Jesus." These words refer to the marks Jesus bore in His body after his arrest, trial, and crucifixion (Mt 27:27-30; Jn 19:1-2; 33-34). The swollen, livid, blood-shot welts and bruises from the Roman scourging left many marks in Jesus' body.

Speaking in a quaint, convoluted 19th century style, one writer has said that the "dishonoring whip" had made the body of Paul's "adorable Lord . . . vile." The crucifixion presented "to open view those brand marks of degradation." Therefore, the Apostle felt in his own heart that he had "in no small measure [been] assimilated" into the very body and sufferings of Christ (Phil 1:29).[12]

In truth then, Paul's own physical torture enabled him to declare to the Galatians, "I bear the brand-marks of Jesus." His use of this "ownership" phrase echoes his familiar declaration that he is continually being crucified with Christ (Gal 2:20).

In describing his suffering thus, Paul showed the Galatians that he had joined himself, in spirit, to Christ—and Christ was enfleshed in him (Jn 1:14). Unlike the clean-cut, well-dressed Judaizers, he could demonstrate that he had fully shared in the bodily sufferings of his Lord. Bearing "brand-marks" for Jesus, he reminded the church, opens heaven to every believer. Therein lay the glory of it all. Jesus' broken, abused body, therefore, soon became His perfect resurrected form.

A CALL TO ARMS

The fact that the Gauls painted themselves for war has been well documented. Additionally, the ancient Celts used branding for at least three classes of persons: soldiers, slaves, and devotees of idols. By claiming to have brand marks, Paul made a final appeal to his apostolic authority. He had served Christ as a soldier, a slave, and a devotee.

Addressing them endearingly as "brethren" (Gal 6:1), he challenged the Galatians to assume, along with him, this triple relationship with Jesus. Surely such a commitment would stir the ire of the Judaizers, for they would not have thought twice about physically torturing the subjects of their proselytizing efforts. Moreover, the Roman authorities (with power over everyone) wanted to preserve the peace at any cost, no matter who fell by the way.

We see the brand-marks of Jesus, then, as a subtle call to spiritual arms in the on-going battle between Good and Evil. Eventually, the Galatian Christians would also bear in their bodies similar signs of suffering for their faith. The brand-marks would, as it were, identify them to the world as a committed family of faith.

At the same time, Paul's message also served notice on the Judaizing Christians who prided themselves on superior sanctity. By means of their legalism and their persecution they defied Jesus Himself. Thus, they robbed one another of their very salvation.

Members of the early Christian Church acquired brand-marks all too easily. Nor is religious persecution unknown in our own times. Besides, the Galatian churches already knew more than enough about war.

Now Paul introduced them to the fierce conflicts of *spiritual* warfare. Knowing what we have learned of the Galatians, we can imagine that they took rather readily to the prospect of becoming once again "painted" people. Lively, courageous adherents who truly knew how to bear brand marks! What Celt ever shrank from a battle in a just cause?

PAUL, A MAN FOR ALL SEASONS.

Paul's letter to the Galatians summons all Christians to find a truly spiritual identity in Jesus Christ. Since humans desire to be indelibly and irrevocably marked, he beckons believers to bear the "brand marks of Jesus." They can literally confer identity, ownership and transparent honesty on the Christian.

To be sure, Paul had paid his dues. He had come through the floods of persecution. He survived the fiery furnace of debilitating disappointments. Some of those for whom he had sacrificed much to win them to freedom in Christ had returned to embrace the legalism of "another Gospel." Now he desired the Galatians and all Christians thereafter to be so recognized.

He offered a triad of significant brandmarks to identify the Christian lifestyle. Believers would be:

1. **Slaves of Jesus.** As the Owner, Possessor and Master, Jesus provides food, shelter, security, a place of belonging and work assignments. Ironically, Christians thus "enslaved," are emancipated from the anxieties that haunt those who refuse to surrender to His claims on their lives.
2. **Soldiers of Jesus.** Soldiers are readily identified by their often-colorful uniforms. A seasoned soldier wears his badges of honor, with pride. A soldier of the cross, however, does not need such advertising, because he/she bears the brandmarks of Jesus. Instead, he/she must fight the good fight (2 Tim. 4:7) and "not lose heart in doing good" (Gal. 6:9).
3. **Saints of Jesus.** Here the mark of genuineness distinguishes the authentic community of the faithful from spurious imitations. Sainthood can move a person from the tyranny of time to the pleasures of heaven, on *this* side of eternity.

This book challenges each reader to acquire those prints of Christ's wounds. We must wear the brand marks of Jesus as prominently as the painted people wore their war paint.

In every human breast lies the innate passion for Life. That same vibrant Life that first drew the Celts to their Christ.

The Tent Maker

His contemporaries had no idea how great a tentmaker Paul of Tarsus really was.

That indefatigable evangelist traveled the sea lanes and cobblestone roads of the eastern Roman Empire.

Thus he erected the wonderful life-giving theological tent of Christianity.[13]

Epilogos

The journey we have taken together in the writing of *The Celt and the Christ* has deepened our own friendship and our relationship with God. Sometimes great intellectual and spiritual adventures have very modest beginnings. This one began in Pastor Hyveth's small Bible study group at Campus Hill Church in Loma Linda, California. At the time, we were walking step by step through the book of Galatians. Dorothy, a newcomer to this congregation, remarked in passing that the Galatians were Europeans (like the French, Spanish, Scots, Irish, and so forth). Not Greek. Not Roman. Not Semitic. Instead, they belonged to the vast community of Celtic culture. Surprise!

Having already delved into her own Anglo-Celtic family history, Dorothy began to study the early Celtic Church. She was fascinated to find how "apostolic" Gaelic Christian beliefs actually were. Indeed, much Gospel light went on shining all through the Dark Ages! Interest mounted until she and Dr. John Jones co-directed a "Celtic Tour of Britain" in the summer of 2001. (Both served on the faculty of La Sierra University.)

Now also intrigued with the topic, Hyveth prepared to join the La Sierra University venture—until family circumstances prevented her. Although she admits to a possible Scottish connection in her family, that is not what first attracted her interest. She plunged into a study of the book of Galatians. The discovery of Paul's subtle recognition of the Galatians' Celtic culture excited her most. What a striking connection between the ancient Gauls wearing their body paintings as a "badge of honor" and Paul's reference to his own "brand marks!" That was just *one* of the discoveries yet to come!

By the time Dorothy returned in July, 2001, our manuscript was just about ready to hatch. For more than seven years we have worked together. Weekly,

Epilogos: Our Spritual Journey

whenever we could manage it. More sporadically, when other responsibilities overwhelmed us.

Increasingly, we came to *believe* in what we were doing. On a business trip to Washington DC, Pastor Hyveth became aware of the powerful revival of interest in things Celtic. Which one of us can overlook the impact of Celtic music and spectacles like "River Dance" and the concerts of "Celtic Women"?

Finally, an invitation to a camp meeting in Alaska (2003) confirmed the fact that we actually *did* have a book that could earn a warm reception in the Christian community.

Then something else happened to us. Something that is difficult to put into words. Spending many hours dwelling on lofty Gospel themes created for us a rich context in which to work. As we blended the chapters together, we discovered strong fibers of faith being woven into our own experience. Personally, we came to understand what "soul-friending" could mean in our busy modern world.

At last, with genuine Celtic enthusiasm, we have come to comprehend the meaning of bearing the "brand-marks of Christ."

A Triad of Blessings from the Authors

May this ancient letter to the Galatians

- Inspire you anew and open one more path to your understanding of Scripture,

- Help you discover the assurance of God's capacity to redeem us, and

- Reveal the true richness of the Gospel.

ENDNOTES

Preface

[1] Eugene H. Peterson, *The Message [of the] New Testament* (Colorado Springs: Nav Press, 1993), p. 388.

Introduction

[1] Philip Yancey, *The Bible Jeasus Read* (Grand Rapids, MI: Zondervon, 1999), p. 38.
[2] See "Chronology of Galatia," Appendix 1, p. 201–205.
[3] Today, Turkey is 97% Muslim and is part of the troubled Middle-East sphere of influence. Yet, as it always has, the land of Old Galatia remains a bridge into (and out of) Europe.
[4] Peter B. Ellis, *The Celtic Empire: The First Millennium of Celtic History, 1000 B.C. – A.D. 51* (New York: Carroll & Graf Publishers, 1990), p. 1.
[5] Today the true inheritors of the first 3,000 years of Celtic culture survive as the Irish, Scots, Welsh, Manx, Cornish and Bretons. Only two million of them still speak a Gaelic language (Ellis, *The Celtic Empire*, p. 2). The Celts retained their own social and political forms with great determination. The German and Austrian tribes lived alongside them but developed their culture separately. The Germanic tribes and the Celts, however, probably came from the same origins. (See Patrick Lavin, *The Celtic World: An Authentic Guide to Ancient Celtic Spirituality* (Scotland: New Celtic Publishing, 1999), p. 6.
[6] Stephen Mitchell, *Anatolia: Land, Men and Gods in Asia Minor*, v. 1 (Oxford, 1993), pp. 23-28.
[7] Christiane Eluere, *The Celts: First Masters of Europe* (London: Thames & Hudson, Inc. 1992), p. 72.
[8] Barry Cunliffe, *The Ancient Celts* (New York: Penguin Books, 1997), p. 83.
[9] Ellis, *The Celtic Empire*, p. 93. In 1937 an articulate travel, H. Wenzel described the high Galatian plateau around Ancyra: "The grey-brown or violet hues of the vegetaation hid themselves from view in the dusty haze of the lower atmosphere. An isolated willow, poplar or wild pear tree serves merely to enhance the impression of a dismal wilderness. Only during the rains of early summer is the picture enlivened, when the wheat fields are freen and the plants of the steppe are in bud. But this adornment is of sort duration. By the end of July . . . the steppe lies as though dead." See Wenzel, *Die Steppe als Lebenstraum* (Kiel, 1937). Cited in Stephen Mitchell, *Anatolia: Land, Men and Gods in Asia Minor*. Vol. I (Oxford, 1993), p. 143.
[10] The high desert plateau of Anatolia, centered in Ancyra, continued to bear their name, *Galli* (Gauls) for many centuries.

Endnotes

[11] Ellis, *The Celtic Empire*, p. 92-93.
[12] Mitchell, v. I, p. 42..
[13] Ellis, *The Celtic Empire*, p. 94-95.
[14] Lavin, p. 1.
[15] Mitchell, v. 1, p. 126.
[16] Steve Rabey. *In the House of Memory: Ancient Celtic Wisdom for Everyday Life* (New York: Penguin, 1999), p, 15.
[17] A Galatian Tomb. www.livius.org/a/turkey/gordium/galatian-tomb-ab.jpg. Photo by Jona Lendering and Marcos Prins. (c Livius)
[18] Ellis. *The Celtic Empire*, p. 9-10. The Celts used the "Ogham" alphabet for rituals and monuments. It was made up assorted straight lines.
[19] We owe most of our knowledge of Gaelic culture to the classical historians/geographers: **Poseidonius** (135-150 BC), a Syrian historian and philosopher; **Strabo** (64 BC-21 AD), the Greek historian and geographer from Cappadocia; **Titius Livius/Livy** (59BC-17 AD), major historian of Rome; **Diodorus Siculus** (90-21 BC), a Sicilian Greek historian; Lucan (39-65 AD), Roman poet born in Cordoba; and **Julius Caesar** (102-44 AD) himself. Not surprisingly, these classical commentaries showed prejudice toward their Gaulish enemies. At the same time, they remained quite consistent in their views.
[20] Mitchell, v. I, p. 84-90; Ellis, *The Celtic Empire*, p. 103.
[21] Cunliffe, p. 85; Ellis, *The Celtic Empire*, p. 96.
[22] See Strabo's discussion of the Galatian Constitution in Book 12, v. 51, 567. Cited in Mitchell, v.1, p. 27. Strabo himself was born in Amasia, Pontus, in Asia Minor. His historical sketches filled forty-seven now-lost books, but his observations on geography still remain. Livy (Titus Livius, of Patavium, Benetia, Italy) was a major Roman historian to whom we are also indebted for our knowledge of Celtic culture.
[23] The form of Galatian government described by Strabo parallels that of the Gauls who met at Lugdunum (Lyons, France)
[24] Cited in Mitchell, v. I, p. 27. The council at *Drynemetos* handed down sentences for murder. Other cases were handled by the tetrarchs and the judges. It seems that the tetrarchies developed in the 2nd-century BC due to the civilizing effects of nearby Pergamum. The division of four, however, is based on the fundamental Celtic pattern for tribal gatherings.
[25] In Gordium stood a pole around which the legendary "Gordian Knot" had been tied. Prophecy had it that whoever could unravel the knot would become the lord of all Asia. In 333 BC Alexander the Great "fulfilled" the prophecy by slashing the knot to pieces with his sword. (Ellis, *The Celtic Empire*, p. 94)
[26] Eluere, p. 72. Kings and nobles from all over the Hellenistic world visited the shrine at Delphi, paying large fees for the prophetic services of the priestess.
[27] Deiotarus consolidated his political moves by conveniently arranging marriages. He had no love for Rome, but he became an indispensable agent for the Empire in Asia Minor. To insure a peaceful succession, he put all of his other sons to death, preserv-

ing only his eldest (Deiotarus II). Then, in 43 BC, he slew his daughter Filia (L "my daughter") and her husband Castor for the same reason. The surviving (first) son served in the Celtic capacity of tanist (co-regent) while his father still lived. (Ellis, *The Celtic Empire*, p. 105.)

[28] Despite his non-Gaelic name, Amyntas was a Celt. Although of a different family, he carried on the Deiotarus Dynasty.

[29] A sept is a social unit a subdivision of a clan, descendants of a common ancestor.

[30] Ellis, *The Celtic Empire*, p. 101-102.

[31] Mitchell, v. I, p. 7.

[32] Ellis, *The Celtic Empire*, p. 104-105.

[33] 2 Phil. 11.33-4. Cited in Mitchell, p. 31.

[34] Peter Beresford Ellis, *The Ancient World of the Celts* (New York: Barnes & Noble, 1998), p. 216-218; Mitchell, v .I, p. 31.

[35] Cunliffe, p. 215.

[36] Mitchell, v. 1, p. 35.

[37] Mitchell, v.1, p. 100-117.

[38] Mitchell, v. 1, p. 23.

[39] Mitchell, v. 1, p. 240.

[40] Mitchell, v. 1, p. 173-174.

[41] Mitchell, v. 1, p. 239.

[42] Mitchell, v.1, p. 189.

[43] Mitchell, v. 2, p. 10, 15, 45.

[44] Mitchell, v. 1, p. 23.

[45] Ellis, p. 108-109; Eluere, p. 74-75.

1. Departing from Tradition

[1] Peter Beresford Ellis, *Celtic Women: Women in Celtic Society and Literature*. (Grand Rapids: William B. Eerdmans Pub. Co., 1996), p. 83.

[2] Ireland was divided into four provinces, ruled by kings chosen from among the *tuatha*. They are now known as Leinster, Ulster, Munster, and Connacht. The High King over them ruled from Tara, the fifth royal province of Meath.

[3] Geoffrey Bibby, "The Celts," *Horizon*, vol VII, 2 (Spring, 1965) p. 23. The author worked in the Prehistoric Department, at the National Museum, in Prague.

[4] Stuart Piggott, *The Druids* (New York: Thames & Hudson, 1985) p. 186-189; Alexei Kondotrieve, *Celtic Rituals: An Authentic Guide to Ancient Celtic Spirituality* (Scotland: New Celtic Publishing (1999), p. 10.

[5] Piggott, p. 186-189; Alexei Kondotrieve, p. 10.

[6] Slave-ownership, unfortunately, continued until long after the coming of Christianity. See Elizabeth Sutherland, *In Search of the Picts: A Celtic Dark Age Nation* (London: Constable & Co. Ltd, 1994), p. 26.

[7] This legal heritage had its roots in Indo-European culture. From the Hittite Kingdom which was at its height in 1600 BC) and the Vedic (Hindu) laws (about 1100 BC). The

Endnotes

Celts had a similar [lunar] calendar, like that of the Indians. (See Donna Peck, "Brehon Law, I & II." Unpub. Manuscript, June, 2001).

[8] Cunliffe, p. 27.

[9] One of the first written copies of the Brehon Laws is to be found in the *The Book of the Dun Cow*. (see "Book of Ballymote," 1391). The Brehon Laws were not eradicated until 1687 AD, when the English monarchy reconfigured Ireland to its own specifications.

[10] Seamaus MacManus, "The Brehon Law," in *The Story of the Celtic Race* (Konecky-Konecky: Devon-Adair Co, 1921).

[11] Trevor Bryce, *Life and Society of the Hittite World* (Oxford University Press); Kenneth W. Harl, *Great Ancient Civilizations of Asia Minor* (Tulane University).

[12] Peck, pp. 2-3

[13] Peck, pp. 2-3

[14] Peck, II, p. 7

[15] Seamus MacManus, *The Story of the Irish Race: A Popular History of Ireland*. Rev. ed (New York: Devin-Adair Company, 1966).

[16] "Brehon Laws," http://en.wikipedia.org/wiki/Brehon_Laws. Themes associated with Ireland's Brehon Laws have been fictionalized in the popular Sister Fidelma novels by Peter Tremayne (pen-name for the Celtic scholar, Peter Beresford Ellis).

[17] A Jewish Baptism near Jericho. www.biblepicturegallery.com./pictures/Jordan/the%20immersion%20of%20thre%20Pilgrim

[18] Josephus, *War*, 11, xviii, vol. 10, xviiii, 2.

[19] "The Acts of Pilate," 2:1. *Interpreter's Dictionary of the Bible*, 2 (Nashville: Abingdon Press, 1986), p. 105.

[20] David Allan Hubbard, *Galatians: Gospel of Freedom* (Waco, TX: Word Books, 1977), p. 58.

2. Ceremonial Obligations

[1] *The Gallic Wars*, Cited in www. Religioustolerance.org/big_juli.,htm.

[2] www.magicwicca.com/wicca/samhain.htm

[3] Ostara (Vernal/Spring Equinox) was the Norse (Germanic) goddess of fertility, her symbols being the rabbit and the egg. Her festival celebrated new birth, as the snow melted and the days became warmer.

[4] Derived from ancient Candlemas rites, "Groundhog Day" was brought to America by Pennsylvania's German settlers. The groundhog is supposed to "report" on the first stirrings of Mother Earth and predict the end of winter.

[5] Midsummer Solstice is the longest day of the year, full of young creatures abroad. It was supposed that at twilight on this day the faeries to came out to consort with humans. In the last quarter of the Celtic year, summer reigned over outdoor celebration.

[6] Lugh was honored throughout Europe as the "God of Many Gifts." He stands for the Celtic inventions of farm implements and metal-crafts. Today, however, he has been reduced to the comical, mischievous Irish leprechaun.

[7] MacNeil, cited in Caitlin Matthews, *The Celtic Book of Days: A Celebration of Celtic Wisdom* (Dublin: Gill & Macmillan, Ltd. 1998), p. 99.

[8] Clinton E. Arnold, *The Colossian Syncretism: The Interface Between Christianity and folk—Belief at Colossae* (Grand Rapids: Baker Books, 1996), p. 107.

[9] Richard Foster, *The Celebration of Discipline: The Spiritual Path to Spiritual Growth* (New York: Collins, 1978), p. 1.

3. Inalienable Rights and Restrictive Regulations

[1] Donna Peck, Unpublished manuscript II (2002), p. 6.

[2] Piggott, p. 44. Some adherents of the British Istrael Movement regard the Celtic-Christian bonds to be so strong that they describe druidism as "the foster mother" of Christianity." (www.asia.com)

[3] Greek *temenos*, "a cut or share of land apportioned to the god. Roman *templum* ("space apportioned to the god. Celt, *nemeton*" "a natural woodland clearing, or a clearing within a grove (Piggott, p. 104).

[4] Piggott, p. 64.

[5] The Honor Price determined that a mercenary soldier would be worth 5 cows (or 600 danars). A craftsman = ten cows (1200 D); a householder = twenty-six cows (2400 D); and a thane/chieftain = forty cows (4800 D). (See David Dunham, "East Talios Orlanthi." www.poppyware,com/dunham/ralios/honorPrice.html).

[6] Ellis, *Celtic Women*, p. 133.

[7] "Sick Maintenance" regulations have been found in the earliest Hittite laws (See Trevor Bryce, *Life and Society of the Hittite World*, Oxford University Press.)

[8] The Celts recognized eight kinds of marriage, the position of the wife varying according to her social rank. Her carefully assessed honor price insured her inheritance, ransom, and compensation for injuries. (Peck, "Brehon Law," II, p. 9). The marriages, in descending order of excellence, were:

    1. Man and woman of financial equality
    2. Woman contributes nothing by way of property
    3. Man contributes little or nothing
    4. Man cohabits with woman in her home (with consent of her kin)
    5. Woman goes away openly with a man (without consent of her kin)
    6. Without kin's consent, woman is abducted by man
    7. Without kin's consent, woman is secretly visited by man
    8. Marriage by rape.

[9] Ellis, *Celtic Women*, p. 124-125, 133.

[10] Cassius Dio (150-235 AD), a Roman senator and prolific historian. Cited in Ellis, *Celtic Women*, p. 102.

[11] When King Alfred, the Saxon (b 849 AD, ruled 871-899 AD), codified his laws, he employed a Celt to do the work for him. An excellent choice, for the latter would have been skilled in law-making.

Endnotes

[12] The Gaelic Mother-Goddess embodied fertility, sovereignty, love, and healing. Maeve, Queen of Connacht, the most celebrated Irish mythological heroine, filled this role (Ellis, *Celtic Women*, p. 41-41).

[13] This Roman idea of Mary as a faithful follower, passive and asexual became a stifling barrier to women in centuries to come (Ellis, *Celtic Women*, p. 37-38).

[14] Albert Barnes, *Notes on the Old Testament: Psalms, Vol 2* (Grand Rapids, MI, Baker Books, 1998) p.129. Lachrymatories (tear bottles) might be made of skins, pottery or thin glass.. They had slender bodies, a broad bottom and a funnel-shaped top. Many of these bottles have been found to tombs and sepulchers.

[15] See Brennan Manning, *Ruthless Trust: The Ragamuffin's Path to God* (2000)

4. Breaking Down Barriers

[1] The Gaelic version of the Queen's name is "Boudicca," meaning "Victorious." This may have been her title rather than her personal name. "Boadicea" is the Latin interpretation of her name.

[2] Client kings received several favors from Rome: military protection, state funding, education and employment. At the same time, the Britons suffered slavery and serfdom. The Iceni tribe occupied the lands of modern Norfolk and Suffolk. Additionally, the client kings of East Anglia occupied parts of Cambridgeshire and Essex. These Celts may have arrived in Britain as early as the 7th or 6th centuries BC.

[3] See http.//www.geocities.com/Athens/Parthenon/7094/claud2.html.

[4] The Final Speeches of Boudicca and Suetonius before the Final Battle of the British Rebellion. See http//www.romans-in-britain.org.uk/his_boudiccan_rebellion_ final_battle. htm.

[5] Colchester became the Roman capital of Britain, after the invasion of Claudius in 43 AD. Hagiographers of the early Celtic church declare that the Apostle Simon Zelotes preached in Britain and that he was crucified by the Roman Catus Decianus during the Boudiccan rebellion in Caister, Lincolnshire (61 AD).

[6] Two-and-a half centuries later (304 AD) the important Roman town of Verulamium (St. Albans, in Hertsfordshire), took on a different image. There the pagan Roman soldier, Alban, became the first Christian convert to be martyred in Britain. The Venerable Bede describes how Alban went to his death after he took the place of a fleeing Christian cleric who had sought shelter in his house.

[7] The statue of Queen Boudicca was created by Thomas Thornycroft (1814-1885). The art work was presented to the City of London in 1902.

[8] Brennus committed suicide after his unsuccessful attack on Delphi, Greece. The remnants of his people, however, went on to colonize Galatia. (Cunliffe, *The Ancient Celts*, p. 194).

[9] It is not clear whether Boudicca poisoned her daughters at the same time or whether they had been killed earlier by Roman soldiers. In any case, all three heroic women passed off the pages of history at the same time.

[10] Vix (Burgundy) was a *oppidum* near Chatillon-sur-Seine, Gaul. The age of the dead princess is estimated at thirty-five, and she was surrounded by a spectacular collection of jewels. www.discoverfrance.net/France/History/DF_prehistoric.html.

[11] Ellis, *Celtic Women*, p. 106.
[12] The Hebrew word *shipha* (meaning "maidservant" indicates a "member of a family with strong blood ties." (Gen 12:16).
[13] Charles R. Erdman, *The Epistle of Paul to the Galatians* (Philadelphia: The Westminster Press, 1976), p. 102.
[14] "Fringe" or "tassel" was generally translated as "hem" or "border" in the New Testament.
[15] Francis D. Nichol, ed. *The Seventh-day Adventist Bible Commentary*, v. 6 (Washington D.C.: Review & Herald Pub. Assn., 1980), p. 962.
[16] In later generations married women were even required to "hide the attractiveness of their own hair." Rosemary R. Ruether and Rosemary S. Keller, eds. In Our Own Voices: *Four Centuries of American Women's Religious Writing* (San Francisco: Harper, 1995), p. 112.
[17] This Jewish restriction becomes the main theme in the film "Yentl." Her tolerant rabbi father began the girl's revolt by allowing his beloved but determined daughter to read the *Torah*.
[18] The very pervasive assumption about women made it impossible for Jewish women to bear witness to an event. The law required two or three persons, but none of them could be women (Dt. 17:6). Commentators conjecture that upon Simon's death, Martha inherited her husband's house.
[19] Erdman, p. 86.
[20] Erwin Gane, *Galatians: The Battle for Freedom* (Boise, Idaho: Pacific Press Publishing Associate, 1990), p. 95.

5. Face-Off With the Judaizers

[1] The apostolic faith and teachings of Celtic Christianity permeated the British Isles under the leadership of: Patrick (Ireland); Columba (Scotland); Gildas (Western England); Cadoc (Wales); Aidan (Northumbria); and Cuthbert (Scottish border country)
[2] Maud O'Neil, "Two Men from Galatia," in *They Took John's Torch: Sequel to the Book of Acts*. (Mountain View CA: Pacific Press Pub. Assn., 1961), p. 1-15.
[3] Himself of Romanized Gaul, Antonius became a believer. Two centuries later, Patrick, the "Apostle to Ireland" would come from this same Celtic group of Christians, Romanized but still proud of their Gaelic heritage.
[4] Brennan Manning, *The Signature of Jesus* (Sisters, OR: Multinomah Books, 1988), p. 36.
[5] See Alvin Schmidt, *Under the Influence: How Christianity Transformed Civilization* (Grand Rapids MI: Zondervan Publishing House, 2001) p. 346. See also the "Epistle to Barnabas" (130 AD) which warned against Judaizers.
[6] Cicero 7.6; *War* II.xvii.10; xviii.2; Magn. 8:1; 10:3; *Acts of Pilate* 2.1. Cited in *The Interpreter's Dictionary of the Bible*, v. 2, p. 1005.
[7] Dinah's name means, aptly, "judgment" or "controversy."
[8] Epispasm, (Gr *epispaomai*, "to draw over as if to efface Judaism"). This increasingly popular—but forbidden—practice (1 Cor. 7:18) was the attempt to replace foreskins by stretching out the remaining skin of the penis.

Endnotes

[9] Clinton E. Arnold, *The Colossian Syncretism: The Interface Between Christianity and Folk Belief at Colossae* (Grand Rapids MI: Baker Books, 1996), p. 184.

6. Liberty Or Death?

[1] Much scholarship has sought out the origins of Merlin, some of which trace him to ancient China! Geoffrey of Monmouth [erroneously] credits him with designing the Stonehenge (See *Histories of the Kings of Britain* (12th c AD). See John Matthews, ed. *An Arthurian Reader*. (Northamptonshire, England: The Aquarian Press, 1988). At last, Merlin was seduced by Nimue (a "Lady of the Lake") who locked him into an endless "living death." Historically, "Merlin" (Welsh, "Myrrdin") seems to be a generic title for wizardry. " Merlins," were, in fact, Celtic shamans.

[2] See also Ambiorix of Belgium and Viriathus of Iberia/Spain (Cunliffe, *The Ancient Celts*, p. 13)

[3] Cunliffe, *The Ancient Celts*, p. 244.

[4] In his *Gallic Wars*, Caesar described these Celtic sites he encountered in his Gaulish campaigns. Vercingetorix occupied the *oppidum* of Bibracte, in the Territory of the Aedui tribe. It stood on a prominent hillside, overlooking an important trade route and covered an area of 15 hectares. Here Vercingetorix was elected leader of the revolt.

[5] Julius Caesar. http://en.wikipedia.org/wiki/Julius_Caesar.

[6] The hill-forts were made of ramparts, trenches, walls and earthworks enclosing a hilltop. They could serve as refuges for whole villages. The Celts built these fortifications throughout Britain and Europe. Between 700 BC and 600 AD thousands of hill-forts were erected.

[7] At the siege of Alesia, 70,000 Gauls died. This event began the decline of Celtic power in Western Europe.

[8] Ellis, *The Celtic Empire*, p. 169-174.

[9] This nomenclature has been given to the Apostle by Professor F. F. Bruce (Rylands Professor of Biblical Criticism and Exegesis Emeritus, University of Manchester, England).

[10] Francis D. Nichol, Editor, *The Seventh-day Adventist Bible Commentary*, Vol. 6 (Washington, D.C., Review and Herald Publishing Association, 1980) p. 978.

[11] Charles R. Erdman, *The Epistle of Paul to the Galatians* (Philadelphia: Westminster Press, 1976), pp. 116-117.

[12] Paul drew on this supreme principle that is embedded in the heart of the ancient legal code (Lev. 19:18). Jesus Himself declared it to be the greatest of all the codes (Mark 12:31).

[13] Erdman, p. 117.

[14] See http://en.wikipedia.org/wiki/Merlin. This illustration is taken from a French manuscript of the 13th century. Notice that an oak tree dominates Merlin's half of the portrait. The monk is sitting in a *scriptorium*, under a steeple and cross.

7. The Solitary Way

[1] *The Rule of Ailbe* was written in Old Irish (8th century AD). A contemporary of King Aengus of Munster, Ailbe is credited with founding of the monastery of Emly. Myth has it that Ailbe could take on the likeness of the people who believed in him.

[2] www.taisbean.com/worldcletic/skellig.htm

[3] Rabey, p. 150-151.

[4] Rabey, p. 151

[5] Bamburgh Castle was built by the Normans in the 11th century AD. It's importance, however, goes back 400 years to the time of King Arthur. The site is said to be the legendary home of Sir Lancelot of the Round Table, "Joyous Guard" (Brit, *Din Giuayrdi*).

[6] Kondratiev, p. 13-14; 21, 25.

[7] This poem was written by an unknown monk in a 9th century Irish abbey. The two decorative cats are adapted from the *Book of Kells* (See Bernard Meehan, *The Book of Kells: An Illustrated Introduction to the Manuscript in Trinity College Dublin* (Thames and Hudson, London, 1994, p. 76). While illuminating their manuscripts, the Celtic monks often gave way to their imagination and humor and inserted many artistic-though-irrelevant features. Such as, two men—legs entangled—fighting and pulling one another's beards. Unnumbered fanciful birds and animals blended into the designs. Then a green lizard appears between the lines for no reason whatsoever. And much more.

[8] Katharine Scherman, *The Flowering of Ireland: Saints, Scholars and Kings* (Boston: Little, Brown & Co., 1981), p. 68.

[9] Rabey, p. 154, 158.

[10] The 19th century drawing of the Monasterboice Cross appeared as an illustration in Henry O'Neill's book on high crosses. A passionate nationalist, he was one of the first antiquarians to make such a study. See Roger Stalley, *Irish High Crosses* (Dublin, Country House, 1996), p. 6.

[11] Clonmacnoise is a picturesque abbey site on the banks of the Shannon River, Ireland.

[12] Scherman, pp. 103, 117, 132

[13] Cited in Rabey, p. 193.

[14] Scherman, p. 116-121.

[15] Rabey, p. 130, 134.

[16] Rabey, p. 191.

[17] Cited in Rabey, p. 192-195.

[18] A very ancient, tiny, one-person boat, the *coracle*, originated among the Celts of Wales. It was also known as a *curragh*. The light frame was covered with animal skins or canvas, impregnated with pitch. A single paddle propelled the round little "tub." Coracles were used in Ireland until the late 1940's.

[19] Cited in Rabey, pp. 201–202.

[20] This ritual is a survival from the pagan festival of Lughnasa. Ancient Celtic farmers dreaded "Hungry July" and would wait for the wonder-working Lugh, "The Shining One." He would overpower the earth god and win the harvest for the people. (See Merle Severy, "The Celts," *National Geographic* (May, 1977), p. 628-629.

Endnotes 189

[21] See http://.en.wikipedia.org/wiki/St_Brendan_the_Navigator. [20] Rabey, p. 163.
[22] Rabey, p. 171.
[23] See http://saints.sqpn.com/saintc17.htm
[24] Rabey, pp. 251, 257, 269.
[25] Rabey p. 260-261. When the Venerable Bede sensed the approach of his own death, he welcomed it eagerly as a "heavenly birthday." Having kept "short accounts" with others and having "practiced confession to God," he had "no huge backlog of unfinished business."
[26] Scherman, p. 73.
[27] Scherman, p. 126.
[28] Scherman, p. 73.
[29] Medallion for the Apostle Paul. See www.chirstusrex.org/www1/vaticano/Sb-Paul.jpg. The medallion of St. Paul is copper with enamel and gilding.
[30] Herman N. Ridderbos, *The Epistle of Paul to the Churches of Galatia* (Grand Rapids: W. B. Eerdmans, 1953), p. 65.
[31] Suetonius, *Life of Nero* (c 120 AD), cited in Bruce, p. 442.

8. The Journey-Quest

[1] St. Columba's baptismal name was *Crimthann* (Irish "wolf") for the wolf-infested forests of Garton where he was born. He had a very high-ranking royal pedigree. Through his father, Fedhlimidh, he was a great-great-grandson of Niall of the Nine Hostages, a 5th-century warlord and High King of Tara. He was also nephew to both Fergus Mor Mac Erca (then King of Scotland) and his brother Muircheartach Mac Era (then High King of Tara). His mother, Eithne, came from the royal family of the Kingdom of Munster. Such was his godly life, however, that his friends later called him *Columcille* (*"Dove of the Church"*).
[2] Severy, p. 626.
[3] Esther de Waal, *The Celtic Way of Prayer: The Recovery of Religious Imagination* (New York: Doubleday, 1997), p. 89. Prayers for traveling mercies were an essential part of every Celtic Christian voyage.
[4] Columba made long journeys into the Scottish Highlands, as far north as what is now Aberdeen. http://reader.classicalanglican.net/?orthodoxsiki.org/Columba_of_Iona.
[5] Schermann, pp. 148-163. King Oswald, who in 635 AD had taken refuge on Iona, called Aidan to preach the Gospel among his Northumbrian [Saxon] people. Then the king gave him the island of Lindisfarne for a monastic site. Modeled on Iona, Lindisfarne had both Irish and Saxon monks. (Kondatriev, p. 30)
[6] Cited in Rabey, p. 24.
[7] See F. W. Fawcett, "Columba: Pilgrim for Christ." In *The Derry Standard, Ltd.* (Londonderry, 1963)
[8] David Marshall, *The Celtic Connection: The Beginnings of Christiantiy in Ireland and Britain* (Grantham, Lincs: The Stanborough Press, 1994) The rule of Columba was fundamental but severe.

[9] Columba is said to have died on a (7th day) Sabbath. "Then he [Columba] said to those who stood around him: 'This day in the Holy Scriptures is called Sabbath, which means rest. And this day is indeed Sabbath to me, for it is the last day of my laborious life and on it I rest. And this night . . . I shall go the way of my fathers.' At the end of the day, when it came time for the Sabbath Vigils (evening prayers), having reached the end of a page, he laid down his pen [and died]. (See John D. Keyser, "Columba of Iona—Sabbatarian and Keeper of the Stone." www.hope of Israel.org/columba.htm-45k) Later copyists omitted Item # 7 ("Sabbath"), or replaced it with "Lord's Day." Aidan of Lindisfarne and other early Celtic Christians were also Sabbatarians.

[10] The pre-eminence of the Celtic Church (Iona) began to decline after the Synod of Whitby (664 AD) when the central power gravitated to the Roman Church of Canterbury, South England. (Kondatriev, p.31)

[11] Kondatriev, p. 29.

[12] De Waal, p. xi. Given their vigor and constant need for expansion, it can be no accident that the chief explorers and empire-builders of modern times sprang from ancient Celtic roots.

[13] De Waal, p. ix.

[14] De Waal, p. 3.

[15] Scherman, p.174-201.

[16] Scherman, p.132-147.

[17] Travelers in the 9th-century attested to the presence of Irish monastic settlements in Iceland.

[18] Rabey, p. 174.

[19] Scherman, pp 132-133.

[20] Kondatriev, p. 58.

[21] The Grail is identified with the Celtic "Cauldron of Plenty." When it was Christianized, it became the sacramental wine cup from Jesus' Last Supper. Tradition has it that Joseph of Arimathea brought it to England where it disappeared.

[22] Bruce, p. 63.

[23] Bruce, p. 456-457.

[24] John Mark, author of the gospel of Mark, was a young cousin of Barnabas (Col 4:10). Some commentators have mistakenly described him as a nephew.

9. The Discipline of the Rule of Three

[1] Traditionally, the village of Bonnaven, lying between the Scottish towns of Dumbarton and Glasgow, is said to be Patrick's birthplace (later named "Kirk-Patrick"). His father, Calpornius, was a deacon in the church and gave his son Patrick a careful education. See August Neander, *General History of the Christian Religion and Church*. Vol. 2 (Boston, 1855), p. 122.

[2] Twenty-two-year-old Patrick left Ireland on a vessel loaded with Irish wolfhounds. Then he trekked across Gaul searching for food and a market for the hounds.

Endnotes

[3] It has been speculated that St. "Patrice" may have been at a family home on the Loire River. Patrice is a common name in France. Also, he may have been a nephew of St. Martin, founder of the Abbey.

[4] Patrick's first church was on the land of Chief Dichu, at Strangford Lough, County Down (*Sabhal Padraic*, Saul). His main church, the power-center of Celtic Christianity, was on a hilltop at Armagh, County Armagh, near Emain Macha. Eventually, it became (temporarily) the religious capital of Europe. Special sites of pilgrimage include: Croagh Patrick, Lough Derg, and Downpatrick (his burial place).

[5] Unfortunately, "The Confession of Saint Patrick" gives us much less biographical information than we would wish to have. Rather, he concerns himself with the spreading of the Word.

[6] Theophilus was a very early Christian leader. The books of Luke and Acts of the Apostles are addressed to him (Luke 1:3; Acts 1:1).

[7] George Arthur Buttrick, ed. *Interpreter's Dictionary of the Bible* (Nashville: Abingdon Press, 1962), p. 711.

[8] Lavin, p. 4. The Celts were constantly preoccupied with threefold arrangements in every phase of their lives. They even practiced a "triune" administration (Ellis, p. 105).

[9] Matthews, p. 72.

[10] Matthews, p. 36, 50, 60, 80, 109.

[11] Ann Ross and Michael Cyprien, *Celtic Britain* (Harrisburg: Historical Times, Inc.), p. 335.

[12] Cunliffe, p. 187.

[13] Erdman, p. 90-105.

[14] Cited in Pennick, *The Celtic Saints* (London: Harper Collins Pub., 1997), p. 55, 78.

[15] Sir Kenneth Clarke, OM, CH, KCB (1903-1983) created the thirteen-part series, "Civilization," for BBC television in 1969. Although the format is common today, he was the first to take us on an epic film journey through Western culture.

[16] From David Adam, *The Edge of Glory* (1985).

10. Raiding and War

[1] Cunliffe, p. 178. Like western European Celts, Galatia determined tribal leadership by prowess in war and personal prestige rather than hereditary privileges. Genealogies of Celtic chieftains are, therefore, unusual. The fact that Ortagion is an exception indicates his political importance.

[2] Ellis, p. 88-89.

[3] Cited in Mitchell, v. 1, p. 43.

[4] Cunliffe, p. 88-89.

[5] Cunliffe, p. 83.

[6] Cunliffe, p. 202. Cuchulain, the ancient Celtic champion of Ireland, once came home with no less than nine trophy heads hanging by the hair from his horse's bridle

[7] *Hist.5.29*. Cited in Ellis, *The Celtic Empire*, p. 21.

[8] Cunliffe, p. 210.

[9] Piggott, p. 42. See Aix-en-Provence and Roquepertuse sites.
[10] Cunliffe, 127-128.
[11] "Evidence Unearthed of UK Cannibalism 2,000 Years Ago," http://unisci.com/stories/ 20011/0228012.htm.
[12] For further details on holy war see *The Interpreter's Dictionary of the Bible*, IV, p. 796-805.
[13] Deuteronomy 20 outlines the Hebrew laws of warfare.
[14] Note the salutation of "Grace and peace" in Romans 1 & 2, Thessalonians, 1 & 2, Cor. 1 & 2, and all of the later epistles. Timothy 1 & 2 are the exception. There the word "mercy" is added.

11. Passion and the Virtues of Commitment

[1] Ellis, *Celtic Empire*, p. 101.
[2] Ellis, *Celtic Empire*, p 102.
[3] The Attalid kings of Pergamum erected several victory monuments in the first period of their artistic awakening (250-200 BC). Attalus I commissioned the bronze figures commemorating his victory at the Springs of Kaikos (233 BC). He put them on the Pergamum Acropolis, in the temple of Athena.
[4] Drawing by A. Chober (1952). Finely carved marble copies of these Galatian figures were commissioned by Attalus I (269-197 BC) and taken to Italy. (Cunliffe, p. 8).
[5] Sculptures of Pergamum (420 BC) are now in the Capitoline Museum, Rome. See also "Galatian Constituency" (p. 106). Another part of the Pergamene sculpture group, "The Gaul and His Wife," features a Galatian suicide. The naked warrior has just killed his wife, who slumps down at his side. With his left hand he supports her body, and with his right he drives the dagger into his own heart. His head turns to the right as he defiantly stares down his enemies.
[6] This Celtic penchant for record-keeping is repeated in the history of America's founding fathers. The Puritans' self-examination served as a means of organizing their personal lives and mapping their spiritual journey. See Gal 5:19-21.
[7] Rabey, p. 39, 41.
[8] Rabey, p. 4.
[9] Cited in Rabey, p. 9.
[10] Rabey, p. 13, 16.
[11] Mead is an alcoholic beverage brewed from barley and honey.
[12] The Greek *praxis* (practice) is written in the present tense to show that this continuing lifestyle is not a one-time event. It is a perpetual pattern of behavior.
[13] Following his enumeration of sixteen vices, Paul lists nine virtues (Gal 5:22-24). Against these, he declared, "there is no law."
[14] Cunliffe, p. 4-6.
[15] Cunliffe, p. 84.
[16] Rabey, p. 5.

Endnotes

12. Boasting and Challenges

[1] The epic work, *Beowulf*, is important as the first European poem recorded in a vernacular language. Written in Old English, it has survived in a 10th-century manuscript. While the tale is believed to have come from the 6th-century AD, the large number of Christian references indicate a later time when the Gospel was transforming pagan Britain. One single manuscript of *Beowulf* remains, having survived Henry VIII's dissolution of the monasteries and the destruction of religious artifacts.

[2] Beowulf is a kinsman and "table companion" of Hygelac, King of the Geats. Eventually, he inherits the Geatish throne and rules for fifty years. Half a century filled with magnificent achievements. He dies, at last, of wounds received in a fight with a fiery dragon.

[3] Beowulf tears off Grendel's arm and carries it to Hrothgar as a trophy, leaving the monster to bleed to death. Then, in a second larger-than-life encounter he kills Grendel's mother who is bent on revenge.

[4] *Geography*, IV.4.2.5. Cited in Eluere, p. 135.

[5] Bibby, p. 29.

[6] Cited in Ellis, *The Celtic Empire*, p. 20.

[7] Lavin, p. 38.

[8] Julius Caesar killed or enslaved two million Gauls. By deception he virtually wiped out 350,000 of the Celtic tribe of the Helvetii (Switzerland) when they tried to emigrate out of the Alpine regions and down to the plains.

[9] We find a striking parallelism, a tragic inequality, between the fight of Cuchulain and Ferdiad and that between Achilles and Hector in Homer's Greek epic, *The Iliad*. The one-to-one encounter between two champions also recalls the swimming competition of Beowulf and Brecca.

[10] Norma Lorre Goodrich, *Medieval Myths* (New York: New American Library, 1977), p. 193.

[11] Mark Edmundson, *Teacher*. (New York: Random House, 2002), p. 128.

[12] Robertson, *Word Pictures in the New Testament*, IV (Nashville: Broadman Press, 1931), p. 311.

13. The Ties That Bind

[1] Ludwig Devrient played King Lear in a French production of the Shakespeare play in 1769 (Galerie Dramatique). See en.wikipedia.org/wiki/Image:King_Lear.jpg.

[2] Having given over his powers and lands to his daughters and sons-in-law, Lear still wants to keep his kingly title and privileges. Given the power of human greed, he has made an unwise decision, and Goneril and Regan immediately start plotting his dethronement.

[3] The centuries-old rivalry between Britain and France explains what is clearly a plan to make a claim on the British throne of King Lear. The Duke of Burgundy refuses to marry Cordelia because she has no land.

4 The fact that the King France suddenly disappears makes one question how much he "loved" Cordelia. He has his own political agenda and will live to fight another day.
5 Cunliffe, p. 108-109.
6 Kondatriev, p. 27.
7 Cunliffe, p. 108.
8 Erdman, p. 90.

14. Help With the Heavy Load

1 See http://en.wikipedia.org/wiki/Brigid_of_Kildare
2 Edward C. Sellner, *Wisdom of the Celtic Saints* (Notre Dame, IN: Ave Maria Press, 1992), p. 69-75; de Waal, p.135-38.
3 This story (and those of many other Celtic saints) comes under the heading of hagiography. That is, the body of biography and miracle stories about the saints. While it contains the threads of facts, it is embellished with legend. Nonetheless, the stories represent the basic beliefs of a culture as it builds its theology. Unlike the Roman Church, the Celtic clergy never formally canonized their saints. That practice evolved only after Celtic practices gave way to Rome.
4 Ancient Egyptian priests, the Persian magi, and Indian Brahmins are all part of the learned class that also includes the Gaelic druids (Piggott, p. 102).
5 Piggott, p. 186-189.
6 While the current, wildly popular Harry Potter series draws on traditional Celtic magic for its content, it lacks most of the *other* wiser parts of the druidic system.
7 St. Patrick masterminded the amalgamation of pagan druidism with Celtic Christianity, establishing connections at several interesting points.
8 After the Synod of Whitby, the Celtic clergy began to blend into what was to became the united (Western) Roman church in the 11th and 12th centuries. It might be argued that if Celtic practices had prevailed, there would have been little need for the Protestant Reformation.
9 In a sense, the soul friend could be seen as a person's alter ego.
10 *Diapedesis* is a hemorrhaging through the pores of the skin. It derives from the Greek *thromboi haimatos* ("great clots of blood"). See Walter M Chandler, *The Trial of Jesus* (Atlanta: Harrison Pub. Co., 1956), p. 31.
11 Bruce, p. 83. Barnabas (Rom 16:10) is credited with writing the *Martyrologies of the Greek Church*. Tradition has it that he joined missionaries from Ephesus in preaching in Britain (42 AD).
12 Barnabas was a "Levite and a native of the island of Cyprus" (Acts 4:36). His priestly family had evidently separated from Jerusalem, and thus Barnabas had a career somewhat like that of John the Baptist. His birthplace makes him a Jew of the Diaspora, a fellow-Hellenist of Saul of Tarsus, in contrast to the Palestinian Jews like Peter whom Luke called "Hebrews" (Acts 6:1). George Arthur Buttrick, ed. *Interpreters Dictionary of the Bible*, v. 1, p. 356.

Endnotes

[13] See Shelley Taylor (Research psychologist at UCLA, California). Cited in Katherine Griffin, "Friends: The Secret of a Longer Life." (*Reader's Digest*, September 2, 2002, p. 114).

[14] Both biblical and extra-biblical evidence shows that Judas originally belonged to the group. At first, Jesus actually formed a unit of four rather than three.

15. Love Never Fails

[1] From the monastic *Book of Cerne* (AD 630). Cited in Matthews, p. 57.

[2] *Interpreter's Dictionary of the Bible*, v. 2, p. 654.

[3] The question of the date of this epistle is not only controversial; it is also significant. It is one of the most complicated issues in New Testament commentary. There are many hypotheses about the date of Paul's first visit and about the writing of his letter. The majority of scholars maintain that his first visit took place prior to the Jerusalem Council (Gal 1:18-2:10) and that the letter was written from Corinth shortly afterwards, between the events of Acts 14 and 15.

[4] *Scorn, loath* (Gr. "to spit on the ground in disgust")

[5] *Despise* (Gr. "to make of no account")

[6] On the evidence we have, it is possible that Paul suffered from the chronic, highly contagious infection called *Trachoma*. The disease was endemic in the Middle East. A person might suffer recurring episodes of infection, until, eventually, he became blind. This inflammation of the eyes was quite revolting, with discharges of tears and foul-smelling pus.

[7] The Celts invented soap and introduced it to the Greeks and Romans. Daily bathing was habitual, usually in the evening before the feast and entertainment. A good host would prepare a bath for his visitors. No questions or negotiations were permitted until these hospitalities had been offered. This reverence for cleanliness blended well with the Celtic skills of the healing arts.

[8] By the age of fourteen, a Gaelic child was expected to make and play their own musical instrument (flutes, whistles, bagpipes, harp, drums, and the fiddle). The bard (Saxon scop) also preserved tribal histories and sometimes served as a "public relations officer" for a tribe. http://celts.mdonn.org/bards.html.

[9] Rev. R. W. Morgan, *St Paul in Britain, or, The Origin of British Christianity*. Abridged from 1860 edition (Artisan Sales, P. O. Box 1529, Muskogee, OK, 74402, c1984). Another book of the same period was written by Rev. George F. Jowett, *The Drama of the Lost Disciples* (London: Covenant Books). These two books stimulated a long lasting interest in the :Celtic church in Rome. The traditions of Joseph of Arimathea arriving at Glastonbury, Britain, shortly after Christ's crucifixion are part of this school of thought. The "British-Israel-World Federation" was also born as a movement in the 19th century and was federated in 1919. The British aristocracy traced their heritage to Joseph of Arimathea and, thereby, to the family of Jesus Christ. Joseph was said to be a great-uncle of Jesus.

[10] Like other Celts of the British Isles, the Royal Family of Caradoc preferred to be known by the more aristocratic title of *Cymri* (a Welsh tribe of Siluria). The Welsh maintained an unstable frontier between themselves against the Romans, and, later, the Saxons. In the time of Caradoc Wales consisted of five provinces: The Silures (south); the Demetae (south-west), the Cornovii (mid-Wales); the Deceangli (north coast); and the Ordovices (mountains of Snowdonia). See Bryan Sykes, *Saxons, Vikings, and Celts: The Genetic Roots of Britain and Ireland* (London: W. W. Norton & Co., 2006), p. 221.

[11] The country estate of Rufus Pudens was in Umbria. There household servants/slaves were born and bred. Four hundred (200 male and 200 female) served in the Roman mansion, evidence of the wealth of the family. Morgan, p. 58.

[12] Roman Historians. See **Juvenal** (1st – 2nd c AD); **Cornelius Tacitus** (55-c120 AD); **Suetonius Tertullian** (155-222 AD), and the Greek geographer, **Strabo** (64 BC-23 AD).

[13] Church Fathers: St. **Jerome** (340-420 AD); St. **Chrysostom** (347-407 AD); **Venantius Fortunatus** (b 530 AD); The Venerable Bede (672-736 AD). See also the Vatican historian, **Caesar Baronius** (1538-1607), *Annales Ecclesiastici*. Jowett, p. 61.

[14] Since the mid-19th century proponents of the idea of "British Israel" claim Biblical proof that the Celts of Britain and northern Europe can trace a lineal descent from the "Ten Lost Tribes of Israel." (www.celts.org.uk) They refer to the apocryphal "29th missing chapter" of Acts to prove Britain as the center of the Ten Lost Tribes. These writers also identify: The Tuatha de Dannan of Ireland (Tribe of Dan); Angles (Ephraim); Jutes (Judah); Saxons (Sons of Isaac); Normans (Benjamin); Members of the Ten Lost Tribes are said to have escaped the enslavement of Sargon II, King of Assyria and to have migrated into Europe. (See E. Raymond Capt, *The Lost Chapters of the Apostles*) Considered the primary sources of "the Jew," there is little comment on the tribe of Judah. Still others point out the similarities between certain British legends and the Holy Land: Joseph of Arimathea of Glastonbury ; The Stone of Scone ("Jacob's Pillow"); The Brythonic (Welsh Genealogies; Brutus (immigrant hero from the Trojan War); King Arthur; British Common Law versus Mosaic Law (basis for England's rejection of the Vatican in Rome); the resemblance of certain Celtic place names to "Hebrew" as in Iberia (Spain) and *Hibernia* (Ireland).

[15] www.religioustolerance.org/anglo_is.htm.

[16] Bruce, pp. 148-149. Mark describes Simon the Cyrene as "the father of Alexander and Rufus" (Mark 15:21).

[17] The argument is that Paul's mother first bore Paul by a Hebrew husband. Then, later, she married a Roman Christian and gave birth to Rufus.

[18] In contrast, the Christian "Church of the Hebrews" (or "Church of the Circumcision") in Rome indicates a different ethnic congregation. Here Priscilla and Aquila were leaders (Rom 16:3). From Pontus, the couple had to leave when Emperor Claudius ordered all Jews out of Rome (Acts 8:2) . See Morgan p. 61-62.

[19] The epigrammatist, "Martial," compared Claudia's height to the "Palatine Colossus" standing in the Roman Forum (Epig. Viii.60).

Endnotes

[20] See http.//en.wikipedia.org/wiki/Claudius. (In the Vatican Museum, The Vroma Project) Emperor Claudius is credited with an extraordinary degree of stupidity. His own mother, Livia, often remarked: "[He/she] is as imbecile as my son Claudius." Fat, with trembling knees and head, he stuttered, foamed at the mouth in anger, and laughed idiotically. His cruelty and cowardice became legendary. Nero succeeded Claudius in 54 AD. See Morgan, p. 41.

[21] Pendragon (Welsh, "*Pen Draig*, "dragon head") was the Celtic title for a military dictatorship. The symbol of the red dragon remains the centerpiece of the Welsh flag today.

[22] Almost incessant hostilities lasted from 43-118 AD, long after Caradoc was gone. The Roman "Caractacus" is the more commonly known version of his name.

[23] As a client queen, Cartimandua ("sleek pony") sold out to the Romans in a power struggle against her ex-husband, Venutius. See "The Histories of Cornelius Tacitus." www.ourcivilisation.com/smartboard/tacitusc'histries/chap11.htm.

[24] Caradoc's speech was recorded by Tacitus, In *Annals*, Bk: XII, Ch.36.

[25] Caradoc was sentenced to spend seven years in Rome, in "custody of surveillance," not unlike the Apostle Paul's later house arrest. See Rev. Richard St. John Tynwitt, *Greek and Gothic: Progress and Decay in the Three Arts of Architecture, Sculpture and Painting* (London: Walter Smith, 1881), p. 192.

[26] Eubulus and Joseph of Armathea are said to have evangelized Britain as early as 39 AD. A wealthy tin-merchant, Joseph had made several journeys to Cornwall, arriving in Glastonbury between 36-39 AD. See Andres Gray, *The Origin and Early History of Christianity in Britain*. Joseph's earliest converts included members of the Silurian (Welsh) royal family. He is supposed to have established the first above-ground Christian church in the world. Gildas of Wales asserted that Christianity came to Britain in 37 AD, the last of the reign of Tiberius Caesar.

[27] Lib.xi, Epig.54; Lib.iv, Epig 12. Cited in Alexander Jones, MD, *The Cymry of '76; Or, Welshmen and Their Descendants* (New York: Sheldon, Lamport & Co., 1855, p. 47. See also Tynwitt p. 193. Martial elsewhere congratulated Claudia for having so promptly started a family: "Thanks to the gods, she (Claudia) has borne many children to her holy husband!"

[28] Jowett, p. 58.

[29] Tynwitt, p. 193. Thus St. Pudenziana became the first Christian Church in Rome.

[30] The two daughters of Rufus Pudens and Claudia, Pudenziana and Praxedes, were mere teenagers when they took part in burying the remains of Christian martyrs in the catacombs. They did so until they themselves were put to death. Praxedes is said to have been Paul's first Christian convert in Rome. The church of Santa Prasseda honors her name.

[31] Seneca was a statesman, philosopher, dramatist and rhetorician. Although he once served as a tutor to Nero, he eventually turned against the notorious emperor who ultimately forced him to commit suicide

[32] The Apostle Paul was at first buried in the Pudens family cemetery, the Priscilla Catacombs, on the Ostian Way.

16. A Flair for Design

[1] "HW" at the end of a text indicates translation from the original language by Hyveth Williams.
[2] *Geography*, IV.4.2,5. Cited in Eluere, p. 135.
[3] Kondratiev, p. 9
[4] Kondratiev, p. 9. Celtic arts also incorporated the styles of Thrace, the Near East, and even India.
[5] Lavin, p. 109; Cunliffe, p. 113.
[6] Top left: A gilded bronze sheld (Bibby, p. 21); Top right: A bronze helmet (Bibby, p. 27); Lower right: The brooch of Tara (8th c AD). It is displayed in the National Museum of Ireland, Dublin (Bibby,); Lower left: The Jewelry of Kings and Heroes (BIbby, p. 26).
[7] Left: The Gunderstrup Cauldron. Right: A wine flagon (Bibby, pp. 25, 30). The Rhone River and later the Danube connected the Celts with Greece.
[8] Cunliffe, p. 57-61.
[9] Celtic cauldrons became the prototype of the legends of the Holy Grail.
[10] Eluere, p.164-165.
[11] Kondatriev, p. 30.
[12] "Cuchulain," cited in Norma Lorre Goodrich, *Medieval Myths* (New York: New American Library, 1977) p. 204-205.
[13] Ellis, *Celtic Women*, p. 52
[14] Ellis, *Celtic Women*, p. 52.
[15] In the midst of his battle frenzy, the Irish hero Cuchulain roams the river and the fords (crossings) fending off war-parties single-handedly. The temptress Morrigan appears before him, a beautiful young woman "dressed in all the colors of the rainbow." Thus he knows her to be "the very highest personage." (See Goodrich, pp. 193–194, and Bibby, p. 29.)
[16] Eluere, p. 65.

17. Bewitched!

[1] "Magus" www.britannica.com.
[2] The drawing of the druid in the oak grove is taken from the title page of *Antiquities of England and Wales, 1773–1789*, vol. 4. By Francis Greene (See Piggott, p. 135). While the druids have used Stonehenge from time to time, it was built long before those Gaelic philosophers reached Britain. Only after coming under Roman influence did the Celts build temples.
[3] Lavin, p. 98-99.
[4] Cited in Mitchell, v. I, p. 27. The *nemeton* (Gallic, "clearing within a grove") was also described by Strabo.
[5] Lavin, p. 102.

Endnotes 199

[6] The confrontation between Simon and the apostles gave rise to the word "simony," which is the buying or selling of sacred objects, church offices, or spiritual favors. For the first three centuries of the Christian Church, simony was not a problem, but it became so as the Church became wealthy and had influence and wealth to bestow—particularly in the 9th and 10th centuries AD.

[7] From the *Clementine Homilies*, which, like the apocryphal Acts, were written for both instruction and entertainment. Therefore, they should be read in that light.

[8] Mankind has always been obsessed with the idea of flying, but first it appeared to be so unnatural an undertaking that only a magician could accomplish it. Simon Magus' alleged attempt appears to based on the story of Daedalus, a legendary Athenian inventor. He claimed descent from Hephaestus, the Greek god of the fire and blacksmiths. In a fit of jealousy over the skills of his nephew, he tried to kill the boy. As a result he and his son, Icarus, fled to Crete. Eventually, weary of exile, Daedalus fashioned for each of them a pair of wings constructed of wax and feathers so that they might escape their island prison. "Do not fly too near the sun," he warned Icarus. Exhilarated as he soared heavenward, however, Icarus disobeyed his father. His wings melted, and he fell into the ocean (now the Icarian Sea).

[9] *The Interpreter's Dictionary of the Bible*, (Nashville, Abingdon Press, 1962), v. 2, p. 404-405.

[10] These types of gnosticism promoted by Simon and Menander, in turn, influenced Jehovah Witness belief as well as Mormonism. (*Interpreter's Dictionary of the Bible*, v. 2, pp. 404–405).

[11] Arnold, p. 57.

[12] "Magic," www.britannica.com.

18. The Painted People

[1] Elizabeth Sutherland, *In Search of the Picts: A Celtic Dark Age Nation* (London: Constable & Co., Ltd., 1994), p. 1.

[2] Cited in Sutherland, p. 41. *Woad* is a mustard-like plant with yellow flowers and leaves that make a blue dye.

[3] Sutherland, pp. xv, 40.

[4]Adapted from a drawing by John White (c1488), in Cunliffe, p. 10.

[4] Severy, "The Celts, Europe's Founders," *National Geographic* (May, 1977).

[5] The influence of Africans in the New World is noteworthy. In the early times of slavery, the brandings and the lashings produced two results. First came the pain of the ordeal. Second was the scarring of their smooth dark skins, something that they highly prized. Contemporary blacks, however, have forgotten this part of their heritage. With their passion for multiple tattoos, they have surrendered to the tastes of their Celtic cousins.

[6] Roman soldiers averaged not more than 5' 6" in height. Hence, their Celtic opponents usually towered over them, sometimes by as much as twelve inches.

[7] Kondratiev, p. 14-15. Mercenaries were professional soldiers who hired themselves out for service in foreign armies.

[8] Ellis, *The Celtic Empire*, p. 20.
[9] Polybius, *History*, 29, 5-9. Cited in Cunliffe, p. 99.
[10] Cunliffe, p. 99.
[11] *The Interpreter's Dictionary of the Bible* v. 4, p. 520.
[12] E. Huxtable, "Galatians," in *The Pulpit Commentary*, v. 20 (Grand Rapids: Eerdmans Pub. Co., 1980), p. 316.
[13] Adapted from Peter Parshall, "The Momentous Mission of the Apostle Paul, *US News World Report* (April 22, 1991), p. 54.

APPENDIX I

A CHRONOLOGY OF GALATIA

Early Civilizations of Asia Minor: Migratory Period

2000-1700 BC	Heavy droughts in the Indus Valley (probably) induced the Indo-European culture to move westward.
1900 BC	The first Hittite Kingdom in Anatolia (Capital: Bogazkoy).
1200 BC	Migrations of Sea Peoples, Trojan War. (Capital: Gordium, in Phrygia).
1100 BC	Milesian invasion of Ireland.
900-600 BC	Emergence of Celtic civilization in Europe (Time of King David & Homer).
753 BC	Founding of the City of Rome.
600 BC	The Celts (Gr *Keltoi*, "the tribes") came out of Scythia, a huge nation of 2.5 million.
700-500 BC	Hallstatt Celtic civilization (Salzburg, Austria, Iron Age).
500-100 BC	La Tene Celtic civilization (Switzerland, Iron Age).

The Beginning of Celtic Expansion Out of Europe

500 BC	Dominance of Persian Empire in Asia Minor.
474 BC	Celts defeated Etruscans in northern Italy.
390-387 BC	A Celtic army led by British princes, Bellinus and Brennus, invaded and humiliated Rome (a ransom paid for Celtic withdrawal).
350 BC	Celtic tribes crossed over into Britain.

335-334 BC	Alexander the Great met Ceiltic chieftains on the Danube, Bulgaria.

Classical Period: The Hellenistic Monarchies of Asia Minor

323 BC	Death of Alexander the Great. Celts swarm through the remnants of his empire. Ptolemies and Seleucids divide Aisa Minor into Five Hellenistic Monarchies (323-325 BC).
301 BC	Kingdom of Cappadocia established under Ariararthes II. Tiberias makes Cappadocia a Roman province in 17 AD.
301 BC	Kingdom of Pontus established under Mithradates I. Mithradates VI (120-64) became an ardent enemy of Rome and solicited aid of the Galatians.
297 BC	Kingdom of Bithynia established under Nicomedes I (278-250). Nicomedes III (91-74) bequeathed his kingdom to Rome.
283 BC	Kingdom of Pergamum established under Eumenes I (263-214). Attalus 1 (241-197) defeated the Galatians. Eumenes II (197–159). Attalus III (138-133) died without an heir and donated Asia Minor to Rome.
280-278 BC	(Tribal) Kingdom of Galatia began as the settlement of three Celtic tribes (The Tolistobogii, Tectosages, and Trocmi) who crossed from Europe into Asia Minor. The first band of Gauls (Tolistobogii under Chieftain Brennus) ravaged Macedonia, defeated the Greeks at Thermopylae, and pillaged the Shrine of the Oracle to Apollo at Delphi, Greece.
279-210 BC	Second Band of Celts ruled Thrace, at Tylis.
278-277 BC	Third Band of Celts (20,000) crossed the Bosphorus into central Asia Minor. (The high desert plateau of Anatolia [Galatia] was named for them—*Galli*, Gauls).
277-232BC	The Galatian tribes terrorized and ravaged Asia Minor, each with its own "hunting ground." Eighty years of Galatian independence (270-189 BC).
276 BC	Galatian tribes settle in Phrygia.
269 BC	Galatians defeated by Antiochus I of Syria at the Battle of the Elephants, south of Thyratira.
232 BC	Galatians attacked Pergamum and were defeated by Attalus 1, who confined them to the high desert plateau of Anatolia (Galatia).

The Chronology of Galatia

225 BC	Rome defeated Celts at the Battle of Telamon, Italy.
222-205 BC	Celts still served as mercenaries in the Egyptian army (since 277 BC) and secured overlordship of Pergamum (197-159 BC).
190 BC	Battle of Magnesia. Galatians defeated (again by elephants).
192 BC	Rome controlled all of Cisalpine Gaul.
189 BC	Galatian defeat. Romans conquered Seleucid king, Antiochus III, and gave all of Asia Minor to Pergamum. The Tolistobogii and Trocmi were defeated at Battle of Olympus and the Tectosages at the Battle of Ancyra.

Galatian Efforts at Independence

181 BC	Rise of Ortagion of the Tolistobogii who attempted (unsuccessfully) to unite the Galatian tribes.
178-173 BC	Celtic languages and customs predominated into the time of Imperial Rome. (Area produced many writers).
148 BC	Macedonia became a Roman Province.
123 BC	Power politics. Galatians formed an alliance with Rome against Cappadocia and a pact with Bithynia against Pontus.
112-113 BC	Germanic tribes (Cimbri and Teutoni) ravaged Transalpine Gaul, beginning with the Boii (Bohemia) and the Noricum (Eastern Alps).
102-101 BC	Rome defeated the German marauders.
88 BC	Mithradates V of Pontus treacherously assassinated sixty Galatian chieftains at a feast in attempt to destroy Celtic leadership.
86 BC	Athens and Asia Minor rebelled against Rome (under Mithradates VI, King of Pontus).
63 BC	Pompey made Deiotarus (Tolistoboii) King of Galatia, ending Celtic tribal organization. He entered into an alliance with Rome and drove army of Pontus out of Galatia.
58-51 BC	Julius Caesar's wrote his own commentary on the Gallic Wars (*De Bello Gallico*). Organization of Gaul laid the groundwork for modern France and Europe.
58 BC	Celtic alliance migrated westward to avoid incursions of German tribes (north-east) and Romans (south-east). Julius Caesar began his campaign in Gaul.
54 BC	Julius Caesar invaded Britain.

46 BC	Execution of Vercingetorix of the Arverni of Gaul. He led an almost-successful revolt against Julius Caesar.
41 BC	Antony first met Cleopatra in the city of Tarsus, Cilicia, Asia Minor (birthplace of Apostle Paul).
25 BC	Last Galatian King (Amyntas) assassinated. Augustus Caesar made Galatia a Roman province.

Early Christian Era

4 AD	Birth of Jesus Christ in Bethlehem, Israel.
9 AD	Beginning of Pax Romana. Roman expansion arbitrarily halted at the Rhine, leaving Germany to the barbarian Franks.
10 AD	Approximate time of the birth of the Apostle Paul.
17 AD	Tiberius made Cappadocia a Roman Province.
33 AD	Crucifixion of Christ.
33-34 AD	The Pentecost experience of Christianity in Jerusalem.
35 AD	Conversion of Paul of Tarsus, Asia Minor, leading to his three-year retreat into Arabia (Acts 8:9).
40-50 AD	Paul preached Christianity in Galatia, made converts, and established house-churches.
55 AD	The Jerusalem Council.
53-57 AD	Paul's Letter to the Galatians.
61 AD	Revolt of Celtic Queen Boudicca of the (British) Iceni tribe against Romans in Britain. Roman slaughter of druids in Anglesey Island, Wales.
67 AD	Death of the Apostle Paul (executed by Emperor Nero) in Rome.
74 AD	Galatia united with Cappadocia as a single province.
82 AD	Rome ruled all Celtic territories from Galatia in the east, to Britain in the west, and to Cisalpine Gaul and Iberia (Spain) in the south. Exceptions: Ireland, Scotland (northern Britain), Wales, Cornwall, and surrounding smaller islands.
122 AD	Hadrian's Wall built against the Celtic Picts.
4th – 7thc AD	Predominance of the Celtic Christian Church in British Isles. Celtic/Irish missionaries went to Britain and Gaul (France) in 4th c.
347-419 AD	St. Jerome found the Celtic language still spoken in Galatia.

The Chronology of Galatia

The Decline of Galatia

350 AD	The Huns invade Europe (373-461).
401 AD	[St.] Patrick of Armagh taken into Irish slavery.
409 AD	Roman garrison abandoned Britain to the Germanic invaders. Fall of the City of Rome to the barbarians.
444 AD	Patrick (385-461), a British Celt, evangelized Ireland, establishing the Celtic Christian Church.
450–600 BC	Great Saxony invasion of Britain (The Angles and Jutes had already arrived in BC times).
570 AD	Galatians lose their Celtic language and identity.
613 AD	Historical "end" of Galatia (Death of St. Theodore of Sykeon). History of Asia Minor remained obscure for the next 200 years.
664 AD	The Synod of Whitby, England. The British Celtic Church began to give way to the rule of the Church of Rome.
714 AD	The Islamic (Turkish) Caliphate of Omayyad (661-750 AD) invaded and subdued Galatia.
793 AD	The Vikings plundered Lindisfarne Monastery in Britain. (The Irish defeated the Vikings at the Battle of Clontarf in 1014). The Roman Church predominates.

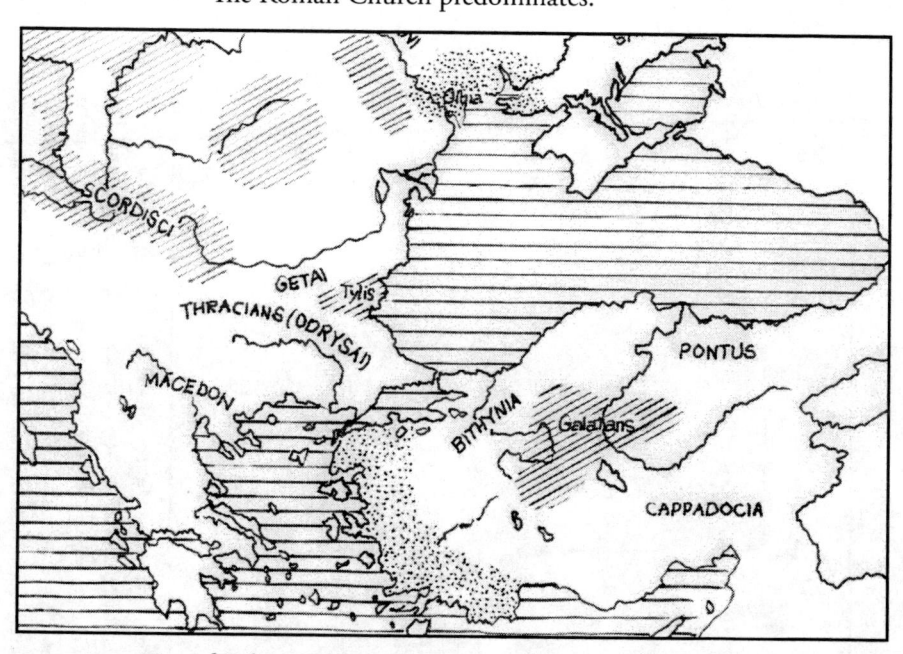

Map of Celtic Settlements in Eastern Europe and Asia Minor.

APPENDIX II

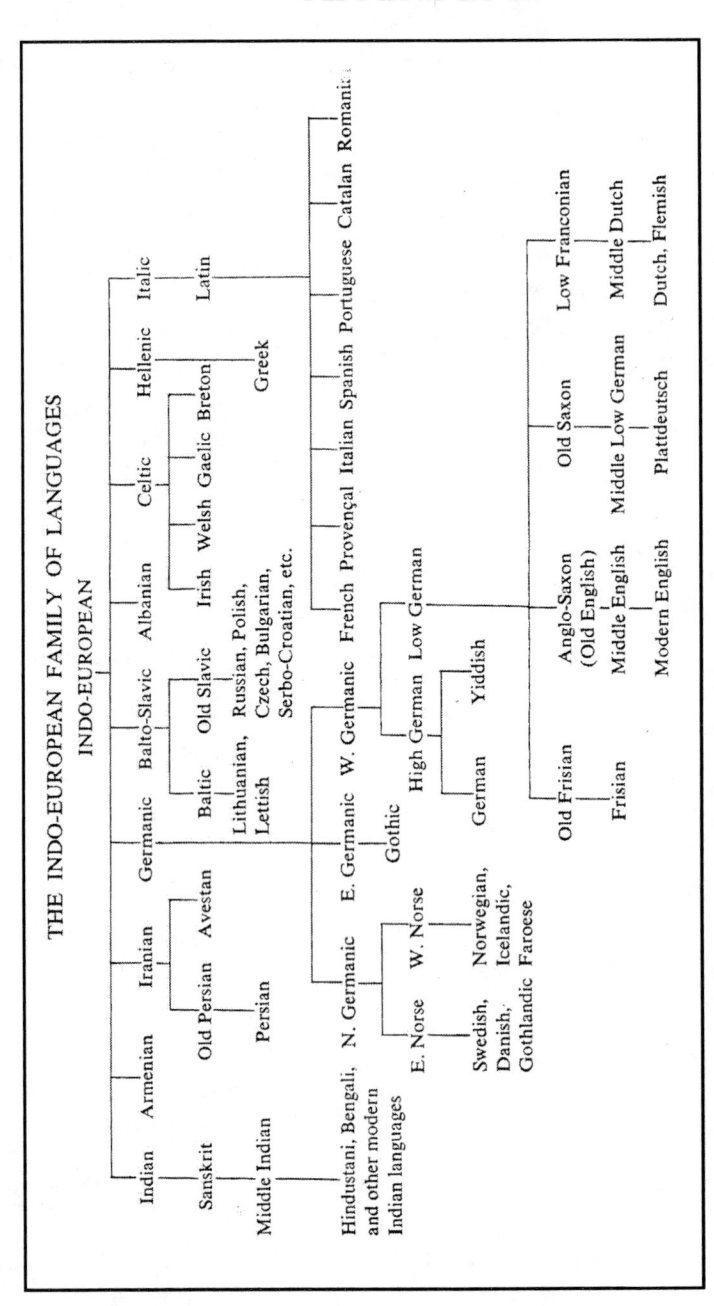

THE INDO-EUROPEAN FAMILY OF LANGUAGES
INDO-EUROPEAN

- Indian
  - Sanskrit
  - Middle Indian
  - Hindustani, Bengali, and other modern Indian languages
- Armenian
- Iranian
  - Old Persian
  - Avestan
  - Persian
- Germanic
  - N. Germanic
    - E. Norse
      - Swedish, Danish, Gothlandic
    - W. Norse
      - Norwegian, Icelandic, Faroese
  - E. Germanic
    - Gothic
  - W. Germanic
    - High German
      - German
      - Yiddish
    - Low German
      - Old Frisian
        - Frisian
      - Anglo-Saxon (Old English)
        - Middle English
        - Modern English
      - Old Saxon
        - Middle Low German
        - Plattdeutsch
      - Low Franconian
        - Middle Dutch
        - Dutch, Flemish
- Balto-Slavic
  - Baltic
    - Lithuanian, Lettish
  - Old Slavic
    - Russian, Polish, Czech, Bulgarian, Serbo-Croatian, etc.
- Albanian
- Celtic
  - Irish
  - Welsh
  - Gaelic
  - Breton
- Hellenic
  - Greek
- Italic
  - Latin
    - French
    - Provençal
    - Italian
    - Spanish
    - Portuguese
    - Catalan
    - Romanian

Sanskrit was the first recorded "mother" of the Indo-European family of languages and was describd as early at 500 BC. Today, like Latin, Sanskrit is frozen in time. This chart was adapted from *Webster's New World Dictionary of the American Language*, College Edition, copyright 1966 by the World Publishing Company, Cleveland, Ohio. Three languages contributed to the development of modern English. Greek and Latin account for more than 50 percent. Most of our "everyday words" and sentence structures, however, come from the Germanic line. The latter group gained a separate identity about 1600 BC.

206

APPENDIX III

A

Aaronic Benediction 34
Adoption 97, 124–125
Agabus 90
Age of Choice 38, 125
Agriculture 7–8, 20
Ailbe, St. 68
Alban, St, of Verulamium 45, 54
Alesia, Hill-fort of Vercingetorix. Gaul 63–64
Alexander the Great 5
Ambassadors 47
Anatolia (Turkey) 5, 8, 12, 64, 100, 153
Ancyra, Battle of 11, 12, 173
Ancyra, Galatia 12, 14
Anthony, St. and the Desert Fathers, Egypt 70–72, 77
Animosity 114

Antioch of Psidia 15
Antiochus I, of Syria...5
Aquila and Priscilla..51
Ariarthese I, of Cappodocia 6
Arthur, King of Cornwall 62, 87
Attalus I 106
Attalus II 110
Auxerre, Gaul 53–54

B

Babylonia 163
Balaam the Seer 163–164
Balak, King of Moab 163–164
Baptism 24
Bards 19, 116, 145, 165
Barnabas...89, 136
Basil, St. of Cappadocia 77
Benjamin, Tribe of 103–104, 121
Beowulf, of the Geats 116
Bewitchment, by Judaizers 168–169
Bimah (Reading room for *Torah*) 99
Bithynia 6
Black Sea 7, 10
Boasting 116–117, 120–121
Body modification 171–172
Boii, Tribe of, Gaul..102
Book of Kells, Ireland..157
Boudicca, Queen of Iceni, Britain.........................44–46, 48, 63
Brand marks of the Celts 175
Brandmarks of Christ 173–176
Brecca, friend of Beowulf 117
Brehon Law, of Druids 22–24
Brendan the Naviagator, of Clonfert, Co Galway, Ireland.................37, 85–86
Brennus of Tolistoboii of Galatians...................................10
Brigit, St. of Kildare, Ireland...............................31, 130–131
Britanni, Celtic Tribe, England..171
British Israelitism 146

Index

Brude, King of Pictland 83
Bunratty Castle, Ireland 130–140
Burial, Ancient 41

C

Caesar, Julius 8, 29, 63–64, 100, 118, 126–127, 171
Camma, Wife of Galatian Chieftain, Sinatos 17–18
Cannibalism 103, 114
Cappadocia 6
Cashel, Rock of, Ireland 28–29
Celibacy 73
Celtiberians of Spain 153
Cerne Abbas Giant (*Dis Pater*), Dorset, England 93
Characteristics of the Celts 15, 16
    Affections 96
    Belligerence and Fighting 12, 36, 67, 77, 101, 105, 107
    Boasting 117–118
    Competitiveness 36, 117–118
    Courage 43, 107
    Despair 108, 110–111, 150
    Drunkenness 113
    Elitism 8, 18–19, 154
    Emotionalism 108, 110–111, 119–120
    Empathy 95–96
    Fashion, love of 153, 157–159
    Feasting, love of 113, 117–118
    Freedom, love of 18, 62
    Gullibility 169
    Healthcare 22–23, 38, 144–145
    Hospitality 139–142
    Instability 15, 115
    Intellectualism 74, 93–94, 96
    Journeying and Love of Travel 3, 74, 86
    Learning, love of 37, 157
    Nature, love of 37
    Pride 95–96, 114, 117, 172
    Vanity 115, 154

Chiomara, wife of Galatian Chieftain, Ortagion 100–101
Cicero 12, 153
Cisalpine Celts of Italy 47, 153
Circumcision 33, 56–59
Circumcision, Spiritual 59
Claudius, Emperor, of Rome 44, 147, 166
Client Kings, of Rome 44, 126
Clonfert Cathedral 102
Clonmacnoise, Abbey of, Ireland 103
Clonard Abbey, Ireland 81
Colchester, England 45
Columba ("Columcille"), St, Monastic Rules of 76
Columban [us], St. of Luxeiuil, Gaul 73, 85
Commandments, Ten 163
Copyright law 81–82
Covenant, New 43, 58
Covenant, Old 47
Crosses, High, of Ireland 72
Cuchulain, Irish champion 157–158

D

Daedalus and Icarus, of Athens 166 (8n)
Dalriada Kingdom, North Britain 63, 83
Damascus 78
Danube River 6
Deborah, Hebrew judge 104
Deiotarus, of Tolistoboii, Galatia 11–12
Delphic Oracle of Apollo 10
Demetrius, Silversmith of Ephesus 111
Derbe 15
Derry, Ireland 81–92
Diapedesis (bleeding through the pores) 126
Diarmat, High King, Tara, Ireland 81–82
Diviners/Seers 19
Divorce 34, 36
Druidic sanctuaries
    Drynemeton, Galatia 10, 37, 165

Index

    Mona, Anglesey 45
    Remi, Wales 63
Druids 19, 31–32, 36–37, 131
Dubthach, poet, father of St. Brigit 130
Dumnorix, Chieftain of Aedui, Gaul 127

E

Edinburgh Castle, Scotland 170
Education, Celtic.. 165
Eithne, wife of Aengus, King of Munster 28
Emperor Cult, Rome... 13–14
Ephesus 39, 111
Epispasm 59
Equites (Craftsman) 19
Eremitism (Hermit)... 70
Eumenes II, of Pergamum 109

F

Faith *versus* Works 27, 41–42, 65–66
Farmers (*Plebes*) 20
Fasting 140
Finian, St., of Molville, Ireland..81
Fosterage..18, 38, 121–122, 124–126
Funeral customs, ancient 46
Funerary treasure 155

G

Gaelic culture..18–20
Galatian Estates, rural 161
Galatian Plateau 7–8, 14–15, 69
Gamaliel...26
Gawain, Sir, of Arthur's Round Table, and the Green Giant.....117–118
Geats, Swedish Tribe 116
Gemara (Talmudic commentary) 41
Ghandi, Mahatma 140
Gideon..104
Gnosticism...166–168

Gordium, of the Tolistoboii, Galatia..5
Gospel of Freedom 64, 65, 66
Government..2, 5, 12
Grail, the Holy..87
Grendel, the monster 116–117
Gunderstrup Cauldron, Denmark 156

H

Hadrian, Emperor 58
Hair style 158, 172
Headhunting and the Cult of the Savered Head 101–103
Health Care, Celtic laws for 144–145
Hebrides Islands, Scotland 83
Hellenism..21, 70, 165
Hellespont (Dardenelles) 5, 101, 114
Hierarchy, Social ranks............................14-17, 32, 65, 116, 124, 164–165
Hinduism...37
Hittite, Kingdom of (at Bogazoy) 5, 21, 37
Holy Spirit 87, 89, 97–98, 111, 137, 145
Holy War 103–105
Honor Price 23, 37–38
Honore, St. of Arles, Gaul 77
Hospitality, Anglo-Saxon 141
Hospitality, Celtic 139–141
Hostages..126–127
Hrothgar, King of the Danes 116

I

Iconium 15
Identity, Jewish (synagogue, etc.) 48
Idolatry 112–113
Ignatius 55
Ilium (Troy)...101
Indo-European culture 4
Indutiomarus, Chieftain of Treverit, Gaul 127
Iona (Hebrides), Monastery of St. Columba..................................83
Isaac, Esau, and Jacob..162

Index

Irenaeus, Bishop of Lyons, Gaul 166
Ita, St. of Limerick, Ireland 85

J

Jerome, St. (342-419 AD) of Ilyria, Dalmatia... 10
Jerome's Vulgate (Bible) 81
Jerusalem Council 56, 143
John, the Apostle 53
Josephus, Jewish historian 55
Journey types 84–87
Judaizers 24–26, 40–44, 47–48, 54–55, 56, 115, 121, 129, 134, 142
.... 144, 146, 168–169, 175
Judaizers, Gentile 55, 60–61
Judaizers, Jewish 55

K

Kaddish (Memorial Prayer) 49
Kells, Book of... 157
Kevin, St. of Glendalough, Ireland 73–74
Kildare, monastic city of... 130
King/Chieftain, Celtic 18, 19, 156
Kings, Client, of Rome.. 126
Kinship, Hebrew 127
Kinship, Celtic 18, 70, 98, 122–123
Kinsman-Redeemer, Hebrew 97, 127–128

L

Languages and Literacy, Gaelic 9, 33, 70, 154
Laoghaire, High King, Tara, Ireland 22
Last Supper of Jesus 141
Law, Anglo-Saxon 141
Law, Brehon (Irish) 22–23
Law, Celtic 18–20, 31, 35
Law, Jewish (*Talmud* and *Mishna*) 40
Lear, King of Cornwall, Britain 122–123, 148–149
Lindisfarne Gospels 157
Lindisfarne ("Holy Island"), Monastery of 157

Livy, Roman Historian 7, 102
London 45
Lovespoon, Welsh 132
Loyalty 18
Lucan, Roman Poet 9
Lydia 15
Lystra 15

M

Macbeth, King of Scotland..141
Macedonia 89
Magi of Chaldea...163
Magic (High/Low, White/Black) 163
Magus, Simon 166
Manuscript Illumination 156–157
Mark, John..89, 136
Marriage, Gaelic 38–39, 47, 112
Martial, Roman Poet 150–151
Martin, St. of Tours, Gaul 77, 165
Martyr, Justin...166
Martyrdoms (White, Green, Red) 73–77, 151–152
Martyrdoms of Paul 77–78
Mead [hall]..116, 139
Mechitza (barrier) 49
Medo-Persia 163
Menander, of Antioch 167
Mercenaries, Celtic...5, 6, 10
Merlin, British druid 62, 131
Metalcraft, Celtic 8, 10, 154–156
Migration, Celtic 11
Minyan (Ten Jewish males)..49
Mishna, Jewish law 34
Missionaries, Galatian 49-50
Missionary Journeys of Paul 82-83
Mithradates V, King of Pontus and Paphlagonia....................13
Modesty, an appeal to..159–160
Monastic Rules of the Celts 84

Index

Monastic Rules of St. Columba 84
Monasticism, Celtic 70–73, 76, 130
Monasticism, Roman 132–133
Moses 42

N

Nero, Emperor of Rome 44, 80, 166
Nicomedes of Bithynia 5

O

Oak Grove, sacred to Druids 33
Ogham writing 17n, 181
Olympus, Battle of 11
Olwen of Wales 157
Oppida (Celtic hill forts) 63
Ortagion, Chieftain of Tolistoboii, Galatia 11, 100–101, 108
Orgatorix, Chieftain of Helvetii (Switzerland) 159
Otherworld, Celtic 87, 103, 112

P/Q

Paschal fire 32–33
Patrick, St. of Ireland 22, 28–29, 32, 91, 145
Patrick, Breastplate of 93
Patrick, Confessions of 91
Paul the Apostle
    Apostolic qualifications 26
    Conversion 79–80
    Gospel preacher 21
    Illness 143–144
    Jewish heritage 21, 26, 174
    As missionary 78, 88, 89–90
    His passion 105–106
    In Rome 78, 80, 146, 152
    Solitude 72–73, 77, 89
Peace 65, 105
Pentecost 21
Pergamum 6, 11, 108

Pergamum, Sculpture of Galatian warriors 106, 108–110
Pessinus of Tolistoboii tribe, Galatia 11, 14
Peter, the Apostle 65, 134–135, 151, 166
Petra, of the Nabateans, Jordan 78
Phylactories 48
Philadelphis 15
Philetaurus of Pergamum 6
Philip the Deacon 166
Philos (Friendship) 134
Phrygia, Empire of (at Gordium) 5, 89
Picts, of Scotland 171
Plutarch, Greek biographer..17, 35
Poet, Itinerant 145–146
Polybius (BC 202-120), Greek historian..101, 173
Pontus and Paphlagonia 6, 12
Posthumus, Roman Consul 102
Prasutagus, King of Iceni, Britain 44
Prayer, Celtic Christian...75, 82, 86, 98–99
Prejudice of Gender 44–46
Prophecy, Gaelic...165
Pudens, Rufus and Claudia 146–152
Pudenziana, Santa, Church in Rome 151–152
Punic Wars...173

R

Raids, Celtic 5, 6, 87, 96–97
Redemption 128–129
Retirement plan, Celtic 19
Ritual, Celtic 29–30
Ritual, Celtic Calendar (*Samhain, Imbolc, Beltaine, Lughnasadh*) 30–32
Ritual, Gnostic..154
Ritual, Judaeo-Christian..32–34
    Agricultural, Jewish 33
    Baptism 33
    Baptism of King Aengus of Cashel 28–29
    Irrelevant practices 41
    Lord's Supper 34, 134–135

Index

Sacrifice 41
Road-building, Asia Minor 6, 8
Roman Catholic Church 94
Rome, Celtic Siege of 159

S

Sarah and Hagar 47–48
Sardis 12
Scholarship, Celtic 81–82
Scythians 171
Seneca, the Younger 152
Sensuality 111–112
Servants and Slaves (Plebes) 20
Shamrock legend of 92
Shechem, Jacob at 56–58
Siculus, Diodorus (BC 90-27), Greek historian of Sicily 102, 118
Simon and Martha of Bethany 49–50
Sinatos, Galatian chieftain 17
Sinorix, Galatian chieftain 17
Skellig Islands, Co Kerry, Ireland 68–69
Solitude 70–73
Soap, Celtic invention of 159
Soul-Friend (Anam-chara) 132–133
Soul-Friend, Apostolic 133–135
Soul Friend, benefit of 137
Soul-Friend, Jesus as 137–138
Spirituality 128–129
Strabo, Roman Historian of Pontus 7, 10, 117
Stigmati 174–175
Suetonius, Paulinus, Roman Procurator in Britain 45, 80
Suicide 46
Suicide of Queen Boudicca 46
Superstition 168–169
Synagogue 143
Syria 5, 78

T

Talmud	40–41
Tara, High King of, Ireland	22, 81–82
Tartans, Celtic	158
Tattoo, Biblical prohibition	172, 173–174
Tattoo, Military	170
Tattoos, Body-modification	171–173
Tattoos, purpose of	172, 175
Tavium, Galatia	10, 14
Tear bottles (Lachrymatories)	40
Telemon, Battle of	173
Tetrarchy, Gaelic	10
Tetrarchy, Galatian Massacre	12
Three, Rule of	92–93
Theophilus of Antioch	92
Timothy	60
Titus	59
Torah, Jewish Law	27
Trade and Commerce	14
Triads, Gaelic	90, 92–93, 162
Triads, Pauline	95–98
Tribes, Galatian	5, 29, 107, 124
Triple Mother – Goddesses	92
Tolistoboii	5, 10, 101
Techtosages	5, 10, 101
Trocmi,	5, 10, 101
Trinity, Christian	92, 96–97, 116

U/V

Urbanization, Gaelic	7, 69–70, 133, 165
Vercingetorix, of the Arverni, Gaul	63–64
Vices	111–114
Vikings	68
Vix, Princess of, Gaul	46, 155
Volso, Roman general	11, 107

Index

W

War 103–105, 118–119, 170
Warriors, Celtic 119–120, 157, 173
Way, The (Christian) 27, 87–88
Whitby, Monastery of 94
Whitby, Synod of 94, 132–133
Wisemen 163–164
Witchcraft 168
Woad, dye 171, 173
Women, Power of 46–47
Women, Legal Rights of 38–39, 125
Word, the Spoken 162, 169

X/Y/Z

Zeus, Altar of, Pergamum 112
Zoroaster, Indo-European god 163

Over the years, **Dorothy Minchin-Comm**, has written many books and articles for and about other people. Occasionally, her name has appeared as a co-author, other times not. The Celt and the Christ has been an entirely different experience. This time she very literally wrote *with* another person. What evolved is a relationship that moved steadily and smoothly from the meeting of two strangers to a point where they can now almost finish one another's sentences. The fact that t hey come from entirely different backgrounds signifies nothing at all. They have, indeed become an efficient team.

Hyveth B. Williams has written three books: *Will I Ever Learn?* (Autobiography, 1996); *Anticipation: Waiting on Tiptoes for the Lord* (2001); and *Secrets of a Happy Heart: A Fresh Look at the Sermon on the Mount* (2004). Also, she has contributed chapters to three other books. All of these were shaped by an editor to fit the theme of the book.

Writing *The Celt and the Christ* was Hyveth's first real experience as a co-author. More than just a "writing together," the co-authors have developed a lifelong friendship.

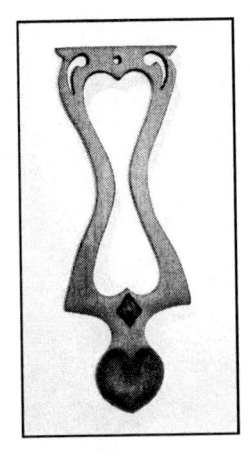

Instead of rejoicing that the task is done, we find ourselves missing the times of study and creative writing. We promise to come up with another project soon! This, after all, seems now to be the natural course of our lives.

To celebrate the completion of this book, we share a Welsh love spoon (hand-carved in Australia). The designs symbolize, very naturally, the essence of the spiritual adventure we have taken. We invite our readers to join us here in yet one more journey of the soul.